THE AMERICAN FAMILY

The American Family
Across the Class Divide

Yasushi Watanabe

Pluto Press
London • Ann Arbor, MI

First published 2005 by Pluto Press
345 Archway Road, London N6 5AA
and 839 Greene Street, Ann Arbor, MI 48106

www.plutobooks.com

British Library Cataloguing in Publication Data
A catalogue record for this book is available from the British Library

ISBN 0 7453 1557 7 hardback
ISBN 0 7453 1552 6 paperback

Library of Congress Cataloging in Publication Data applied for

10 9 8 7 6 5 4 3 2 1

Designed and produced for Pluto Press by
Curran Publishing Services, Norwich

Printed and bound in Canada by
Transcontinental Printing

I admit that I saw in America more than America. … I wanted to understand it so as to at least know what we have to fear or hope therefrom.

Alexis de Tocqueville, 1848

Contents

Acknowledgments

This book is based on my dissertation, *Nurturing A Context: The Logic of Individualism and the Negotiation of the Familial Sphere in the United States*, submitted to the Department of Anthropology, Harvard University, in 1996. I am deeply indebted to my former advisors, Professors David Maybury-Lewis and Nur Yalman, for encouraging me, as a student from Japan, to investigate such "mainstream" America as the middle-class White Americans. I am not one who holds that a student should refrain from doing fieldwork in his or her country of origin. Jean-Jacques Rousseau once remarked that "to study man one must look from afar." Yet, I believe that the "afar" could be found in one's close vicinity, and it is possible and important to identify "others" in oneself and oneself in "others." Nevertheless, to me, it was very precious and enlightening to be able to experience this fieldwork at a younger stage of my life, especially in the place where I spent most of my twenties as both a student and a resident. My respect and appreciation for these two advisors, of great integrity, truly liberal minds and extraordinary charm, will never fade.

Memories of my informants make me nostalgic for all that occurred throughout those years. I confess that I felt almost choked with tears when I re-read my field notes about those who had passed away, wishing I could see and talk with them even one more time. I will never forget the words that J. C. wrote to me before his demise: "A man is weak and fragile, but every man has something to shine about, and we must respect it." I sometimes meet my former informants when I return to Boston. Every time I do so, I realize that they and I keep changing, in both sensitivities and values, as years go by. The ethnographic present that I put forward here is, therefore, also subject to change, in terms of both interpretation and signification, as we live our lives. I strive to accept and appreciate that change.

If reducing and instrumentalizing "others" is the business of the powerful, it is a scholar's task to uncover their complexity and constructedness. I hope that this book makes a modest contribution to this task. Such a hegemonic nation as the United

States needs our close scrutiny to avoid hasty generalization or simplistic personification.

I should like to offer my thanks for the generous financial support of the following institutions that allowed me to engage in this pursuit: the Matsushita International Foundation, the Mellon Foundation, Harvard University, the Japan Society for the Promotion of Science, Keio University, and the Japan Foundation.

I acknowledge with gratitude my colleagues at various institutions, including, but not limited to, Keio University, Harvard University, the University of Cambridge, the University of Oxford, the Japanese Society of Cultural Anthropology, the American Anthropological Association, the Royal Anthropological Institute of Great Britain and Ireland, the Japan Association for American Studies, the American Studies Association, and the British Association for American Studies, who have inspired me in both scholarly and personal terms. I have simply found it too difficult a task to list all those names here.

I am also deeply appreciative of Susan Schmidt for proofreading the manuscript so conscientiously and diligently. Only someone truly bilingual in the Japanese and English languages, like Susan, could understand and work on the little nuances I meant to convey.

Last but not least, I would like to thank Roger van Zwanenberg and Julie Stoll of Pluto Press for their heartwarming encouragement and invaluable guidance for the successful completion of this manuscript as a book.

To them go all the credit, to me the responsibility for any errors.

Yasushi Watanabe
Boston, Massachusetts
February 2004

1 Introduction

Scope of research

An unpublished letter from Alexis de Tocqueville to Jared Sparks, then President of Harvard, was recently discovered in the Harvard University Archives. De Tocqueville had known Sparks for two decades since they first met during his sojourn in Boston in September 1831. The letter acknowledged with gratitude an honorary degree of Doctor of Laws awarded to him by the university in 1852. At the same time, he made plain his apprehensions about America's increasing international belligerence and adventurism, which he had encountered firsthand in 1849 when serving as French Foreign Minister:

> America has nothing more to fear except from herself, from the abuse of democracy, from the spirit of adventure and conquest, from the sentiment and exaggerated pride of her forces, and from the impetuosity of the youth. ... Do not pick quarrels lightly with Europe ... since these could lead to grave difficulties for you, and could have many repercussions on your internal affairs that are difficult to anticipate in advance (*Harvard Magazine*, January–February, 2004, p. 84).

The passage is truly insightful and suggestive, especially in light of the current situations of international affairs of today.

De Tocqueville is known for communicating his concerns, in his 1848 classic *Democracy in America*, about the possibility of negative consequences of individualism in the United States: "Each man is forever thrown back on himself alone, and there is danger that he may be shut up in the solitude of his own heart" (1969, p. 508).

I had felt uncomfortable with an easy, sound-bite labeling of "America" and an opportunistic use of it, but this line had remained heavily on my mind through the course of my stay and study in the United States. There was no way that I could ever possibly match the caliber and insight of such intellectual giants as de Tocqueville. However, I wished to understand as best I could what he meant by the fine line I have just quoted, and that was the primary drive for me to undertake this whole project. This book is, therefore, a record of a three-year struggle by a foreign anthropologist from Japan, with de Tocqueville in mind, in the Boston area where he stayed for four weeks in 1831.

The method I chose to pursue this exploration was by furnishing an ethnographic comparison between two distinctive social groups in the Boston area: first, the descendants of one of the oldest and most distinguished aristocratic groups in the United States, the so called "Boston Brahmins", and second, the descendants of immigrant workers from Ireland, or the so-called "Boston Irish."[1] Interestingly enough, John Forbes Kerry, a US Senator from Massachusetts and the Democratic candidate for the 2004 US Presidential Elections, is closely linked to the Boston Brahmins, with a grandmother from the Winthrops and a mother from the Forbes. South Boston, where I conducted most of my fieldwork among the Boston Irish, was featured in such popular films as *Good Will Hunting* (1997) and *Mystic River* (2003) and includes the districts that a *US News & World Report* in 1994 called the "White underclass capital of America." I intended to capture and compare the ways in which these Americans in such different sociocultural milieus make sense of, and live out, the complex, oftentimes distressing, transfigurations of postwar society. In other words, I wished to illuminate the dialectics between the structural and historical constraints in which these social actors are located and their maneuverings to create and nurture a context for a stable identity and social lives in late-modern (or postmodern, transmodern, supermodern, hypermodern) America.

Alice Kessler-Harris, in her presidential address to the American Studies Association meeting in 1991, proposed that "[a]s students and scholars of American Studies, we are called on to engage in, to facilitate, the conversation that occurs in the public marketplace by ensuring the perpetuation of a processual notion of America" (1992, p. 311). This research subscribes to that "processual notion of America" which, instead of presupposing "America" as a cultural unity with fixed boundaries and primordial values, is more receptive to the complexity and constructedness of "America" in both historical and social terms. The ethnographic approach, with its tradition of "thick description" (Geertz 1973) and first-hand scrutiny, has a proven advantage in uncovering the contested and emergent properties of culture as it is lived, and thus addressing the vexing question of cultural identity and achieving a better understanding of a processual America.

Setting the stage

I had already spent a few years in the Boston area as an international student from Japan. There a series of culture shocks had both bewildered and entertained me, ultimately broadening my perspectives on life and on the world. Boston's culture, history, and people had furnished me with a window on American society, which I had begun studying as a college student in Japan. I preferred building my fieldwork upon the personal experience and knowledge that I had accumulated at first hand. From a more pragmatic point of view, the Boston area was well suited for securing research funding, for locating informants, and for implementing fieldwork and follow-up research in a timely fashion.

I have been interested in the family for as long as I have in social anthropology, but there was a personal dimension as well. One thing that puzzled me greatly in my early observations of American society was the seemingly contradictory realities of domestic life. On the one hand, I was extremely impressed by what David Schneider (1968) calls the "diffuse, enduring solidarity" of the American family that I witnessed in the street and in my personal interactions. In Japan, I had encountered numerous cases in which the family appeared to be almost besieged – by forced relocations of fathers to remote posts, the routinization of overwork (even to the point where it resulted in death in extreme cases), high suicide rates, obsession with test-coaching schools for children (even those at kindergarten), strict imposition of hyper-rigid school regulations, social stigmatization of divorce, and the unequal status of women, among many other elements. In the United States, conjugal relationships seemed to me more equal and affectionate, parent–child relationships more casual yet authentic, and family life as a whole more warm hearted and nurturing.

At the same time, I was dismayed by the "dilute, ephemeral solidarity" of the American family, which occasionally entailed a substantial degree of both emotional and physical pain. The high rates of marriage breakup and of children born out of wedlock certainly captured my attention. Reports from journalists, scholars, civic groups, and public organizations informed me of tragic cases of domestic violence, sexual and child abuse, drug addiction, and other phenomena that were often associated with dysfunctional families. As a student of kinship and family, I strained to remind myself that these issues needed epistemological and methodological care in definition and interpretation; yet the sense of crisis articulated in American public discourse on family life lingered in my mind. I became more convinced of the acuteness and magnitude of this public feeling by the debates and rhetoric during the campaigns for the Presidential elections in 1992, which placed heavy emphasis on these issues (as the subsequent campaigns of 1996 and 2000 were also to do).

Those election campaigns indicated to me that my personal struggle over how to make sense of the exemplary – yet problematic – properties of the American family that I had noticed was also their struggle, even if their memories of the past, diagnoses of the present, and prescriptions for the future were different and contested. Thus, the family as the institutional concern of this research came into focus at the intersection of what I (the semi-outsider) found enigmatic in American society and what I observed the Americans deemed cardinal and pressing in their lives. It was the winter of 1992.

I spent several months contemplating how to approach this large issue through small-scale fieldwork in the Boston area, the northeastern corner of the country. There were innumerable paths that I could have taken in exploring this issue, but conversations with my American acquaintances as well as my preliminary readings of Boston history gradually aroused my curiosity about two social groups that represent contrasting cultural histories and social realities in the Boston area: the upper to upper-middle class, Anglo-Saxon, Protestants (the Boston Brahmins), and the lower to lower-middle class Irish Catholics (the Boston Irish).[2] By comparing these two groups in different sociocultural milieus, I aimed at elucidating the diversity of experience and culture even within what is generally categorized as "White, middle-class" America, while at the same time extracting from such diversity some common logic or theme that might be applicable to other Americans in different sociocultural contexts of which the family is a part.

White, middle-class Americans are among the most understudied groups in the anthropology of the United States, despite (or perhaps because of) their hegemonic presence in society. It is worthwhile to study this group because cultural "others" are often constructed by reference to them, and because they often represent "America" in the eyes of foreigners. My ethnography is probably most distinctive in presenting an account of the little-studied elite segment of this group, in scrutinizing the experience of this group from the different perspectives of two opposite segments in the same regional (urban) setting, and in analyzing the trajectories of their lives in the light of intergenerational mobility within a broad span of history since the Second World War. To the best of my knowledge, mine is one of the first ethnographies of White, middle-class America by a non-native anthropologist, and the first of its kind among these particular segments in the Boston area.

It was theoretically possible to narrow these two social groups further by using a more rigid cluster of social attributes but I avoided doing so, partly because I was unsure of how realistically the field opportunities would open up for me, and partly because I preferred to follow my informants' own theories in emphasizing any specific attributes. Similarly, I did not apply any quantitative criteria in determining whether a family falls into either category in a rigid fashion, partly because I was unsure whether local people actually perceived these categories with such rigid and mathematical precision, and partly because I was curious about "deviant" cases among these two groups as a clue to understanding what is considered normative in society and in their lives. Many friends and acquaintances warned me, illustrating with various anecdotes, that these groups could be exclusive, protective, and elusive. "The Brahmins will not be interested in you." "You might be beaten up by those rough bosses." Fair enough. I resolved to focus on these two groups anyway. It was the spring of 1993.

Boston, or the "hub of the solar system"

Boston, the capital of Massachusetts, is the largest city in New England: in 1990 the population of its 48.4 square miles was 574,000, and by 2000 it had grown to 589,000. In 2000 it ranked 20th in size among American cities and joined New York City as one of the only two older cities in the US northeast and midwest to gain in population between 1980 and 2000. However, Greater Boston – the metropolitan area whose boundaries are indefinite but broadly encompass the city of Boston and nearly 100 smaller cities, towns, and villages – is inhabited by more than 3 million people in its 1,100 square miles, and is one of the most densely populated areas in the country.

The city of Boston itself consists of 17 small but tightly knit and distinctive neighborhoods such as Charlestown, South Boston, Back Bay/Beacon Hill, and Fenway/Kenmore. Its early history, beginning with the settlement of the Pilgrim Fathers in Plymouth (1620), includes the declaration of a "City upon a Hill" by John Winthrop (1630), the foundation of the first institution of higher learning in the country – later called Harvard (1636) – triumph in the War of Independence (1775–83), the prosperity of shipping and textile industries, the blossoming of the American Renaissance in the mid-nineteenth century, the Emancipation Proclamation (1863) and other historic documents, and an uncountable number of the heroes and heroines of "American" narratives. Boston's hegemony in the spheres of politics, economics, and culture led Oliver Wendell Holmes, Sr. in 1858 to state to the *Atlantic Monthly* that the "Boston State-house is the hub of the solar system." The wealthy Brahmin families were the heirs of the Puritan "aristocracy of saints," often descendants of New England's "first families," and the leading figures in the political, economic, intellectual, artistic, and charitable domains of social life in the "hub."

Yet the Industrial America that accompanied the Civil War shifted the locus of economic power away from New England to New York City, and into the hands of such rising capitalists as the Vanderbilts, Rockefellers, and Carnegies, who pursued a more aggressive and materialistic style in their construction of "empires" in steel, railroads, and venture capital. The Brahmin virtues of good breeding, frugality, and civic-mindedness became a pallid anachronism in the culture of the "Gilded Age," and their traditional combination of shipping and textile industries became powerless and obsolete in the face of the new regime of the "survival of the fittest."

In addition, the physical face of Boston was transformed from that of an old colonial town to that of a metropolis. Over the half-century from 1825 to 1875, the area of the city was expanded about 30 times, to 24,000 acres, by a series of land reclamations of flooded areas, and the population increased almost seven times, to 314,000, partly due to a huge influx of Irish immigrants fleeing the Potato Famine of 1845–50 in their homeland. By 1855, nearly a third the total population of Boston was Irish. The Yankees' fear and suspicion of the "Catholic menace" was politically exemplified in the organization of "the American Party" by the so-called "Know-Nothings" and socially epitomized in the famous phrase "No Irish Need Apply." O'Connor (1995) conjectures:

> If there had existed in the nineteenth century a computer able to digest all the appropriate data, it would have reported one city in the entire world where an Irish Catholic, under any circumstance, should never, ever, set foot. That city was Boston, Massachusetts. It was an American city with an intensely homogeneous Anglo-Saxon character, an inbred hostility toward people who were Irish, a fierce and violent revulsion against all things Roman Catholic, and an economic system that precluded most forms of unskilled labor. ... Other major American cities, to be sure, shared many of Boston's social, cultural, and religious characteristics, but few to the same extent and none to the same degree (pp. xv – xvi).

The Civil War mitigated these antagonistic sentiments, partly because the Yankees' concern was diverted from the Irish to slavery in the South, and partly because of the Irish contribution to the Yankee cause in the Union army and in war-related industries and services. Also, the emergence of a powerful national economy in the United States attracted hordes of immigrants, mostly from Eastern and Southern Europe (Italians, Jews, Poles, Portuguese, Greeks, and others), whose sociocultural traditions were so different as to make the polarity between the Yankee and the Irish less distinctive and salient. The other reprieve for the Irish came from a massive demand for the civil servants and utility workers needed for the modernization of the city and the state after the 1880s. These new contexts moved the Irish not only out of the slums but also further up the political ladder. Hugh O'Brien, in 1885, became the first Irish mayor (1885–8), and thereafter the Irish "bosses" and "machines" consolidated their political predominance and altered the power structure of Boston.

The turbulent social fluctuations precipitated by rapid modernization and the social maelstrom of the Great Depression enforced a moderately managed and socialized form of capitalism ("the welfare state") in the United States, and the federal government's "new deal" gradually curtailed the patronage system and the power base of such old-style Irish mayors as John Fitzgerald ("Honey Fitz," 1906–7, 1910–13) and James Curley (1914–17, 1922–5, 1930–3, 1946–9). A new electorate came of age, even among the Irish (especially those of the middle-class), that embraced an ideal of justice, rationality, and clean government on the political level; and the financial power of the Brahmins and the political power of the Irish could find a common ground after the mutual antipathy of almost half a century.

The aspiration to achieve a progressive society was epitomized in the landslide victory of John Hynes over Curley in 1949 (and on the national level in the inauguration of John Fitzgerald Kennedy as US President in 1961). As Mayor throughout the 1950s, Hynes took the initiative of launching the Boston Redevelopment Authority in 1957 for urban renewal projects covering 11 percent of Boston's land. Mayor John Collins (1960–68) implemented Hynes's ambition in the construction of numerous complexes, skyscrapers, and parks in an atmosphere of constant criticism and resistance against bureaucratic vandalism and insensitivity.

Mayor Kevin White (1968–83) successfully shifted the locus of projects from mega-development to the revitalization of historic sites and buildings, yet the municipal population decreased by a third in the three decades following the Second World War (before leveling off at today's figure). This exodus took place partly because of the development of suburbs in the postwar era, partly because of the increases in rents and real estate prices inside the city, and most importantly because of the new racial tension in the neglected outer neighborhoods. The influx of Blacks into urban areas in the North during the postwar era, along with the growth of minority and immigrant populations, kindled a sense of crisis among working-class Whites, who fought to protect their spatial boundaries, social entitlements, and occupational opportunities. The craving for a progressive society, upon which the Civil Rights movement in the 1960s was grounded, rationalized a program of school busing in 1974 of about 80,000 school children to integrate Blacks and Whites in classrooms.

The chaotic and tragic consequences of the busing program created a backlash, and as a result Raymond Flynn, an active anti-busing city councilor, was elected and later re-elected as Mayor (1984–93). The racial turmoil calmed down significantly, but the late 1980s witnessed a transition from the "Massachusetts Miracle" to disillusionment caused by economic recession on both the national and international levels. Flynn's departure to the Vatican as the US Ambassador in 1993 made way for Thomas Menino to succeed him as the first Italian mayor in Boston history. Mayor Menino (1993 to present) increased the number of police officers, worked to improve the public schools, revitalized business districts, and succeeded in attracting the 2004 Democratic National Convention to Boston. The city's crime statistics showed marked improvements in all areas compared with 1990, and President Clinton in 1997 described it as a "nationwide model in crime prevention." However, the number of homeless people jumped 61 percent, to well over 6,000 in the 1990s, a decade of unparalleled wealth, as a result of the severe lack of affordable housing, changes in welfare programs, and other factors.

Today, Boston's economy rests primarily on such service industries as high tech, venture capital, education, medicine, entertainment, and tourism. There are more than 50 colleges within a 30-mile radius of the city center, attracting more than 250,000 students from throughout the world. This so-called "Athens of America" boasts 17 major hospitals (and nearly 100 medical facilities in Greater Boston), dozens of National Historic Landmarks, and myriads of well-known cultural institutions and business enterprises. Boston, like other major cities in the United States, has been undergoing a process of diversification since the enforcement of the 1965 Immigration Act, which opened the gates wider to new immigrants from Asia, Africa, Latin America, and the Middle East as well as from European countries. Between 1990 and 2000, the racial composition of the city changed: the White population fell from 59 to 49 percent of the total, while the Hispanic/Latino proportion rose from 10.8 to 14 percent, and Asians/Pacific Islanders from 5.2 percent to 8 percent; Blacks/African Americans moved from 23.8 to 24 percent, and Native Americans from 0.3 to 0.2 percent.

Greater Boston reveals a similar demographic transformation. Bostonians claiming Irish ancestry still form the largest group, but decreased from 21 percent in 1990 to 16 percent in 2000, while the percentage of those of English ancestry dropped from 6.3 to 4.5 percent in the same period. With the fastest growing racial groups being Asians (Vietnamese, Chinese, Asian Indians, and Koreans in particular) and Hispanics (Central and South American and Mexican groups in particular), Boston, home to around 150 languages, has finally reached the "minority as majority" status (as have other major cities in the US).[3]

At the same time, however, with the entry of national enterprises and global corporations (for example, the *Boston Globe* is now owned by the New York Times Company, and Jordan Marsh Department Store by Macy's), the city has become more gentrified and less distinctive in local colors and flavors. Boston thus shares its characteristics with those of other urban centers in wider society, and my research aimed to capture how the current generations of the Boston Brahmins and Boston Irish were making sense of, and living with, these larger processes at work in late-modern (or postmodern) America.

Method of research

The summer of 1993 was spent probing the realistic possibility of doing this fieldwork. I was particularly apprehensive about the accessibility of Yankee families because of their allegedly snobbish and elitist exclusivity. My reading of historical literature had acquainted me with specific family names that might appear in my interview list, and I was able to identify most of those names in the *Yellow Pages*, the *Social Register*, and Harvard University's alumni records, but I was fully aware that direct calls or letters out of the blue would be far less productive or courteous than referrals. Therefore, I sought advice and help not only from my personal acquaintances and friends in the Boston area but also from several professors at Harvard and various staff members at the Beacon Hill Civic Association, Boston Athenaeum, the Japan Society of Boston, King's Chapel, the Massachusetts Historical Society, the Mayflower Descendants Society, the New England Historic Genealogical Society, and nine other cultural institutions that were supposed to be have long-standing connections with the old, wealthy Yankee families. Strict codes of confidentiality prohibited any disclosure of their membership records, but all of them were extremely conscientious and cooperative, and I was given several referrals on a personal basis.

A mixed feeling of strain and anxiety, amplified by my own shyness, resulted in occasional procrastination in making contact, yet the list of names itself became longer in a geometric progression as time passed. My objective at this phase was to socialize with potential research subjects, to ascertain their willingness, commitment, and candor, and to extract what they deemed significant in their family histories and present lives. Some of them were experts in the social sciences, and our conversations were often shaped by sociological jargon. Some were only too happy to turn over long bibliographical lists for my bedtime reading, including the works of Levi-Strauss, Charles Wright Mills, de Tocqueville, and Weber. Some of them, having donated their Oriental paintings to the Museum of Fine Arts in Boston or elsewhere, were far better acquainted with Japanese history and culture than I was, to my great embarrassment. Edward Evans-Pritchard, in his 1940 classic *The Nuer*, related that the lives of the Nuer people of Africa were not controlled by autonomous time, and ended with the famous phrase "The Nuer are fortunate." However, nearly six decades later, it seemed to me that Evans-Pritchard was also fortunate! From the Bostonians' point of view, it may have felt strange to be the "specimens" studied by a student of anthropology from the country of The Chrysanthemum and the Sword, who perhaps should have been off studying a remote tribe or a minority group.

This preliminary research enabled me to correspond with a total of 29 individuals from 21 families for an average of four hours per person over a five-month period. I singled out 16 families from this group for my official fieldwork on the basis of their availability and willingness. The *Social Register* (1993, 1994, 1995) and resources at the New England Historic Genealogical Society were referred to later for information on the general background of these families. Three families eventually declined to participate further: one because they had to take care of a parent with Alzheimer's disease; another because they considered their own family life essentially a "private" matter; and the third because one member was socially in a highly delicate position.

Several informants later speculated on three reasons for this still very high rate of cooperation: first, my affiliation with Harvard, with which many felt a strong affinity; second, that I was not an American citizen and my intentions were purely scholarly; and third, the ongoing dislocation of the Brahmins from the center of the power structure in Boston society.[4] In any case, I was relieved that the Brahmin families were far more amiable, outspoken, and hospitable than a whole set of stereotypes and anecdotes had led me to believe.

I faced more difficulties with the Irish families, because I had no clue how to approach them except by going through various organizations in South Boston, the so-called "Irish neighborhood." My inquiries covered the Gate of Heaven Church, the Historic Society of South Boston, the Laboure Center, St. Augustine's Church, St. Brigid's Church, SS. Peter and Paul Church, South Boston Neighborhood House, South Boston Public Library, and eventually 14 other cultural institutions, extending to such adjacent neighborhoods as Charlestown and Dorchester. My project was publicized in some church bulletins and similar publications with an invitation to participate, but I received only one response. However, the principle of geometric progression functioned here as well, and various intermediaries enabled me to communicate with a total of 22 individuals from 13 families for an average of three hours per person over a three-month period.

As was the case with the Brahmin families, my being a foreigner who, with no political interests at stake in their lives and introduced to them by intermediaries, would eventually go home might have worked positively to lower their wariness of me. Also, as many informants in both groups related to me and intermediaries, it might have been a refreshing experience for them to hear what a foreign researcher found interesting about their lives or American society in general. However, it did not take long for me to perceive this group's deep skepticism towards outside journalists and academics, who, according to nearly all of my informants, had a propensity to characterize them only as "bigoted," "insular," "barbaric," or "impoverished." Therefore, I had to define my position and objectives more explicitly than I did to the Yankee families in order to gain their confidence. In the end, they were all extremely outspoken, affable, accommodating, and courteous, and I did not hesitate to solicit their further participation in my project – except for one family whose life appeared too hectic and one elderly lady whose health concerned me greatly (yet she graciously sent me a card wishing me good luck and Merry Christmas). Imbued with all sorts of frightening anecdotes of my friends and acquaintances, I used to leave South Boston with hurried steps after sunset in the early days of my fieldwork, though I can now look back on it as a funny story.

The first several months of 1994 were spent preparing my prospectus defense (the examination of a doctoral candidate's proposal for fieldwork), which was due in early May. My preliminary fieldwork, based on open conversations over the preceding months, had given me a sense of some of the key issues and events that seemed to have a central significance in my informants' social realities and cultural histories, but my notes were too devoid of "facts of life" for analytic purposes, and I was urged to tailor my official fieldwork more to an open-ended interview based on a list of questions. I drew up a list that consisted of 50 clusters covering such specific facets of my informants' actual social lives and relationships as neighborhood, social clubs, social services, work, cultural taste, kinship, friendship, love, marriage, divorce, division of labor at home, childrearing, care of the elderly, finances, and inheritance. In so doing, I referred to the list produced by Elizabeth Bott (1957) in her classic study of urban families and their social networks in London, as it was highly comprehensive in its scope.

After the defense, my schedule was flooded with appointments with my informants. I used to be puzzled by the ambiguous symbolism behind the American art of not calling back (an implicit "no, thank you"), but now bustling urban life seemed to have made cancellation of appointments a habit not only for my informants but sometimes even for myself. Roughly one out of three appointments had to be rescheduled, and the answering machine became an indispensable instrument for this urban-based fieldwork. (It took place before the advent of e-mail and cellular phones.) Interviews were carried out mostly at the informants' homes or workplaces, in nearby restaurants, and (very occasionally) over the phone, with or without the presence of other family members. The question list was constantly revised and frequently improvised in its order and phrasing, and was essentially used as my own reminder of the basic information that had to be collected. Otherwise, the interviews were mostly Socratic, in the sense that I openly contested the informants' views in order to secure clarification of their thoughts, and we often engaged in long dialogs.

Each interview lasted from one to two hours, and in most cases I had between eight and 15 sessions with the primary informant in the family, followed by interviews lasting one or two hours with other family members when they were available. I had a constant fear of being asked not to come back. As it turned out, however, the generosity of my informants enabled me to participate in and observe even such family occasions as Thanksgiving, Christmas, weddings, commencements (graduation ceremonies), funerals, memorial services, and recreational activities. I also had a few chances to show *Boston: The Way It Was* (1995) – a special video by local TV station WGBH that depicted Boston in the 1930s and 1940s – to my informants, and to hear their responses to the historical representation in the video.

My investigation also incorporated insights and comments from lawyers, schoolteachers, government officials, genealogists, home helpers, social workers, journalists, and many local residents. In addition, I strove to visit various places that were frequently mentioned in my informants' testimonies so that I could visualize those contexts more clearly. The official fieldwork was technically wrapped up in June 1995 with the presentation of a modest gift as a token of gratitude and friendship, but the follow-up investigation continued until the completion of my dissertation in the autumn of 1996. In other words, I have known these informants for nearly three years (with the sad exception of a few who have died).

Most of the informants allowed me to record their responses, but my intuition told me that this would incline them toward "correct" answers, and therefore the recorder was often turned off when it came to delicate issues or, on occasion, completely dispensed with. This prevented me from quoting at length, but direct quotation itself was a very sensitive matter, for even a word could reveal the identity of my informants. As is often the case with this sort of study, I have modified – insofar as it does not affect my analytical context – some attributes of individuals and families to preserve their anonymity.[5] This principle was followed particularly in the case of the Brahmin families, who tend to be in rather conspicuous positions in Boston society. Others involved in this project were of course sworn to absolute confidentiality regarding all informants. I promised to obtain the interviewees' permission before describing anything sensitive about their lives in my dissertation, and to publish it only after several years' (as some informants jested) "grace period." I returned to Boston at least once a year even after I left the United States in 1997 and spent my sabbatical leave (2003–4) there. I have updated some data and literature here insofar as they do not affect the context of the original fieldwork.

The issue of inter-subjectivity was persistently in my mind, since both participant observation and interviewing are essentially highly subjective exercises: my curiosity and interpretations could be predisposed by my own background, experience, personality, intentions, and interest; the respondents' answers and reactions could vary widely in different contexts; and our new frame of reference would be constantly in the making throughout the course of the fieldwork. After all, even a little smile could mean much, and we had to strain to read its nuance. During my preliminary fieldwork, for instance, one family hosted a live-in student from Japan. As that person constantly spoke to me in Japanese (which none of the family understood), pointing to various spots in the house, the family seemed to feel they were intruded upon by an outside inquirer and became increasingly passive and protective. To the very end I was unable to erase their suspicion, and I had to abandon

[15]

the idea of asking their formal participation in this project. In a contrasting case, one of the sons gradually developed an interest in his lineage and heritage as I asked those questions, and now runs a homepage about his whole family.

How honestly are the respondents expressing themselves? How deeply am I penetrating their lives? How correctly am I reading them? Am I fair in describing them? Am I not "othering" them too much? These questions were (and still are) of concern to me, especially because I was neither born nor bred in the United States, and had never visited it nor lived in an English-speaking country until I entering graduate school at Harvard. This background impeded me from understanding colloquialisms, slang, and vogue words (especially those of young people) or distinguishing subtle nuances and elaborate euphemisms among Americans who were, according to a common stereotype in Japan, supposed to express themselves quite straightforwardly, even too bluntly or self-righteously. I had to project all of my possible preoccupations, prejudices, and ignorance onto the actual field situation, and avoid indulging in navel-gazing and self-reflexivity. After all, such research is a whole learning process between two individuals: a permanent dialog or dialectics that would never reach the point of "complete" understanding in a strict sense. It is perhaps no different from any other human relationship.

And it is probably the same even with one's own self. I feel I am conducting an internal dialogue and learning about myself every day (and will be, as long as a life lives through me). I feel, in this sense, as Claude Levi-Strauss once reflected:

> I never had, and still do not have, the perception of feeling my personal identity. I appear to myself as the place where something is going on, but there is no "I", no "me." Each of us is a kind of crossroads where things happen. The crossroads is purely passive; something happens there. A different thing, equally valid, happens elsewhere. There is no choice. It is just a matter of chance.
> (Radio interview, Canadian Broadcasting Company, 1977)

As I re-settle in Japan, visit other parts of the United States (or the world), gain more experience, and grow older, some apparent differences between "others" and my own self seem to fade away in my mind, while new ones emerge.

On numerous occasions, I have been asked about my experience of being a Japanese anthropologist in the United States; I am somehow expected to possess a genuinely unique "Japanese" perspective. However, I am rather dubious about whether there are any primordial and essential properties of "Japaneseness," or to what extent I embody them even if any exist. It is true that I am a Japanese anthropologist and that I wrote down what I found interesting about my informants' lives or American society at large at this particular moment in my life. I leave it to each reader, however, to identify or construct anything "Japanese" (or "Asian," "masculine," "young urban," "Harvard liberal," or whatever) about my observation and analysis.

In terms of methodology, the sample of my informants is fairly limited; in a sense, it is restricted by the fact that I might have been referred only to those families whose lives were relatively secure, crisis-free, and not dysfunctional. Although I was warmly invited to stay over at informants' homes on several occasions, it must be admitted that my reports emphasize what they said more than what they actually did. There was also a limit, both ethical and practical, to the extent that I could inquire into their lives, especially in the case of such highly private matters as money, sex, illness, and death. Politics could have been one of those sensitive topics, because the tension between liberals and conservatives, or Democrats and Republicans, seem to me very acute and far-reaching on both the academic and public levels in the United States. However, my informants were all unequivocal about their feelings and opinions concerning the government, abortion, homosexuality, foreign policy, and other topics.

The long-term commitment needed for this fieldwork made it difficult, even impossible, to bring in and scrutinize the younger generation, whose lives tended to be more hectic and mobile than those of their parents. As a result, nearly 60 percent of my informants turned out to be the parents of baby-boomers (those born between 1946 and 1964). Their sharp memories and vivid testimonies enabled me to trace a broad span of history since the

Second World War and see the evolution of habits and mentalities over the past several decades. This could not have been achieved by focusing on the younger generations, and it is well in phase with my project of understanding "processual America."

All these contingencies, inter-subjectivities, and technical constraints of my fieldwork inexorably allow me to furnish here only a partial reality of my informants' lives. The reality I perceived should be incessantly contested, compared, and thus refined by future scholars for the sake of "ensuring the perpetuation of a processual notion of America," as Kessler-Harris proposed.

Yet, on the other hand, every single aspect of the processes and phenomena that emerged in the course of this fieldwork – stereotyped ideas about my informants, skepticism of my investigation, the process of relationship-building, problems of confidentiality and "private" matters, the frequent cancellation of appointments, the relative inaccessibility of the baby-boomer generation, and the sensitized demarcation between "liberal" and "conservative" – furnished me with valuable insights into their microcosms, on which I will elaborate in the following chapters after briefly outlining a theoretical groundwork of this research.

Theoretical background

The natives' theories of their own cultures

For a long period, the analysis of kinship and family has been preoccupied with a formal approach, evinced most notably in descent theories (functionalism) and alliance theories (structuralism), which seeks to extract a set of behavioral patterns and categorical formulas. This preoccupation eventually led Rodney Needham (1971) to criticize not only the logical and epistemological looseness of the descent and alliance theories themselves but also to question the validity of the very concept of "kinship" in his now-famous statement:

> The term "kinship" is what Wittgenstein calls an "odd-job" word ... and we only get into trouble when we assume that it must have some specific function. ... To put it very bluntly, then, there is no such thing as kinship (p. 42).

What is missing in Needham's hyper-formal analysis and accompanying conclusion is the simple fact that local people nevertheless reflect upon and argue over "kinship" and "family" in their social discourse and practice. There is no reason to assume that local people use these categories (or idioms) in their everyday life with the same rigid and automatic precision that Needham does. As a matter of fact, these categories are used very flexibly, and their applications are by no means mechanical. Yet this does not justify the view that kinship and family are inappropriate for anthropological analysis. The question is what is behind the use of these categories and ideas (or ideologies). "Kinship" and "family" would become easy prey for "epistemological hypochondria" (Geertz 1988) if they lose vitality by being detached from people's own experiences and their sociocultural contexts.

David Maybury-Lewis (1979) shares Needham's criticism of descent and alliance theories, but follows quite a contrasting avenue guided by this recognition:

> [K]inship systems are ideological matrices and that their integrative or linking functions are so important that they cannot profitably be analyzed on their own. ... That is why we have attached such importance to *the natives' theories of their own cultures*, for it is through these that we have tried to understand the logic of their classifications and the meanings and use of their kinship systems (pp. 310–11: italics added).

This "meaning-centered" approach, in contrast to a formal one, is valuable both in illuminating the flexibility (i.e., indeterminacy, contingency, manipulability, and multivocality) of categories and in elucidating ideologies or themes that still inform and appropriate – not to say dictate – those idioms. In other words, the meaning-centered approach is open to the analysis of kinship and family "in culture" – in their interactions and transactions with other domains of social structure, process, and ideology. Such an approach would also benefit us in exploring a processual property of "America" in a more close and vivid way, as is intended in this research.

The analysis of kinship and family "in culture"

In this respect, David Schneider's cultural account of American kinship (1968) is an innovative one in conceiving kinship as a "system of symbols and meanings." Yet his work also provides us with another lesson for formulating and justifying a theoretical groundwork of this research.

His approach is a radical attempt to conceive kinship "in its pure form," without relating it to other social relations or actions. As a consequence, his analysis of kinship is devoid of any social dimension. Schneider concludes that love or the "diffuse, enduring solidarity" of kinship is a cultural product of the American preoccupation with biological facts: "[L]ove is what American kinship is all about" (p. 40), and "kinship is biology" (p. 116). While his insight into kinship as a social idiom fabricated on biological facts resonates with and encourages a constructionist view of kinship and gender, it does not supersede Raymond Firth's concept of kinship as "fundamentally a re-interpretation in social terms of the facts of procreation and regulated sex unions" (1936, p. 483), nor does it indicate how distinctively biological facts are signified in the American folk theory of kinship.

Similarly, his notion of American kinship as an affective domain corresponds closely to the general thesis on the modern family, but does not inform us further. Discourse on the affective dimension of family life has become conspicuous among the bourgeoisie since the late fifteenth century in European society. The eighteenth century witnessed a magnification of the discourse which emphasizes the pre-eminence of "love" in the familial sphere, especially between husband and wife (Shorter 1975), as well as parents and children (Aries 1960).[6] This "sentimental revolution" (Shorter 1975) sharpened the distinction between public and private spheres, as is well reflected in the proliferation of "private" rooms in the residential space, in the restriction of sociability with non-family members inside the house, and in the spatial and temporal seclusion of family life in the suburbs in eighteenth and nineteenth-century European society (Aries 1960; Sennett 1977). Elizabeth Badinter (1981) extracts the ideology of family love and femininity that is appropriated in the thoughts of social philosophers of that era (most notably in Jean-Jacques Rousseau's *Emile*) and associates this idealism with the prevalence of the modern bourgeois family. The modern state undertook to espouse and embrace this ideology by restricting factory labor by children and women, by raising the wages of male laborers, and by tightening corrective controls on dysfunctional families (Donzelot 1979; Lasch 1977).

These new developments concentrated families' investments in boys as future competitive laborers or resourceful entrepreneurs and in girls as prospective good wives and worthy mothers, and thus sustained the reproductive process of capitalism and family life. The connotation of "housewife" was transfigured from its pre-modern definition as a female supervisor of servants, nurses, and cooks in a larger familial community where domestic and private domains were far less segregated (Segalen 1983) to its modern version as a woman who finds meaning in housework, and this new concept was much applauded among the bourgeoisie and the working class (Badinter 1981; Lasch 1977; Oakley 1974; Smelser 1968). The tight link between family and affective sentiment in the United States, which Schneider characterizes as "diffuse, enduring solidarity," can be construed more as a product of these broader and complex socio-historical processes in the modern Western world than as the quintessence of the American family.

Nor is it a primordial archetype in the history of the United States. It is more a historical product, especially in the process of modernization that followed the Civil War. Robert Bellah et al. (1985) exemplify the encompassing ramifications of modernization in

> the division of life into a number of separate functional sectors: home and workplace, work and leisure, white collar and blue collar, public and private. This division suited the needs of the bureaucratic industrial corporations that provided the model for our preferred means of organizing society by the balancing and linking of sectors as "departments" in a functional whole, as in a great business enterprise (p. 43).

The departmentalization of life widened, naturalized, and ossified the polarity between the instrumental, "masculine" world of competitive work and the altruistic, "feminine" world of nurturing domesticity.[7] It was during this period that love and domesticity increasingly became sentimentalized as a "haven in a heartless world," as symbolized in the distinct contrast between the suburban residential ambiance of peace, morality, and concord and the urban industrial surroundings of calculation, competition, and negotiation.[8] It was also during this period that "Mother's Day," which had originally been a vehicle for celebrating the organized social and political activities of mothers outside the household, became sentimentalized and commercialized as a special day for commemorating mothers' roles inside the home (Coontz 1992).

This social interpretation of biological difference reinforced, and was reinforced by, the departmentalization or nuclearization of the family by the state. According to Stephanie Coontz (1992), American social policy in the nineteenth century was particularly designed

> to free the nuclear family from its former entanglements with kin and neighbors and to concentrate previously diffused economic and social responsibilities for children within the nuclear family. Courts invalidated colonial laws establishing minimum ages at marriage and requiring parental consent or public announcement of marriage banns. Legislators lowered marriage fees and authorized increasing numbers of officials to perform marriages. These actions made it easier to form a nuclear family without consulting kin or community (p. 128).

The state's generation and empowerment of autonomous, departmentalized, and nuclearized families against an extended-kin network, community associations, and local rulers helped not only to stimulate the process of modernization, but also to augment the preponderance of objective, universal principles of the public sphere over subjective, particularistic relationships in the private, domestic domain.[9] The family as an arena of "diffusing, enduring solidarity" is thus a political invention with complex consequences rather than a primordial archetype.

Michel Foucault (1978) critically maintains that modern society accorded eternal and transcendental power to love. The ascendancy of love is appropriated in the name of "sacrifice," "disinterest," "dedication," "understanding," "trust," and "commitment." Ivan Illich (1981) demonstrates that there are a good number of laborious but uncompensated tasks that must be undertaken as a token of love for all family members, and these "shadow works" often comprise obligations, duties, and responsibilities in the familial sphere.[10] The externalization of domestic functions (e.g. dietary, educational, and nursing roles) to outside agents often has a propensity to make the expression of love from the family (mothers and wives in particular) more demanding and quintessential, which is well exemplified in the commodification of family leisure activities, in incessant debates about parents' overprotection of children, and in hypersensitivity about childrearing techniques.

As Jean-Louis Flandrin (1979) illustrates by detailing the relation between marriage for love and rates of divorce, the glorification of love is often accompanied by the possibility of disillusionment. This was certainly true in the United States, where the ascendancy of emotional and erotic intimacy came to excuse the termination of a relationship that had ceased to stimulate or provide romantic solace and promise (Hochschild 1983; May 1980, 1988; Peele 1976; Sennett 1977). By the end of the nineteenth century, the United States had the highest divorce rate in the world (Mintz and Kellogg 1988). This is ironic when love is supposed to be a cornerstone of "diffuse, enduring solidarity," but Schneider fails to delineate the potential instabilities and conflicts of family life that are precipitated, or concealed, by the ideology of love. This oversight is the result of his mode of analysis, which aims at understanding the meanings underlying the kinship system in isolation from people's particular social experiences and actions.

Schneider's approach thus paradoxically proves that a "system of symbols and meanings" of kinship cannot be profitably analyzed in its "pure form." For a more sophisticated understanding, kinship needs to be conceived in culture, without isolating it from the wider sociocultural and historical contexts in which it is situated, and from the patterns of social actions. In this sense, Sylvia Yanagisako's observation that "a good many Americans think about family and kinship relations in terms of cultural-historical categories" (1985, p. 285) has a theoretical significance in denoting the relevance and necessity of further advancing the

meaning-centered approach. My research is grounded in this theoretical track and aims to scrutinize the construction and practice of
the family and kinship in their interactions with the wider social
structures, processes, and ideologies in the United States in the
postwar era.

Denaturalizing the American family

This approach shares a conceptual and methodological framework
with that of gender studies as advanced and elaborated by feminist scholarship. Their notion of gender, as a particular way of
viewing and ordering relationships between men and women as
shaped by sociocultural factors rather than by biological facts per
se, is well represented by Yanagisako and Jane Collier (1987):

> [T]here are no "facts," biological or material, that have
> social consequences and cultural meanings in and of them-
> selves. Sexual intercourse, pregnancy, and parturition are
> cultural facts, whose form, consequences, and meanings
> are socially constructed in any society, as are mothering,
> fathering, judging, ruling, and talking with the gods
> (p. 39).

This concept mirrors the constructionist perspective of kinship
offered by Firth (and later propagated by Schneider) as a social
idiom fabricated on the genealogical grid, but it was not until recent
years, as they argue, that the inseparable tie between kinship and
gender came to be widely recognized and proclaimed in ethnographic scholarship (Yanagisako and Collier 1987; Yanagisako and
Delaney 1995).

Underlying this new direction towards a unified analysis of
kinship and gender is a criticism of Parsonian structural-functionalism. Talcott Parsons (1954) emphasizes the structural predominance and functional pre-eminence of the structurally isolated
conjugal family in an open-class, advanced industrial society like
that of the United States. The conjugal family is assumed to
approximate the most functional form of domestic arrangements
for fulfilling the structural necessities (childrearing, socialization,
and the psychological needs of individuals) in capitalist industrial

societies; all the strains and contradictions in the domestic sphere tend to be dismissed either as negligible side-effects or as the unexpected stimulus for the functional adaptation and integration of the social whole. The division of family labor by sex and the specialization of women in the home and in family activities are naturalized, vindicated, and advocated in the name of maximizing function and efficiency.

However, it should be remembered that such strong convictions about the supremacy of the family had an effect in the form of what Bourdieu (1977) terms "symbolic violence," imposing a particular norm on people's thoughts and behavior. Most of the American women who wished to continue to participate in the public sphere after their wartime employment were granted few options but to retreat to housewifery or to downgraded, lower-paid "female" jobs (Hartmann 1982; McLaughlin et al. 1988; Milkman 1987). Women who did not embrace "mom-ism" and "creative homemaking" were stigmatized as perverted, neurotic, or schizophrenic. Bachelors and spinsters were considered immature, self-centered, deviant, or pathological (Ehrenreich 1983; Hartmann 1982; Miller and Nowak 1977; Mintz and Kellogg 1988; Warren 1987). In addition, the ideology of the family as the "haven in a heartless world" encouraged the nuclear family to isolate itself by developing a series of codes of prohibited and expected behavior (Eisler 1986; Pleck 1987). Linda Gordon (1988) argues that it was not until the feminist movement in the 1970s that women could possibly disclose cases of incest and sexual abuse. According to Coontz, "one-quarter to one-third of the marriages contracted in the 1950s eventually ended up in divorce; during that decade two million legally married people lived apart from each other," and "[m]any more couples simply toughed it out" (1992, p. 36; see also Pleck 1987).

More American housewives, especially young mothers, felt "trapped" in their feminine roles (Chafe 1986; Crawford 1978; Friedan 1963; Miller and Nowak 1977; Mintz and Kellogg 1988). Coontz continues, "[t]ranquilizers were developed in the 1950s in response to a need that physicians explicitly saw as female: Virtually nonexistent in 1955, tranquilizer consumption reached 462,000 pounds in 1958 and soared to 1.15 million pounds merely a year later" (1992, p. 36). Men also felt "trapped" in their identity and self-image in masculine roles, and developed a sense of discontent and exasperation with their commitment (Ehrenreich 1983). This symbolic violence afflicted and stigmatized the poor and minorities in particular, as they had too little access to resources and privileges to be able to espouse the white middle-class family image (Barnouw 1975; Danielson 1976; Patterson 1986; Stack 1996; Taylor 1989; Wilson 1996).

Inherent in Parsons' model is an optimistic conservatism that rationalizes, instead of problematizing, the potential instabilities and conflicts of family life, and an unquestioned perpetuation of the essentially arbitrary boundary between kinship and gender as an axiom. Bourdieu (1977) maintains that every established order has a propensity to produce the naturalization of its own arbitrariness. It might be said that Parsonian structural-functionalism is mystified by the seemingly self-evident and stable institutional orders without denaturalizing the "naturalizing power" (Yanagisako and Delaney 1995) of social structures, processes, and ideologies in the domains of kinship and gender.

An investigation of the contemporary American family requires particular attention to this point. Industrial expansion, the increased cost of living, the diffusion of new home appliances, and the drop in fertility, among other factors, demanded the accommodation of women, single and married, in the labor force. Between 1940 and 1950, the number of women at work increased by 29 percent. By the end of the 1950s, 40 percent of women over the age of 16 held a job. The number of women working outside the home rose by 39 percent in the 1960s and by 41 percent in the 1970s. This amplified involvement of women in the labor force stimulated increased college enrollments for women and the postponement of marriage and childbearing among couples, which in turn spurred women's further participation in the public sphere and re-examination of their roles and identity in the private realm.

Between 1940 and 1960, the number of working mothers increased by 400 percent, and women with children under the age of 18 comprised nearly a third of all women workers by 1960 (Chafe 1991; Easterlin 1980; Kessler-Harris 1982; Harrison 1988; Ryan 1975; Van Horn 1988; Weiner 1985). Housewives, who until the 1950s had been "supposed to find their moral meaning, political significance, and societal worth in clean laundry collars, new curtains, and creative cookery" (Coontz 1992, p. 164),[11] thus acquired options and incentives, not only for themselves but also for their husbands, to discontinue unfulfilling relationships in the interest of personal social rebirth (Matthews 1987; Stacey 1990; Van Horn 1988). The frailty of marriage conversely resulted in driving more women to work (Cherlin 1981; Gerson 1985). An inflation rate that was higher than the average rise in incomes in the 1970s made two wages per household vital for any continued improvement in real income, and this compelled more women, especially mothers of young children, into the labor force (Coontz 1992; Van Horn 1988).

These transformations have provoked a public reflection on the "traditional" boundaries between man (public) and woman (private) as fabricated and perpetuated in particular times and places rather than as natural, universal, or timeless. How do people experience this shake-up of dichotomies in their practice of social relations, and what in turn does this re-examination of dichotomies do for social relations? These issues would be most profitably analyzed by denaturalizing kinship and gender in culture – in their interactions and negotiations with social structures, processes, and ideologies, which is the aim of the meaning-centered approach and a good means for "ensuring the perpetuation of a processual notion of America."

Guided by this approach, Chapters 2 and 3 furnish ethnographies of the Boston Brahmins and the Boston Irish respectively. A special emphasis is placed on elucidating the ways in which these two groups internalize and appropriate the rapid and complex transfigurations of postwar society in constructing their own cultural histories and social realities and in undertaking the actual practice of everyday life and engagement in social relations. Chapter 4 compares these two groups in a contrasting sociocultural milieu, extracts from their differences some common features, and contextualizes the ethnographic present in a northeastern city within larger processes of late-modern (or postmodern) America.

The families portrayed in the following chapters do not represent statistical averages or norms. Rather, these families attracted my special attention because of their intense engagement with an art of life within their social contexts. They are "ideal types" in the most symbolic sense.

2 The Yankee family

A contested society

Competing voices

"Flattening of the pyramid": that is how Theodore Lowell Appleton, a lawyer, characterizes the social transformations that he has witnessed at first hand during his lifelong, nearly half-century residence on Beacon Hill – the symbolic capital of prosperity and prestige in Boston.[1] "Flattening" here indicates a "process of democratization in which privilege has become less accessible" and there has been a "massive movement towards the American dream of egalitarianism." He vividly recalls a day in the mid-1950s when he was terribly shocked to come across a Black person for the first time in his wealthy, WASP-dominated neighborhood. This incident revealed to him that society was becoming highly complicated because of the influx of "newcomers" from different sociocultural backgrounds. By the end of the 1960s, holding open house on Christmas Eve ceased to be a tradition, not only for the Appletons but also for other Yankee families in his circle on Beacon Hill, due to fear that strangers might steal items or take advantage of their hospitality by, for example, making long-distance telephone calls.[2] The erosion of social homogeneity and the accompanying reduction of cultural barriers caused the residential eligibility in his neighborhood to be determined increasingly by the principle of economic Darwinism: the survival of the richest. Whereas previously only "proper" Bostonians had houses on Beacon Hill, anyone with enough money is now able to live there. At the same time, the opulent living style of many old families has declined. The Appletons employed and housed seven full-time, live-in maids until the 1950s, but the soaring costs of real estate and personnel today allows them to keep only one live-in and one part-time helper.

The boundaries of exclusivity and privilege have become less clear cut for Theodore Appleton than they used to be. He provided me with several examples of Brahmin families that had left Beacon

Hill because they did not feel comfortable living in this changing social environment and ethos in the postwar era. He sounds both critical and sympathetic of the "newcomers" who are "functioning in no context or in a context in which they have never been before." According to him, the complexity of social contexts makes it hard for the American public to appreciate the mores and customs of society, inclining people to live by a principle of "hyper-individualism" that negates a sense of duty to society or to family. Popular discourse on the "family in crisis" is misleading, in his opinion, because it is the fact that "values are in crisis" which is a more fundamental and pressing issue in American society today. "'If you don't like it, just leave it' – there is no limit to such a mentality in our society!"

William Lyman Saltonstall, a banker as well as a neighbor and contemporary of Theodore Appleton, construes the "disintegration of boundary and connectedness in society" as a repercussion of the rapid socio-demographic transfigurations in the postwar era, and associates this unboundedness with what he perceives as the "breakdown of prohibitions of conduct." He admits that there is a positive side to this – for instance, in the informalization of family life, which he illuminated with examples of his relatives in former generations who had to leave Boston to secure their marriages with "outsiders." This kind of pressure is, according to him, "unthinkable today except for some very stuffy people." However, he regrets that "informality" is oftentimes confused with "discourtesy" and "irre-sponsibility," feeling as if the values that he has grown up with – respecting elderly people, appreciating the perceived notion of goodness, refraining from using "dirty" language in front of women, among many others – have become almost anachronistic today. Having spent his life in different parts of the world, he is particularly apprehensive about two distinctly "American" prob-lems: the fragility of residential stability and the existent prejudice against other generations (both above and below one's own) as being essentially incapable and useless; this latter, he believes, creates a lack of historical continuity and the preoccupation with a "feel for piety only for one's own interest just ahead."

Samuel Adams, a college professor in West Cambridge in his early fifties, offers a more positive interpretation of the "democrati-zation" and "rationalization" of the postwar society that he has witnessed with Theodore Appleton and William Saltonstall. He exemplifies the Yankees' "fall from grace" by pointing out the declining number of Brahmins on the boards of trustees at prominent institutions, in the *Social Register*, and on the alumni records of prestigious schools, and by elucidating the current preponderance of multi-ethnic organizations over their predominantly Yankee counterparts. He maintains that "each group should have a time in the sun" in American society, and therefore the "twilight of Yankee hegemony" is quite "fair." The "breakdown of prohibitions of conducts" that bothers William Saltonstall seems more liberation than decadence to Samuel Adams.

This feeling is magnified especially when he recollects all sorts of stories that his father used to tell – in a derisive tone – about the old Yankee culture. Adams's father was raised by his maternal relatives, a family of great prominence, after the suicide of his father. He and his brother became increasingly hostile and defiant in reaction to a series of "suffocating" and "snobbish" codes of behavior in the Brahmin family, only to be pigeonholed as the "Wild Adamses" by members of his maternal family. His rebellion against the prescribed lifestyle led him to opt for Massachusetts College of Art instead of Harvard College, which was deemed *the* college and attended by his friends and kin of his age. Later, during his tenure as a federal senator, he repeated to his staff: "I am not a Harvard graduate. Don't ask me why!"

He acknowledges the inheritance of his father's abhorrence of the Brahmin culture in himself; and as such, even with a slight regret for his father's overemphasis on the "nuclear type" of relationship in his own family, confesses that he is still prone to view his family history rather negatively. "I feel I am trying to 'graduate from' or 'transcend' the provincialism of Yankee culture," he says, and "I feel I am becoming more and more myself in this process." However, he simultaneously speculates that this iconoclastic mentality might ironically be the very expression of traditional Yankee culture, in light of the fact that "New England conservatism is more liberal than that of blue-collar liberals, or the so-called 'Reagan Democrats.'"

He shares the concerns of Theodore Appleton and William Saltonstall about the "me-ism" and "narcissism" in our society that are "glorified by the mass media" and "symbolized by New

York City," but he believes this phenomenon is an expression of a "social pendulum," and that American society has a proven ability to "reinvent" itself. Samuel Adams wonders if what Mr. Appleton calls "hyper-individualism" is worse than the social despotism of "what you are" and "what you must do" that tortured his father.

Diana Appleton Sears, an English teacher in Beverly Farms and a contemporary of the above three informants, echoes Samuel Adams in her celebration of the postwar emancipation from "compliance with the prescribed way of life." The prescription here comprises "being preoccupied with a 'good' marriage, judging people by class, maintaining tradition, remaining a 'proper' Bostonian, and being clubby." She claims she has "actively avoided the kinds of people that she should have embraced" and that her daughter "has none of the social functions that my mother had." Ms. Sears was enchanted by the opened-up "freedom to do something else – going to college, meeting 'other' people, and staying away from the weak and de-spirited Yankee boys" that she discovered in the 1960s. This sense of "claustrophobia" does, in her opinion, go beyond her own experience – having reflected on, and been intensified by, the prevalence of such communicative instruments as cars and telephones in the postwar national culture. Her parents' lifestyle appears "too much enclosed, limited, and narrow to embrace," and she surmises that this impression is widely shared by her siblings and friends. "I am sure my parents got so appalled, disgusted, and disappointed [with us], but I feel they are also envious."

In reality, her mother was very reluctant to expound on the culture of her younger days, declaring that "those days are all gone, and I simply don't care about it any more!" Diana Sears agrees that people are having a difficult time relating themselves to a larger society. "People don't understand what they are doing for what." "People are unclear about what men and women are meant to be." "Self-fulfillment" is, according to her, a "fairly recent concept in American history," and as such "people are confused about what it exactly means." She predicts that "American society will be more fragmented, having so many people from so many backgrounds with so many different notions of 'society' and 'family.'" However, she adds, "that's fine with me. People can stick to the kind of people they like. At least, that's better than being 'dictated' to by others, isn't it?"

Common voices

Interestingly enough, the above four informants – all graduates of Harvard or Radcliffe College in the 1960s who were born and brought up in the Boston area – share an observation that social ethos and cohesiveness have been undermined and fragmented in the postwar era, enlarging the sphere of individual freedom and autonomy.[3] Theodore Appleton and William Saltonstall emphasize the negative consequences of such individuation or individualism by expounding on the disintegration of "context," "mores," "prohibitions," and "continuity" that Samuel Adams and Diana Sears would see as constraining and moralizing. Mr. Adams and Ms. Sears, in contrast, accentuate the positive ramifications of this process by elucidating the "liberation" from social "dictation" and the prospect for developing the real "self" that Mr. Appleton and Mr. Saltonstall would deem deceptive and solitary.

It is perhaps an exaggeration to place Mr. Appleton and Mr. Saltonstall in the pessimistic-conservative camp and Mr. Adams and Ms. Sears in the optimistic-liberal camp. Their interpretations and sentiments appear to be more mixed, ambivalent, and contingent, and as such could be articulated with a high degree of flexibility in other circumstances. Yet their answers and reactions embrace the polarity within which nearly all my other informants could be located, regardless of several social variables that could have had decisive impacts on their experiences and viewpoints. While comprising a multitude of differences in facts and nuances, this polarity itself seems to demonstrate that the dichotomy between individuals and society is highly sensitized to the frame of reference, and that my informants are seeking a balance by making their own diagnoses of the status quo.

There are three other commonalties in their observations and discourses that seem to be central to their construction of reality. First, the image of a "flattening of the pyramid" is shared by all the informants that I interviewed, and is articulated in such expressions as "decline of Yankee hegemony in terms of value, economy, politics, and culture," "endangered WASP species," "loss of a sense of security," "breakdown of boundaries between social groups," "opening up of society," "democratization," and "rationalization." Here again, their interpretations of and feelings about this perceived transformation of society fall within the sphere of ambivalence and contestation, yet the very recognition that they no longer embody the cultural hegemony of American society seems hardly disputed. The erosion of the Brahmin economic base by the Great Depression, the intensification of the idea of meritocracy, the intensification of competition, the decline of the extended family and nepotism, and the relativization of Anglo-Saxon Protestant culture through demographic diversification and the Civil Rights movement – all these phenomena are unanimously mentioned by my informants to substantiate the perceived "downward slope" in their social map. "Society is not so simple and cannot be taken for granted anymore." This perception sharpens their sensitivity to the terms used to describe people of their social standing.

I am using such phrases as "Yankee," "WASP," and "Brahmin" in this book as a kind of shorthand to refer to those who belong to the upper/upper-middle class, Anglo-Saxon, Protestant (usually Unitarian or Episcopalian) segment of society.[4] However, these terms sometimes carry such negative connotations as arrogance, oppression, elitism, and snobbery. This being so, some informants admonished me to be cautious of using these phrases in front of other people who might feel uncomfortable about them. They testify that such nuances came to weigh on their minds at the time of the Civil Rights movement in the late 1960s. How then should one name them in a politically correct fashion? "Old families in Boston" is the expression that I found most convenient during actual communication with my informants, being indicative enough without suggesting more than I intended. In any case, all these details could be seen as evidence that the legitimacy of these families' pre-eminence in society is being questioned and contested to such an extent that even their referential names are sensitive issues.

Second, most informants openly expressed their reservations or lack of confidence in accounting for their experiences and theories in reference to a larger context, or to other segments of American society. Their comments on American society were accompanied by such preambles as "I am perhaps wrong, but ...," "I don't think I can talk about society beyond Boston or New England, but ...," and "I am not sure if we can talk about the 'American society' today, but ...". Some found it impossible to characterize even the case of Boston, acknowledging their unfamiliarity with "other" kinds of people in the area and their lives. Some drew on bits and pieces of facts and viewpoints that they recollected from books, newspapers, radio programs, friends, and relatives, only to realize the difficulty of encompassing the extraordinary complexities and multiplicities of the American mosaic. All these can be construed as an indication of their modesty, delicacy, and sincerity, yet at the same time as an exemplification of the fact that American society is perceived as too multiplex, heterogeneous, and segmented to be "imagined" (Anderson 1983) as a synthetic context or connected whole.

It is perhaps too hasty to use this phenomenon to demonstrate that American society is in reality fragmentary and divided. In a sense, the society is more connected and condensed than ever by an expansion of the national economy, by a web of highly elaborated communication and transportation systems and by a process of "democratization" in which the possibility of interactions beyond one's own sociocultural boundaries and categories has been magnified. Mr. Appleton, for instance, today appreciates congenial friendships with several Jewish people, which he asserts would have been "quite unbelievable" to his parents' generation. My informants are having a difficult time not so much in actually encountering others as in describing others properly without revealing their possible ignorance and prejudice. This becomes a more salient issue when the ideological difference between "liberal" and "conservative" is highly sensitized and the WASP-White hegemony is called into question. The picture of society as a whole is therefore too opaque an abstraction, and talking about "others" (and consequently "themselves" as well) is too perplexing and delicate a task.

Finally, the perceived social changes in the Boston area were articulated, in most cases, by illustrations from their own families as a point of reference. This can be interpreted as a manifestation of the fact that the family is an integral part of their social universe. It is often claimed that the family has lost importance in modern society, and this seems to be correct in the sense that the family no longer possesses continuous, complete, and governing power in social structures and functions. Yet my informants made it explicit that the family is the matrix of their explanatory scheme, or the center of their cognitive map, of society. If the family is thus "good to think" in Levi-Straussian terms (1963), then it should be worth scrutinizing. In the following sections, I will elaborate on the "politics of culture" – how these perceived social changes in the postwar era (the fragmentation of social boundaries and cohesiveness, the intensification of individualism, the de-centering of the Yankee hegemony, and the complication or abstraction of the larger social picture) are all grounded, exemplified, and appraised in my informants' actual lives and experiences.

The intergenerational transformation

As mentioned in Chapter 1, the contacts with my research families were made possible by referrals. Although I made my curiosity explicit concerning "old families in Boston" to the intermediaries, I did not request any particular variables or rigid criteria in their selection of specific families because I was interested in what kinds of variables or criteria the intermediaries themselves would apply in their own interpretations and definitions of the category. As a matter of fact, I found their definitions were formulated with a high degree of flexibility and subjectivity, but by no means in an uninformed manner. They usually legitimized their selections by emphasizing such points of "distinction" (Bourdieu 1984) as residential area, occupation, education, wealth, club membership, and family genealogy. There seems to be a multitude of subtle distinctions and hierarchies within each element, but it appears that their selections had more to do with their own intuitions about the overall "images" of the families than with a careful calculation of such subtlety exemplified in reality.

Such families as the Adamses, Appletons, Cabots, Coolidges, Eliots, Forbeses, Gardners, Lodges, Lowells, Peabodies, Saltonstalls, Welds, and Winthrops were often imagined as being at the core of the "circle" of old families, while others were perceived as being more marginal to the essentially ambiguous boundaries of the circle (or category).[5] The geometrical progression in family size makes it impossible to speak about the Coolidges as one category;

one informant told me that there exist approximately 2,000 Coolidges in the world today, who are "mixed up with all sorts of people." However, as far as this research is concerned, I am dealing only with the specific Coolidges who are perceived as embodying the "image" of the old Boston families. A methodology that relies on "images" (although by no means wild speculations) might be disadvantageous because it results in a certain fuzziness of the research boundaries, but is beneficial in dealing with the ambiguities, intricacies, and contestations of the social realities and lived experiences of these families. In this section, I would first like to delineate the intergenerational transformation of social backgrounds by taking up the cases of four families identified as "Brahmin families" in two books – Cleveland Amory's *The Proper Bostonians* (1947) and Mary Crawford's *Famous Families of Massachusetts* (1930) – that my informants often recommended for my reference.

Downward mobility and diversification

Francis Hancock's ancestors immigrated from England around 1630 and settled in Watertown, in the vicinity of Boston, as what he calls "middle-class, religious radicals." The Tories' retreat during War of Independence opened up the opportunity for the younger sons of previously middle-class families in the vicinity to fill the vacant positions of the upper-class stratum in Boston. A couple of generations down, Francis' grandfather lived in the heyday of the Brahmin hegemony, becoming a well-established lawyer, marrying the "richest woman in Boston," and raising five children, three of whom became Harvard professors, one an ambassador, and one a lawyer. Francis' father was an astronomer at Harvard and a father of eight children, including two Harvard professors and other "high professionals" in business, medicine, and law. Francis, now in his early eighties, has served as a professor of archaeology at Harvard, director of Harvard's Peabody Museum, vice-president of the Society of American Archaeologists, and president of the Peabody-Essex Museum.

Until Francis' generation, virtually every upper-class Boston boy was educated at private schools and at Harvard College and then married a "proper" woman in the same social circle, while girls were expected to marry "proper" men after attending day schools and then to engage in charitable activities. Francis however, like Mr. Adams, highlights a "tradition of non-tradition" in the Anglo-Saxon culture, and illustrates such iconoclasm or "eccentricity" by many examples. For instance, "astronomy" – the subject that his father pursued – was deemed to be "very radical" in those days, when such humanistic disciplines as archaeology, art, history, literature, and philosophy were more conventional and apposite. In another example, Francis was the only person who voted for the implementation of affirmative action for Black applicants to the Peabody-Essex Museum. Yet, as he admits, such a "tradition of non-tradition", in most cases, existed within orthodox institutional frameworks.

Francis, however, reflects that such orthodoxy itself has gradually become a part of the non-tradition of the postwar era. For instance, the average number of children per couple decreased from "several" to "a few" in his generation. Francis perceives this as symbolic of some pivotal transformations in the "old" culture. From an economic perspective, declining fortunes made it difficult to afford maids to take care of many children or to ensure sufficient financial support for their education through college. Francis himself longed for a "simpler life" after being heavily involved in building a Catholic church for his Irish maids at his summer home in Vermont. From a cultural point of view, the decrease was induced by skepticism or antagonism to the custom of childrearing by nannies and by the permeation of the ideal of the nuclear family and parental love. Francis speculates that these two factors, economic and cultural, reinforced each other, and that the prevalence of family-sized cars since the end of the First World War was stimulated by, and has perpetuated, these new developments. The orthodoxy of the large family thus ceased to be a tradition in his generation.

In addition, family composition became more diversified. Francis has spent nearly two decades outside New England for teaching purposes, and the recession in Boston and the nationalization of the job market have placed his siblings in similar circumstances. This mobility has "enlightened" his generation by lowering their emotional barriers to other Americans and foreigners. Francis notes that his neighborhood off Brattle Street, a "proper" street in Cambridge, became significantly diversified after the First World

War, due in particular to the influx of professionals not only from other parts of the United States but also from overseas. As a matter of fact, Francis' sister and her daughter were the first in the family to marry foreigners (both German). All these circumstances have inclined Francis to stay away from "proper but uninspiring" Bostonians and even to relinquish his membership at one of the most prestigious social clubs in Boston.

According to Francis, his offspring are still predominantly Protestant (either Episcopalian or Unitarian), and are married to Anglo-Saxons. However, recent years have seen several Hancocks marrying Catholics and Jews, which Francis imagines would, in his grandparents' generation, have been possible only at the risk of disinheritance. Francis openly acknowledges his "unexpressed expectation for his granddaughters to get married to 'similar kinds'," but he emphasizes that the "capacity of affection" should not be impeded by such social factors as religion, race, ethnicity, education, and class. Admission to Harvard has become more difficult for the elite families in recent years because of Harvard's merit-based decision making and affirmative action. As a consequence, a majority of Francis' offspring, male and female, have pursued their college educations at such places as Stanford, U.C. Santa Barbara, Rochester University, and the University of Colorado, and continue to be dispersed all across the nation.[6]

High academic accomplishments still enable them to continue to engage in "high professional" occupations at private schools, universities, museums, and private companies; but Francis notes the emergence of craftsmen among the descendants of his wife's family of local prominence. His offspring seldom belong to social clubs, partly because they do not have sufficient resources and partly because they simply have no inclination to participate in that exclusive, old-style culture. Francis' house off Brattle Street is worth more than a million dollars, but he is thinking of selling it soon because he suspects that none of his offspring can afford it. He has many pieces of art, both in his home and at museums, and some of these are worth more than $30–40,000. He also used to own a 36-bedroom summer house near a lake in Vermont, but it was sold outside the family several years ago for about $1 million. All these assets would undoubtedly leave a substantial inheritance to his offspring, but Francis has little doubt that it will be far from enough to live on, and that his family fortunes will continue to decline.

I was able to interview Francis' daughter, Susan, then in her mid-fifties, who used to be a graphic designer at the *New Yorker* magazine and is now a painter. She divorced a "proper" Bostonian and now cohabits with her boyfriend in Michigan. Her testimony corroborates Francis' observations. As she reflects, she was raised in period of transition from "old" to "new" Boston. She acknowledges with gratitude her father's iconoclastic cultural orientation (including the abolition of such family rituals as Christmas dinner) and strong insistence on the "self." "My mother and father shared a great reluctance to make one's own capital by using the family name. I am very proud that my accomplishment was due not to who I am but to what I did." Having been raised in Chicago, Washington D.C., and New York, she has little attachment to Boston, and has no intention to live there. Her stories reminded me of a day when Francis told me that one of the most dramatic changes at Harvard that he has witnessed over the past six decades is the striking increment of "nervous breakdowns" among students because of escalating competition and pressure to succeed. My conjecture is that Francis himself well recognized the transition of the "old" culture to the "new" one, in which ascribed status is less significant than self-achievement based on the principle of tough competition, and the process of democratization in which the prosperity of the Hancocks is gradually fading. The value of "self-help" needed to be underlined to ensure his daughter's success.

* * *

A grandfather of Thomas Winthrop acquired great wealth in the China trade in the 1860s and founded one of the most prestigious social clubs in Boston. He used to spend winters on Beacon Hill, springs and autumns in Dedham, and summers in Southwest Harbor – all in the "proper" areas. Thomas's father was a "typical upper-class man," being the president of a bank in Boston that survived even the hardest days of the Great Depression, a leading figure in charitable activities that included financial assistance to Jewish immigrants, a recipient of decorations from such countries as China and the United Kingdom, and the author of nearly 60 books. Thomas's mother was educated at Radcliffe College, where she met her husband, who was then attending Harvard. Widely known for her musical talent and charm, she was a "center of high society" not only in Boston but also in New York, Philadelphia, London, and Paris. Thomas's parents also resided seasonally at various "proper" locations in New England. Up to this generation, the family background bears a close resemblance to that of Francis Hancock: everybody was educated at private schools and married to the "same kind" – Anglo-Saxon, Protestant (usually Episcopalian or Unitarian) Bostonians – with the exception of Thomas's mother, who originally came from Philadelphia; virtually all the boys were educated at Harvard and engaged in high-ranking professional occupations.

Thomas, now in his mid-seventies, however, testifies to some salient transformations of family traditions in his generation and thereafter. He is quick to reveal his unpalatable sentiments towards his parents: "I never loved them." He is truly grateful to them for having provided him with precious opportunities for education and travel, and certainly respects his father's liberal mind and his mother's social skills. However, he still finds it difficult to feel affection for them because of his negative memories.

Thomas was raised by nannies because his parents had their own things to do. He seldom saw his father, and his mother spared only a couple of minutes for him before his bedtime. He vividly recalls a day when he was "appalled" at witnessing his mother's sudden dismissal, over a fairly trivial matter, of an Irish maid who had been working for the family for more than 20 years: "My mother was a bitch." His father, an "extraordinarily authoritative" man, was already 50 years old when Thomas was born.

Thomas often suspected that his father was "manipulating" him, and he was "sick of being 'told' to do something." "My father was always an old man." These experiences served only to consolidate Thomas's resolution concerning parenthood: "The main part of childrearing lasts only for 15 years, until kids become high school students. Why don't you enjoy that short period with them? Be friendly with them. Rely on their own judgment. Let them do what they want to do." Thomas sent all his children to a "liberal" prep school, for he felt suffocated by the "confining" and "restrictive" atmosphere of St. Paul's, which had been the family school for the Winthrops.

Thomas is also perplexed by his father's remark that "Marriage is just like a bus. As long as you ride on it, that's fine." His parents' married life appeared to Thomas a "hypocrisy" or a "convenience." "You shouldn't take your marriage for granted. You must carefully watch where the bus is heading!" Tired of serving as a "peacemaker" in the home, Thomas left home after finishing Harvard, and went to Princeton to do his graduate work, on the G.I. Bill. His frustration and indignation towards his parents and "high society" were channeled constructively, but his brother's suicide shortly after the Second World War was, Thomas felt, closely tied to his parents' restrictions; his brother's will indicated that he felt "trapped" by the customs and values of the society that he was born into. Thomas described to me similar incidents that occurred in other Bostonian families in the 1950s and 1960s, and interpreted these cases as a representation of what *Atlantic Monthly* described in the 1950s as the "Boston Disease": Boston males' inability to create a life of their own.

Thomas obtained his Ph.D. in Chinese history and taught at Yale for five years, but in his forties, during the early 1960s, he decided to concentrate on building a family museum by renovating his grandfather's house in Dedham. The museum reached its spatial limit, and he transferred some of his collection to Boston's Museum of Fine Arts in 1987. It was not until 1976 that his family museum produced a "marginal profit," but his family assets have provided him with financial security. He now lives in a "two-family house" in a wealthy "upper-middle-class, professional" neighborhood in Cambridge and receives a monthly rent from his tenant. He used to rent out another house he owned in Cambridge, but recently sold it for approximately $800,000 after being frustrated by the abuse of the "rent-control" system by rich tenants. Further, he has disposed of part of his family collection for about $300,000. Because of his enthusiasm for the arts, he retires to his study to work after dinner, and enjoys giving lectures at various museums around Boston.

Thomas is a member of many intellectual and political institutions, but does not belong to any social clubs in Boston as he considers them "a bit narrow." His five siblings, all graduates of

Harvard or Radcliffe College, still maintain a kind of "upper-middle-class" life in the Greater Boston area, especially in Pride's Crossing, one of the popular residential spots among old families in Boston. Thomas feels that his siblings in the suburbs tend to be slightly more "conservative," "closed," and "clubby" in terms of their social consciousness and relationships. However, he observes that faith in religion and in "endogamy" have been somewhat enfeebled in his generation. Thomas and his siblings are technically Unitarian, but they never go to church, whereas their parents were strict churchgoers. "We are the so-called Home Baptists!" His siblings all married people of the "same level," but one Jewish Pole and one Briton have married into the Winthrop family.

His wife is a graduate of Radcliffe College, and comes from a wealthy, Anglo-Saxon family in New York. One of their two sons transferred to a public school, worked at a construction company after graduation, then ran a real estate company in Concord with his cousin, and now works for *Time* magazine on a part-time basis while enrolled at the New Jersey Institute of Technology. He is engaged to a social worker from a middle-class Jewish family in Boston who is now pursuing her graduate degree at Columbia. The other son withdrew from Brown, worked in Wall Street, enrolled at Georgetown where his wife was a medical intern and received his Ph.D. in European history from Cornell, where he now teaches. He converted to Judaism at the age of 18 or 19, even before he met his wife, who is from an upper-middle-class Jewish family in New York City. The couple recently adopted two children from Korea, who now enjoy Thomas's lavish affection. "They are pioneers of the global family!" It is a little too early for him to expound on the family life of this generation, but he presages that this process of "diversification" of family traditions in terms of residence, occupation, education, marriage, and genealogy will not be turned back, even by other branches of the suburban Winthrops.

Referring to de Tocqueville's *Democracy in America*, Thomas maintains that the absence of primogeniture has accelerated the decline of entrenched fortunes and has thus promoted egalitarianism in American society. As he reflects, few Brahmin families are immune to this process, and all those of the younger generation in these families have had to work, not only for self-accomplishment but also for financial security. "New money is striving to follow our traditional path by sending their kids to prep schools, living on Beacon Hill, and so on. They need to do so to ensure themselves in society. ... Old money is striving – just to survive!" Thomas does not resent this propensity at all. "New groups always replace old groups. Our society always wants this. We have less desire to perpetuate a group. We have to change." However, Thomas is highly indignant over the paradox that the ideal of egalitarianism is overshadowed by the reality of the widening inequality in society. He mentions the case of his friend who recently built his fifth house in California at a cost of $18 million. "It's ridiculous! There should be a cap after certain amounts! What happens if we don't invest more in our next generations?" "Americans are very religious, but their religion is money!"

What can he leave to the following generations? It might be a feeling of historical continuity. Thomas organized a family reunion several years ago, gathering together more than a hundred relatives, and also donated 43 rolls of family correspondence that he discovered in his museum in Dedham to the Massachusetts Historical Society for better safekeeping. He is now writing his autobiography, to pass his insights, wisdom, and traditions down to the next generations.

* * *

Tomoko met her husband, Jonathan Cabot Shaw, in the late 1960s on her way back to Japan after visiting her sister in New York.[7] She joined the Shaw family in 1969 when she was in her late twenties and Jonathan in his early forties. His ancestors had emigrated from England to Concord, Massachusetts, in the seventeenth century. Jonathan's grandfather, while making a great fortune from the China trade, established himself as a nationwide authority on insects. Jonathan's father was engaged in the import of spice from India, and served as a state senator around the 1920s. He had four sisters, two of whom were educated at a finishing school, one at Smith College and one at Radcliffe; they all made "proper" marriages. Jonathan graduated from Harvard College, worked for advertising companies in New York, Toronto, and Tokyo, and returned to Harvard as a graduate student in East Asian studies, only to be bewildered by the increased number of "pluggers" (students interested only in grades and exam scores). Although his fortune had been undermined by the expenses of bringing up the three children of his former, Brahmin-descended, wife, it was still possible for him to start a new family with Tomoko on his trust income.

After completing his Master's degree, he was employed at Boston's Museum of Fine Arts. Extra income from the Museum and the lease of his Lancaster house enabled the couple to afford a high social life at a few of the most prestigious clubs in Boston. After a short while, Tomoko volunteered for the Museum, partly because she wished to enhance cultural understanding between the United States and Japan, and partly because she perceived a growing social consciousness that a truly "capable" woman should be able to express herself even outside the domestic sphere. In 1979, Jonathan sold his Concord house and purchased for cash a $300,000 house in Milton where some of the Sturgises, Jonathan's mother's family (also of Brahmin descent), had settled.

Jonathan's son entered a prep school, transferred to a public school, graduated from an art college, and now earns his livelihood as a mechanic and salesperson of Japanese cars. He resides in a Boston suburb with his Jewish wife. One daughter graduated from a public school, studied stained glass at an art college, married an "ordinary" (middle-middle-class) man, and now lives in Seattle. She most ferociously refused to be a debutante. The other daughter graduated from Winsor, majored in the performing arts at Bates College, and married (later divorced) an "ordinary" man. She now cohabits, as her siblings all did, with her partner in New York and is determined to become an actress.

Although these three children benefit from the family trust, and eventually will inherit about $350,000 each, they still need to work in order to maintain a middle-class lifestyle both now and in the future. Tomoko recognizes the downward mobility of the Shaws, and conjectures that public school graduates might outnumber graduates of prep schools in her grandchildren's generation, that they will be more dispersed across the country, and have spouses from more diverse sociocultural backgrounds. As a matter of fact, Tomoko recently welcomed two Korean women who married into the Shaw family. A sense of "culture in transition" comes home to

Tomoko in a most acute form when she witnesses her children's somewhat detached attitudes towards Yankee tradition. Her husband spoke with a British accent and was proud of it; he wore a tie when receiving guests at home, and served traditional American fare at parties; those customs are now superseded by a "California" accent, no neckties, and Mexican or Italian dishes.

Tomoko infers that these processes of diversification and fragmentation of Yankee tradition are far-reaching, even affecting the Brahmin families in her circle who are better off and more conservative. Her observation, which was in accord with my fieldwork, suggests that even those families are susceptible to these processes because nowadays "passion for love" and "personal integrity" are more highly valued than socioeconomic factors when considering marriage. Tomoko also speculates that these processes reflect a collective insurgency against the highly authoritarian and constraining modes of life that have preserved the cohesiveness and distinctiveness of the Brahmin culture. She recalls a few male in-laws who became enormously resentful and critical of their family backgrounds. As teenagers in "hippy" clothes they might have been agitated by the anti-establishment movement during the Vietnam War, but she now reflects that their behavior was also a revelation of their insecurity, fomented by a lack of communication with parents whose lives tended to be centered on the public domain, an absence of goals or ambitions for bettering their lives, and a dearth of confidence that they could transcend their much-celebrated parents. Today, those teenagers have all become "perfect" fathers who are anxious to change their babies' diapers and to feed their kids, even if they employ caregivers.

Tomoko's children can no longer afford membership in social clubs, and her grandchildren might indulge in the "barbecues" and "bowling" that her husband regarded as the perfect symbol of "middle-class" America. As a matter of fact, Tomoko intends to donate most of the valuable paintings in the Shaws' collection to local museums, partly because she does not think they will fit the decor of her children's "middle-class" homes and partly because the donation will lessen the children's inheritance tax. While sorry that those items of symbolic capital are gradually being lost, Tomoko is delighted to observe some growth in the children's "pride" in their past. This by no means indicates a return to a past when a spouse from Wisconsin was discriminated against by the family, or when Jonathan's Jewish friend was denied admission to his social club. It stands for the amicable atmosphere of the family, as symbolized by the football game in which all the members, elderly or young, participated at a Thanksgiving celebration. It denotes the liberalism (or eccentricity) that accepted not only a Japanese marrying into the family but also Jonathan's conversion from Unitarianism to Buddhism. It signifies a lifestyle that is not guided by materialism and consumerism. Tomoko believes it would be difficult to find such attitudes in her native country or in other segments of American society today, and it is in this sense that her son is adopting "Sturgis" as his middle name.

Jonathan, having informed his friends and family that he was suffering from cancer, was finally defeated by it in 1986. There were a couple of relatives for whom his death marked the end of their association with his immediate family. According to Tomoko: "I could tell which relatives really cared about us." Yet, Tomoko still maintains her "diffuse, enduring solidarity" (Schneider 1968) with a wide spectrum of her relatives, lineal and collateral. Besides being a frequent visitor and caller, she is an active participant in family gatherings that occasionally draw as many as 150 members. She is working to track down the location of 120 pieces of Victorian china that have been scattered among various branches of the family. Her great affection for those relatives is strong enough to persuade her to remain permanently in the United States. "I once heard that one of [Jonathan's] cousins suspected that I married him because of name and money. That cousin is a good friend of mine now!" Her immediate frustration is that even the small coffee table that symbolizes the happiest memories of her married life had to be inspected and priced by an outside agency for the purpose of taxation at the time of her husband's demise. "It is a bit strange, isn't it?"

* * *

Margaret Forbes, in her mid-fifties at the time of my study, met her British husband, David Watson, when both of them were attending Harvard in the late 1950s. Her great-grandfathers were notable bankers and businessmen who made their fortune in the China trade in the nineteenth century. As was often the case with Brahmin families, those ancestors were all in genealogical proximity. Her grandfather was a teacher at Phillips Academy, and was married to an extremely wealthy Anglo-Saxon woman from New York City. They resided on Brattle Street in Cambridge, and embraced upper-class tastes. Her father was a graduate of Phillips Academy, Harvard College, and Harvard Medical School; he became an established surgeon and an active member of a social club in Boston. Her mother was born to a wealthy Anglo-Saxon family in New York City and was raised almost exclusively in Boston. She was the first female in either her own family or the Forbeses to obtain a college degree from Radcliffe College. However, unlike her female offspring, she never worked outside her home except for a very brief period before her marriage. The family belonged to the Episcopal Church, but both Margaret and her parents were atheists. They lived on Walden Street, which is off Brattle Street not only geographically but also socioeconomically.

"A break in generation," however, was experienced in the most conspicuous manner by Margaret's generation. Margaret and her two sisters were so "adventurous" as to make trips to Mexico with a group of Quakers and to stay with a working-class French family. "Different peoples with different languages" stimulated their curiosity to such an extent that her parents finally decided to educate all of them at Shady Hill, a local private school which had a reputation as an ultra-liberal establishment. One sister transferred to St. Paul's, graduated from the University of Pennsylvania, and Yale Medical School, and is now a psychiatrist who lives with her Jewish husband in Washington D.C. The other obtained her degree from Wellesley College, taught in Paris, married a Frenchman, and now lives in Maine.

Margaret received her doctorate in multicultural education from the State University of New York at Albany, and now runs a non-profit organization aimed at "developing in Americans a much greater tolerance for gender, race, ethnicity, religion, and sexual orientation." Margaret reflects that her interest in this theme was inspired in her mid-teens when her closest, Jewish friend was denied participation in a formal party. While sending a written protest, she wondered "why people hate each other for being different." The incident made her aware of the discriminatory dimensions of the old Yankee culture and the "false elitism" of some upper-class WASPs whose intellectual scope of mind was extremely narrow.

David graduated from Rugby School in England, received his B.A. from Cambridge, M.A. from Harvard, and Ph.D. from the University of Pennsylvania, and now works at an M.I.T.-affiliated research institute. The couple's joint annual income (approximately $100,000), other resources such as stocks and bonds, and Margaret's family trust constitute what Margaret classifies as a "middle-class" standard of living. Their careers took them to Pennsylvania, New York, California, and Maine for twenty years, before they purchased a $300,000 house several years ago on Clifton Street in North Cambridge, a district which is inhabited mostly by "lower-middle-class" White ethnic groups and abuts a "working-class" multi-ethnic neighborhood. This is the area where in the past Margaret used to "venture" with her sisters, and the change of residence from Brattle Street to Walden Street to Clifton Street appears to Margaret to be somewhat symbolic of the "downward mobility" of the past three generations.

One of Margaret's daughters graduated from a private school in Maine and the University of Maine, works as a product manager of a gardening magazine, and lives in Maine with her husband, a clinical psychiatrist. Another daughter attended a public school in New York and then Columbia University, and works as a municipal officer in New York City in charge of the street environment in Manhattan. The third daughter graduated from a public school in New York and Hampshire College, and now runs a non-profit environmental organization with a friend in Oregon. Margaret's college education was paid for entirely by her parents, while her graduate study was subsidized by her trust. In the next generation, the children's trust income (approximately $10,000 a year each) basically covered their tuition while their room and board was taken care of by their parents.

The Forbeses own four cottages and a theater in a one-mile-square compound in Maine, a property that was only retained after a long legal dispute with a local developer. One of these cottages has been inherited by Margaret, but the high expenses of taxes, maintenance, and insurance (a total of approximately $16,000 per year) make it difficult for her to retain it, and she now proposes to offer it for sale for $500,000 in the near future. Margaret, however, is aware that her two unmarried daughters wish to have their weddings there, as their sister did, and is therefore refraining from disposing of it until then. Reflecting on the significant impact that the cottage has had on her children's consciousness of kinship, Margaret suspects that its loss will indubitably alter the kin relationship in future generations. The Forbeses also own some property on the North Shore, but Margaret confessed that she was "sick of" one of her cousins who was very particular about the management of the land. This property seems to have little significance as a land of memory, that is to say, as a symbol of family identity.

I was able to interview Josephine, the daughter in Oregon, when she was back in Boston during Christmas vacation. Now in her mid-twenties, she enthusiastically remarked that she would love to tell her future children about their grandparents and to take them to the cottage in Maine even if it has been sold by then. Her motivation is not to impress them with her family's "grand past," but to nurture their "spirit of soul" and "passion for life." She openly states that she does not, and will not, capitalize on her family name. The fading of the family's great history does not dishearten her at all. She only wishes to pass down a strong sense of historical continuity so that her children can appreciate the sense of place in their lives. Josephine maintains that such a feeling is amplified by observing a kind of "fierce individualism" among her former classmates, who seem "lonely" and "wandering" with no connection to their family and community.

Her diagnosis is that such individualism is predicated on "economic oppression," "divorce of parents," or "escape from the excessive pressures for 'success' from the family and society." "I am very lucky," she says, in that "my extended family has no record of divorce," that "my family is relatively well-off," that "my parents supported my project [an environmental non-profit organization] with no objections," and that "I could intermingle with my kin in Maine every summer even when my family lived in New York."

David confesses that he is still amazed by the "connectedness" of Margaret's kin. Margaret still maintains a close relationship with the descendants of the family that one of her ancestors founded after moving back to England. Margaret and David went to England to meet those distant cousins during the period of my fieldwork. David is also impressed by the web of social relationships that has been fabricated by intermarriage, or what Thomas Winthrop metaphorically calls "endogamy," among the old families. Yet David remarks that the declining fortune has eroded their overall interest in the family history. He informed me that the Forbeses used to update their genealogy at the time of family gatherings in Maine, but no revision/addition has been made since 1925. In other words, Margaret's generation indeed marks "a break in generation," as Margaret diagnoses.

External and internal drives

These four cases demonstrate that such referential symbols as residential area, occupation, education, wealth, club membership, ethnicity, religion, and genealogy, which have defined the distinction and identity of the old families in Boston, have become more ambiguous and volatile over the past several generations, and that such indeterminacy and fluidity well expose the process of downward mobility and diversification that these families have undergone in varying degrees. There are families that still appear to embody the whole image of Brahmin tradition in their lives, yet both my informants' observations and my own investigation suggest that such a case is more exceptional than typical in the younger generations. "Less privileged, less money, spread more, spouse of more diverse background, and more modest life" – this is how one informant who has served as the Admission Chair at one of the most prestigious social clubs in Boston over the past decades portrays this intergenerational mobility and diversification, and I did not encounter a single informant who attested otherwise.

It would be hard to explicate these phenomena as a coincidental consequence of individual actors' spontaneous voluntarism. They seem to be more informed and guided by both structural and ideological forces in the wider society. First, these families are constrained by a progressive tax system in which primogeniture is not observed and the perpetuation of wealth is not encouraged. My informants endeavor to "play the game" (Bourdieu 1977) with this legal stricture by establishing family trusts, investing in venture-capital enterprises, and seeking tax exemptions through donations to cultural institutions. Yet few can transcend the destiny of declining fortune in the long run, and this tendency is exacerbated by the growing number of inheritors, by soaring price indices (especially in real estate and education), by conservative financial management, and, in some cases, by the financial obligations incident to divorce.

Second, the growth of the national (and even global) economy, the spread of urban areas (especially in the West), the consolidation of legal and bureaucratic structures, and the improvements in transportation and communication systems in the post-Civil War period (and particularly since the Second World War), have curtailed the necessity of depending on consanguineous ties or community networks for trustworthy services and information. Frederic Jaher (1982), comparing the vicissitudes of the urban establishment in Boston, New York, Charleston, Chicago, and Los Angeles over the past centuries (especially in the nineteenth century), argues that "American capitalism contained strong structural biases toward a competitive, open, and rational market where affective and ascriptive considerations eventually placed the patriciate at a disadvantage when challenged by businessmen unhindered by tradition, kin, or reference group" (p. 88). These structural environments have stimulated geographical mobility and the diversification of family traditions.

One ideological impetus, which is closely related to the above structural influences, is that the process of "rationalization" and "democratization" of society has reinforced the principles of competition and meritocracy.

> ... Boston, the home of the bean and the cod,
> where Lowells talk only to Cabots,
> and Cabots talk only to God.

This passage, originally read at a Harvard alumni party in 1905 (Amory 1947), was quoted by most informants as a metaphor for the Brahmin hegemony of the past, which was tightly interlaced with "proper" family names. However, many informants today sense that their "first name talks better than last name." Entrance to Harvard is no longer guaranteed.[8] Old Bostonian names can rarely be identified among the list of Harvard students and staff.

Most of Harvard's exclusive "final clubs" are presided over by people with only weak bases in the Boston area. These phenomena can be seen as the logical consequence of Harvard's emphasis on rationality, efficiency, practicality, expertise, and diversity in its administrative and curricula policies since the mid-nineteenth century, which certainly transformed a provincial, traditional, and upper-class college into one of the greatest cosmopolitan institutions of higher education in the world (Jaher 1982; Story 1980). Yet this has also been a process in which the offspring of the old families who did not adopt such a mode of rationality and aggressiveness lost a reliable set of credentials for nearly automatic recruitment into high society.

Jaher (1982) explicates the impairment of their competitive edge in the larger society by expounding on the cultural impediments implicit in their high social status:

> Ascription may encourage trust and stability, but inventive and speculative skills are difficult to pass on. Inheritance enhances imitation of conventional practices and may blunt the desire for material achievement, thus making the men less competitive. It constricts the social mobility necessary for an adequate supply of new talent and capital while ensuring posts for those who might ordinarily be eliminated by the exigencies of the marketplace (p. 46).
>
> … Against the modern demands for efficiency, mobility, adaptability, innovation, objectivity, achievement, and coordination, the genteel objectors raised the claims of loyalty, sentiment, inheritance, tradition, community, and authority. But these defenders of the past, fighting with weapons from another age, were doomed to defeat in a society committed to the present and the future (p. 120).

Not a few informants articulated their indignation over the excessive self-centeredness of today's society. However, a certain level of egoism and aggressiveness needs to be strenuously pursued in order to cope with a more competitive and meritocratic environment. At least, that is the name of the game, as is well exemplified in the words of Nelson Aldrich, an author and old money insider:

This is a country that belongs to men of confidence and to confidence men. Self-forgiving, self-forgetting, self-asserting, self-improving, every man's a king in America's kingdom of means: means of change, means of possibility, means of making oneself and everything else new and better (1988, p. 266).

The other ideological drive, as mentioned by some informants, is the relativization and dislocation of their own cultural tradition, particularly in terms of its prescriptive, exclusive, and elitist aspects. The recognition of provincialism has been fortified by increased interaction with "others" at school, work, and club, and in the neighborhood; by a heightened consciousness of alternative ways of life; and by the witnessing of their replacement in socioeconomic pre-eminence by newcomers. The "Boston Disease" – Boston males' inability to create a life of their own – can be grasped as an indication of the lost paradigm of their lives, and the suicide of Thomas Winthrop's brother, who felt "trapped" by the old culture, is indeed a most tragic consequence of this disease. I was told of several other cases in which lives were lost for similar reasons, but also of cases in which social actors' agency is exerted in a more positive direction by celebrating the opening-up of society. As a matter of fact, some of my informants actively maneuvered to avoid the reproduction of their cultural tradition by avoiding the kind of people whom they were expected to embrace, by refusing to be debutantes, by resigning from social clubs, by leaving Boston, and so on.

All these strategic acts reveal that one dominant type of social "taste" has been nullified, rather than being automatically inherited and reproduced, by the social actors who are embedded in, and entitled to, that particular taste in their actual lives. This "defiant" dimension is missing in Bourdieu's (1984) presupposition that taste itself should be reproduced and perpetuated by social actors who incessantly invest their capital, material or symbolic, to embody specific tastes, and thus to safeguard their place or distinctiveness in society.[9]

Katherine Newman (1988) investigates downward mobility as it is experienced by middle-class Americans, and illuminates the fact that the ideology of "success" prevents them from being well equipped with rituals, symbols, and vocabularies for making sense of the painful transition to a lower social position. In the case of the descendants of the Brahmin families, the pain of downward mobility seems to be somewhat alleviated by their still comfortable socioeconomic condition, especially among the older generations. "New groups always replace old groups. Our society always wants this. We have less desire to perpetuate a group. We have to change." "I feel I am trying to 'graduate from' or 'transcend' the provincialism of Yankee culture." They can still legitimize the dislocation of their social position for the sake of idealism in the larger society, or in the name of liberation from the dictates of high society. I suspect, however, that Newman's thesis will be more and more relevant to the younger generations whose resources, material or cultural, seem to be becoming obsolete and mediocre.

Thus far, I have delineated how once visible and functional collectivities anchored in a similar geographical, vocational, educational, economic, organizational, ethnic, and religious background have been diversified and complicated over the past generations by both structural and ideological forces in an open, capitalist society. Their family names are engraved on street signs, campus dormitories, museum wings, hospital operating rooms, and nature preserves. Yet it seems that the communal tradition and memory woven into their "thick" (Aldrich 1988) web of social relations cannot easily be transferred to and perpetuated by the younger generations. In the following sections, I would like to scrutinize, in greater detail, the way the transfigurations of social environments and family backgrounds both sensitize and reflect the "politics of culture" in more specific facets of my informants' actual social lives and relationships – for example, neighborhoods, philanthropy, social clubs, kinship, friendship, work, cultural taste, love and marriage, divorce, childrearing, care of the elderly, family life, finance, and inheritance.

Neighborhood

Nearly 80 percent of my informants reside on Beacon Hill, in West Cambridge, or on the North Shore (Hamilton, Pride's Crossing, Beverly Farms, and Manchester-by-the-Sea in particular), and these areas are identified as popular nests of old families by both insiders and outsiders. It would be fair to contrast the "urban" and "liberal" social ambiance of Beacon Hill and West Cambridge with the "pastoral" and "conservative" cultural spirit of the North Shore. However, it would be misleading to differentiate the character of my informants in any polarized fashion on the basis of their residential affiliation. Most of the workplaces, social activities, and cultural interests of my informants on the North Shore are centered in Boston; and all the informants on Beacon Hill and in West Cambridge have second houses or close relatives on the North Shore.

Nineteenth-century brick townhouses, courtyards, cobbled streets, and iron streetlights furnish Beacon Hill with a physical distinctiveness anchored in the silence of time. With the Massachusetts State House on the top of the hill, designed by Charles Bulfinch (1763–1844) and famous for its golden dome, this neighborhood is one of the nation's foremost historic sites, and resident are basically not allowed to alter the exteriors of houses. An emblem of prosperity and prestige, the hill has attracted the *nouveaux riches*, who seek to legitimize their acquired status by emulating the cultural tastes of Brahmin Boston (Jaher 1982). This tendency, according to the testimonies of local realtors and long-time residents, has been consolidated since the massive exodus of Brahmin families who were severely hit by the Great Depression, who were fearful of the soaring crime rate in the city, or who felt "encroached" upon by outside political and commercial interests as well as by the influx of newcomers.

Today, according to my informants, there are only a "handful" of old families living on Beacon Hill (although others still own properties there), and all of them dwell on the "sunny" side of the hill, a high-class residential area between Mt. Vernon Street and the Boston Common. The "dark" side of the hill, once inhabited by those who provided various services for Brahmin families, is today populated mostly by young professionals and middle-class families, and my informants have very little contact with them. On the sunny side, my informants perceive no tangible tension between the old class (like themselves) and the new. The new class's similar socio-economic status and their appreciation of the historical and cultural flavor of Beacon Hill seem to facilitate intercourse and friendship between the two groups. Large single-family homes have been remodeled into condominiums since the mid-1950s due to the shrinking of families and the soaring costs of real estate.

Brattle Street in West Cambridge was once known as Tory Row after the wealthy Tory supporters who lived in the mansions. Even today, strict zoning restrictions preserve some of the most dignified old houses along the wide, tree-lined avenue. This street is a link between the tumultuous vibrations of Harvard Square and the sequestered atmosphere of Mt. Auburn Cemetery, a "proper" burying ground for old families. Property value has increased by 20 times over the past three decades (30 times since the end of the Second World War), as has been the case with other "proper" spots on Beacon Hill and the North Shore, and prices range from $500,000 to $2,000,000. Residents in the Brattle area today comprise new money groups of Italian, Irish, German, Swiss, Jewish, and Chinese families, among others. The high density of society-conscious intellectuals and professionals in this neighborhood appears to be the pride of my informants. The residents' upper-middle-class status and liberalism or moderate conservatism seem to render ethnic and religious attributions less problematic today.

The North Shore features a magnificent coastline, tranquil beaches, inland farms, and wildlife; but it is perhaps more than scenery alone. At the end of the 1960s, the *Washington Post* reported that four-fifths of soldiers in Vietnam associated the image of their home country with that of a New England village: a white-colored church, its adjoining red-painted school, and green lawns. The North Shore still embodies that New England or "American" flavor in a tangible fashion. In the past, the area was composed of small communities in which "year-round people" (the lower-class) provided miscellaneous services to "summer people" (the Bostonians). However, the establishment of highways reduced the driving time from Boston from 2.5 hours to an hour, which resulted in a doubling of the population. The North Shore today, especially the areas inhabited by my informants, is generally identified as an "upper-class" or "upper-middle-class" bedroom suburb for commuters to Boston, although there are also some blue-collar districts. "In the past, there were no Blacks and few Asians; now there are few Blacks but more Asians." Yet diversification is a fairly slow process, and I found it very rare to come across people of color in the neighborhoods of my informants. One female informant testifies that the Yankee accent, which was quite common until her parents' generation, has certainly been dropped, but that she seldom hears Midwestern or Californian accents in her neighborhood.

Despite these variations in social ambience, Beacon Hill, West Cambridge, and the North Shore share similar propensities and phenomena. First, all my older informants reminisced about the old days, before the Second World War, when most of their daily foods and commodities were delivered to their houses or peddled door to door. Those services gradually disappeared with the advent of a more competitive market and the prevalence of automobiles. My informants are generally satisfied with the quality of the supermarkets and chain stores in their proximity, but are somewhat perplexed by the aggressive, sometimes entrapping, advertisements and business practices of recent decades. The proliferation of temporary, part-time staff at these stores has a tendency to hinder my informants from conceiving their relationships with such stores in other than economic terms. My informants prefer local shops for everyday shopping (e.g. medicine, wine, household goods, dry-cleaning, and food) because of their more personal and congenial atmosphere.

Second, the principle of economic Darwinism has entailed, and has been intensified by, an erosion of social homogeneity, which resulted in demographic diversification. This process of demographic dilution and diversification has often been accompanied by resistance and opposition. Several local realtors openly admitted to me that they once made "conscious efforts" to prevent the intrusion of outsiders by relying exclusively on their "inside network" to fill vacancies, and by conveying the neighbors' suspicions and preference straightforwardly to outside inquirers. The Holy Trinity Armenian Church in West Cambridge faced strong opposition from the neighbors before it was built on Brattle Street in 1961, as did many other ethnic and religious organizations in the past. A series of legal codes has been implemented since the early 1970s to safeguard minorities' rights. Today none of my informants perceive the existence of anti-Semitism, but some elderly people appear to me somewhat suspicious of, and uncomfortable with, "colored" people in their neighborhoods.[10]

Third, "community" seems to be too strong a word to characterize the social ambiance of Beacon Hill, West Cambridge, and the North Shore. My informants know who lives where in their neighborhoods, and they occasionally enjoy chatting with their neighbors in the street. However, their relational intensity is far from that of the "fictive kinship" that Carol Stack (1974) identified in a Black community. The combination of neighborhood economic security and adequate public services makes it unnecessary for my informants to develop leadership or forge a strong collective bond. "Last October I hosted a cocktail party for a family who moved in this neighborhood, but it was just for getting to know each other. When we were living in a wealthy neighborhood in Philadelphia, there was a cocktail party in rotation. Each month one family hosted it. I didn't like that kind of too much artificial creation of communal bond and tradition. I am glad that we don't have such 'mid-Atlantic vanity' here."

Fourth, city politics stirs little interest, and ethical propositions could be construed as imposing or intervening. This being so, none of my informants affirmed the existence of "leaders" in their neighborhood, claiming that "much is being taken care of by governments" and that "there is simply no need to rely on, or invent, those figures." During the course of my fieldwork, a woman strove to dominate the neighborhood, only to be resented by other inhabitants. Community organizations such as the Beacon Hill Civic Association, Architectural Design of Beacon Hill, and the Cambridge Historical Commission are designated to oversee the preservation of the area, but my informants do not acknowledge the existence of, or necessity for, any particular guiding figures in the neighborhood.

However, these facts by no means imply that people's attentions are directed only outside of their neighborhoods. My informants are well acquainted with the names and personalities of their neighbors. Nearly all the informants in the baby-boomers' generation (or above) are affiliated with local museums, historical societies, libraries, choral clubs, hospitals, schools, community newspapers, and other organizations in their neighborhood. One informant, an elderly widow, formed a support network with others in similar circumstances. Another informant, a retired male, sometimes asks his home doctor to visit his elderly, single, female neighbor to ensure her wellbeing. These informants on Beacon Hill, in West Cambridge, and on the North Shore certainly maintain more or less self-sufficient and self-contained niches of their own, and they perceive no major threats to their local neighborhood and therefore feel no immediate necessity for "inventing" community and leadership there.

Philanthropy and social clubs

Philanthropy

Philanthropy and social clubs have nurtured a Brahmin identity over generations, and some informants are still actively involved in these spheres. The spirit of philanthropy is exerted through such institutions as the Boston Athenaeum, Boston Symphony, Museum of Fine Arts, Massachusetts General Hospital, Harvard University, Trustees of Reservations, International Conservation Center, and many other smaller organizations in education, art, history, literature, conservation, and medicine. My impression of the motives involved is congruent with that of Jaher (1982):

> Calculations of self-interest and social control weighed heavily in these (charitable) undertakings, but nobler motives were not absent. Civic pride, the stewardship of wealth, concern for the less fortunate, regard for intellectual endeavor, awareness of the obligations of hegemony, and even guilt over the accumulation of vast wealth made *noblesse oblige* more than an instrument of class defense (p. 63).

Tax deduction is undoubtedly an incentive, and the accumulation of "symbolic capital" (Bourdieu 1977) and its accompanying perpetuation of class or "distinction" (Bourdieu 1984) might be an intended consequence. However, it seems an exaggeration to conceive of these philanthropic commitments merely as "social control" or "class domination" per se. The financial contributions can be substantial, and decisions are made on the basis of both personal moral convictions and professional legal/financial advice. One male informant elaborated on his passion for a children's summer camp program in which he has been involved for decades; his will pledges a donation of more than a million dollars, the great majority of his inheritance, to the program. Thanks to his active fundraising and administrative coordination, the two-week program costs each participant only $75, whereas an ordinary (commercial) program charges $4,000. "I feel so good when I see the happy smiles of children – whether they are South Boston Irish, Blacks in Dorchester, or poor Yankees in Lowell."

Several informants cited the example of the late Thomas Dudley Cabot (1897–1995), a dedicated conservationist, who donated a 176-acre forest in New Hampshire to the New England Forestry Foundation and purchased an uninhabited island in Maine in order to conserve its landscape: "He is the model for us." As a matter of fact, I came across many situations in which my informants implicitly or explicitly condemned some families and individuals for neglecting their contribution to society. "It is politically and ethically imperative for humanity's sake and for the descendants' sake." None of my informants objected to the expression of civic virtue by donating to charitable organizations, and even those among my acquaintances and informants who are highly antagonistic to "Brahmin culture" could hardly repudiate the merits of *noblesse oblige*, even if they can be jealous of it.

Declining fortunes make it more difficult for many informants to be as generous as Mr. Cabot, but they are cultivating other avenues for committing themselves to society. Some do so by sitting on the boards of trustees at local museums, historical societies, libraries, hospitals, and schools; others by serving as ballot-counting overseers in their neighborhood, teachers of English to foreign students, or organizers of choral clubs.

Social clubs

Social clubs are a more delicate and contested subject. As mentioned above, some of my wealthy informants, especially younger ones, opt not to join these clubs, seeking a more casual, egalitarian, and informative social ambiance. Yet half the informants still hold memberships at such notably Yankee-dominated clubs as the Algonquin, Brookline Country, Chilton, Essex County, Myopia Hunt, Somerset, St. Botolph, Tavern, Tennis and

Racquet, Union, and Union Boat clubs. Each has a distinct flavor, providing an opportunity for its members to appreciate their shared interests and taste in politics, literature, science, sports, music, and fine arts over sumptuous repasts.[11] Generally speaking, membership requires between five and ten testimonial letters from current members, making it too high a hurdle to clear for an outsider, even one who can afford initiation fees ($3,000–5,000) and yearly dues: $1,000–2,000 in the case of a top dining club. Aldrich (1988) wittily captures the insider-ethos of these clubs, which my informants seemed reluctant to explicate to an outsider anthropologist:

> [T]he greatest blessing of Old Money club life is its removal, not to say aloofness, from the unattractive strains and dangerous disappointments of a middle-class world bent on "making it." ... Here it is considered bad form even to introduce oneself (one is supposed to know), and actually offensive to identify one's job or standing in the world. ... Above all it is a refuge from the ugly world outside, with its pleading, cajoling, sleeve-plucking, breast-thumping strivers and strugglers swirling through the streets in every town and city in the land (p. 51).

An informant's wife, who came from a different cultural background, recollects her first dinner in a club, during which she was warned by her husband "not to look back" during the meal. She has now acquired a technique for crossing subtle prohibitory boundaries without a hint of a broken stride. For instance, she reads a person's social standing by asking whether he plays polo or not, where he has traveled recently, where he spends his summer, and so on. At the least, these questions reveal whether he is a "self-made man" (new money) or a "got-it-made man" (old money). All these ingenious – refined or snobbish – codes of behavior add depth to the social thickness of the old money world, shielding it from the intrusion of the "market time" of the "New World where anything [good] can happen, where anything [good] can be made to happen" (Aldrich 1988, p. 53).

Yet, just as Aldrich (1988) observes, the Old World is being challenged:

All this peace and propriety is threatened now. The strivers in the street want in, badly. Some of them always have, of course, but in the last ten years or so there have been crucial changes in the public's perception of what goes on in there, changes that will force the doors, and disturb the tranquility, of the honor'd number (p. 51).

Some informants assume great responsibility for making important decisions about the direction of their clubs, including the revision of the admissions policy. "If I say 'no'," the applicant cannot get in." They confess to a growing political pressure to open the doors, especially after the Civil Rights movement in the late 1960s. One of their clubs, for instance, has accepted 15–20 Jews, four or five Blacks, and "a very few" Irish Catholics among its 600 members, whose average age is 67. This club is known for having rejected Joseph Kennedy, although one informant recalls it was not because of his ethno-religious background but because of his "unlikable and self-imposing personality." The club's White, male members, mostly pre-baby-boomers, have wives who are of White, Anglo-Saxon, Protestant background, apart from 2–3 percent who have Jewish or Catholic spouses.

All these alleged facts manifest a still conservative and protective disposition. There was strong opposition among its female members when the club was politically pressured to admit the wife of a Black comedian. Also, an enormous controversy arose over whether the club should admit a male, new-money applicant who violated the law by extending the fence of his house in Beacon Hill by five inches. One informant speculates that "it would have been no problem if he were a Cabot or a Lodge."

One informant has received a series of harassment letters written by an anonymous group of "Frustrated Four" in his own club for having married to a woman of modest, "blue-collar" background:

We have not forgotten you. Yes, you are still very much in our thoughts especially since we have learned you are selling Brattle Street and moving to Newton. ... We wonder if you now might continue in your Rolls westward on Route 9 to the "blue-collar town" of Framingham where you and your "blue-collar family" will find a more egalitarian and congenial life with your peers. Think about it.

In truth, you live by a double standard clearly evident to all of us. But – because of your distorted perception of reality – you actually believe you are immune to accountability. How prophetic [*sic*] ... how ludicrous!

We all took a major hit in social esteem and respect from our peers.

The couple stressed that this kind of explicit harassment was rather exceptional, and that they were warmly treated by the members of the club in general. Yet memories of the subtle insults that she had received from some members of the club and her husband's family made her break down during my interview. Her husband asked me to give her a rest, and while she was regaining her composure in another room he confessed that my question hit the "most sensitive issue" in their current life. He acknowledged how difficult it is to protect her from "too many insults." According to him $10,000 is the standard price for a wedding ring among his circle, but he had to spend $25,000 to emphasize to his friends and family how greatly he valued this marriage and to enhance his wife's dignity. Also, the couple is wondering how to describe her modest background (especially the name of her college, a state university in Maine) in the forthcoming *Social Register*. As indicated in the above letter, he intends to move out of West Cambridge, but he claims that he is "confident and secure enough not to be 'trapped' by the so-called 'Brahmin tribalism.'" "Some people ... are still dreaming about their grand past without being able to accept the changing reality!"

In a sense, this kind of "tribalism" has sheltered their enclave, but it is also this normative code that has made these clubs more susceptible to criticism and mockery from both insiders and outsiders. "Is it worth spending lots of money and time there?" This question seems to be asked more and more often, especially by the younger generation of those old families, who have more freedom and choice in their weaving of a social web and wish to include those who cannot qualify for club membership both in financial and in social terms. In an interview with the *Boston Globe* (March 25, 2001), Massachusetts Historical Society director William Fowler, a patron of the St. Botolph Club, states that the scarcity of young members from Brahmin families is apparent. "When I look at the roster, I don't see a Brahmin among the younger names."

In the past, there was a local paper, the *Boston Evening Transcript*, that embraced a wider audience among Yankees in old Boston. Many informants referred to the high quality of the paper (no gossip or scandal), likening it to the *Christian Science Monitor*. This paper was considered to be the "proper" paper, and many informants recollect a lesson for "females" given by both their parents and teachers: "Your name should appear only three times in a paper: when you are born, when you marry, and when you pass away. Die in the *Transcript*, not in the *Globe*!" A male informant cited the case of his mother, who was from California. The *Transcript* reported that his father married a woman from a "background unknown." This paper was, in a sense, a community media in that it aroused people's "imagination" (Anderson 1983) about what their society was like, or ought to be like. In other words, the paper enforced a kind of social control by describing what "proper" Bostonians were doing. However, the *Transcript* went bankrupt in 1941, as did many other local papers in American metropolises, after losing its urban readers to the suburbs.

Kinship and friendship

Kin network

The *Transcript* was known for publishing a most elaborate column on genealogy. This very fact is illustrative of the old families' curiosity about kinship: where they came from, what they are, and where they are going. Indeed, my informants' extensive knowledge about their ancestors and kinfolk and the actual genealogical proximity among the old families constantly astonished me. The degree of recognition varies, but it was not unusual to find a middle-aged informant who could easily identify almost all the names of his grandparents' siblings as well as his first cousins' spouses, along with their residential, educational, and occupational backgrounds.

Some informants could demonstrate a rough delineation of the genealogy even before their ancestors immigrated to the American continent. Such historic figures as John Winthrop, Paul Revere, John Adams, Thomas Jefferson, and Abraham Lincoln are included among the ancestors of several informants. "Be proud of it, but don't show it." "The family name speaks for itself. Don't use it explicitly" – this seems to be an axiom of the old families.

I often discovered such things as that Mr. A's father's first cousin was Mr. B's father as well as Mr. C's father-in-law, or that Ms. X was a second cousin of Mr. Y, whose best friend, Mr. Z, was a husband of Ms. X's sister. In a sense, the very fact that they are genealogically related is not so surprising, because Boston society was much smaller in size and more enclosed and intense in content until a few decades ago. The high frequency of intermarriage ("endogamy") among the old families was, my informants conjectured, not only a reflection of "conscious efforts" but also a "natural consequence of limited social contacts" in those days. Yet their knowledge of these complicated relationships itself impresses not only me but also those who married into these families from different sociocultural backgrounds.

Such knowledge is nourished, to some extent, by history books, genealogical documents, and everyday conversations. In fact, I came across a couple of cases in which the genealogical record is assiduously updated on my informants' computers. The depth of their genealogical knowledge facilitates a feeling of affinity even with a member of the old families met for the first time. "Boston's old families are very much connected. For example, whenever I come across any Gardners or Welds, I will feel like their kin."

Certainly, these families are "well connected" not only on genealogical charts but also in their actual relationships. During my fieldwork, I endeavored not to expose who else I was interviewing to my informants, but I sometimes found myself in awkward situations when they mentioned, "I didn't know Muffy was your specimen. She is my second cousin!" "I belong to the same club with Ted Appleton," or when I saw a couple of informants chatting together at weddings or memorial services. It was not uncommon to witness a wedding party with 300 guests and a Thanksgiving family gathering with 150 in attendance, and social clubs, charitable organizations, and funerals furnish incentives to consolidate their lived knowledge and connections.

Abigail Trafford, an author and insider of the Brahmin world, has expounded on what she calls "WASP Rot Syndrome" – the process of "How the American Upper Crust Crumble" – in the *Washington Post* (February 21, 1993). Yet even she responded to my interview questions by saying that there are still among Bostonian families certain boundaries, although loosened. These old families are nuclear in form but extended in substance. As a matter of fact, I was often impressed by the fact that even those from different backgrounds were very knowledgeable about their in-laws and their genealogy. Some openly admitted to me that they had to make some extra efforts to familiarize themselves with those matters in order to be better accepted by their spouse's family.

However, this particular segment of American society is by no means immune to the wider social processes that have been diluting the density of kinship. Business practices are highly formalized, communication systems are better developed, nepotism has been superseded by bureaucratic rationalism, family members are more dispersed, and social welfare is ensured. Nearly all the informants testify that dependency on kinship is a delicate matter today because it could be viewed negatively as evidence of an inability to take care of one's own affairs. "People rely on kinship when they don't have enough resources. That's not the case with old Yankees families. Kinship basically provides emotional security for us." As far as I observed, job hunting seems to be the only area in which dependency is more permissible, although my informants were cautious in approaching and receiving favors from their relatives. Relying on kinsfolk for business transactions or charitable fundraising is always accompanied by the danger of insulting them.

The social functions that kinship once assumed have thus been curtailed, transforming the way in which social relations are constructed. A female informant in her mid-seventies joined some of the other informants in maintaining that the common stake of kin in old families today is chiefly in the summer house and the family trust. However, as has been demonstrated, the high expenses of taxes, maintenance, and insurance make it all the more difficult for these families to justify retaining their summer houses.[12] The geometrical proliferation of inheritors and the decline of fortunes tend to diminish each individual's share of the family trust. In addition, the divergence of genealogical lines and the dispersion of kinfolk make it technically impossible to keep informed and connected. Several Shaws, for instance, admit that they are in touch with only 5 or 6 percent of the family (who number approximately 1,700 today), and those are mostly the ones within their own social circle.

The density and cohesiveness of a kinship network is also contingent upon such chance factors as the fitness of "chemistry," shared tastes, and the existence of connecting relatives. One informant is on amicable terms with his cousins – a carpenter and a taxi driver – because they all share a love of music. Another informant affirms that his kinship has been solidified ever since he acknowledged warm emotional support from his relatives at the time of his brother's suicide. On the other hand, one informant is quite explicit:

> Most of our summer houses in Maine have been sold off. We are losing symbols. I am not sure if my children will be able to recognize their second cousins when they grow up. Well, we have the trusts, so, at least, you can tell where they are and we maintain minimum contacts with them. But there is no closeness beyond that. I don't have any burning desire to get closer. We don't have so much in common to talk about, and sometimes the difference with our personalities is too vast. In fact, I haven't spoken with some of my first cousins for more than 20 years. They are real nuts!!

Another reflects: "I am less close to my kin than I was supposed to be 50 years ago. It was my choice. Why? As I grew up, some kin didn't interest me at all." This informant underscores the importance to him of his colleagues who share similar intellectual tastes. His knowledge about his nephews and nieces is rather scanty, while he is very well acquainted with the details of his colleagues' children, to the extent that he even telephones them on their birthdays. Several informants testified to the fragmentation and disenchantment of the kinship network after the demise of connecting relatives, leaving it more up to individuals to associate themselves with other kinfolk.

Interestingly enough, I came across a couple of relatives of (then) Governor William Weld, a proper Bostonian, who declared to me that they would not vote for him in the 1996 US senate election. Such an act of "treason" was unthinkable in the past, but seems more acceptable today. "It is an anachronism to cling to kinship for this sort of matter." Most people still consider it "natural" to support their relatives on such an occasion. However, the above case suggests that "nature" is being contested and denaturalized, and that the sphere of personal freedom and choice has expanded in my informants' relationships with kinfolk.

Intimate friendship

In general, an informant has around three to five relatives with whom he or she reciprocates cards, phone calls, and visits on a regular basis. As a matter of fact, those close relatives are sometimes perceived as intimate friends, who usually number between four and eight. These close friends are basically of a similar age to the informant, include both males and females, are well-educated, and professional, and are known from school (especially college), work, and community activities. The friends are mostly Anglo-Saxon Protestants, but it is fairly common to find Catholics, Jews, and Blacks. There are a couple of cases in which an intimate friendship has been continuing since the grandparents' generation. Most informants have close friends in different parts of the United States, and the "diffuse, enduring solidarity" is seen as transcending geographical constraints. Many informants maneuver to preserve their long-distance friendships not only by reciprocating telephone calls, gifts, and cards, but also by organizing joint travel and summer camping.

> As I grew up, I realized that friendship is the most precious thing. You know, my best friend came all the way from California last week. She stayed at our summer house. And we talked about everything – about our own kids, common friends, foods, Paris, politics, the O. J. Simpson trial, even about money and sex!

Some informants live in "non-proper," blue-collar dominated neighborhoods like Charlestown and Chelsea, although their particular blocks are more middle-class. They moved there exclusively for the convenience of their jobs. These informants have very little knowledge about their neighbors and "no intention to get involved in all those mobs." "I am living here only to sleep." They do not participate in any social clubs or charitable activities. Yet the web of intimacy that they are weaving among their friends (including close relatives and colleagues) seems to safeguard these informants from feeling part of the "lonely crowd."

The "breakdown of community" is a popular American topic (Bender 1978). Indeed, if "community" is defined on the basis of locality and institution, it became a highly vulnerable and fragile entity in the mobile and fluid society that emerged in the United States in the post-Civil War (and especially the post- Second World War) era. However, it seems that an alternative community or network that transcends geographical, institutional, ethno-religious, and genealogical boundaries is emerging more and more commonly in the face of the fragmentation and emasculation of "community" in the conventional sense. This can particularly be the case in the Internet age, although my fieldwork took place before e-mail became a common medium of communication among my informants.

Work

Job

A sense of place in society is harnessed also by the engagement with work. Nearly all my male informants are associated with professional occupations in business, medicine, law, and academia, and being a "professional" is construed as an integral part of being a member of the upper-middle strata of society. The symbolism of the upper-middle class seems to lie in the fact that it is neither "new money" (upper class) nor "no money" (middle-middle class or below). "The upper class is too materialistic and conspicuous. You know Ross Perot and Donald Trump. They are very aggressive with no hint of intellectual and philosophical depth." "You can find the [middle-]middle class in ugly shopping malls in the suburbs. They are rootless, having no knowledge about where they came from and what they are. They are struggling to hang on – with a bottle of whisky in their hands!" The connotation of being "upper-middle class" is that of being liberated from the "cult of fetishism" and the "culture of non-culture." Many informants expressed their expectation that their offspring would maintain the upper-middle-class or professional lifestyle because "that allows you to appreciate your 'freedom' in the most balanced way."

My informants spend (or used to spend) eight to ten hours a day (seldom after dinner) on their own work, and take six to ten-week vacations. Salaries vary significantly, from zero (volunteer work) to around half a million dollars a year. Nobody feels over-worked or frantically concerned about advancement, enabling them to relax at home, visit (or invite) friends, and take part in various social activities. The synthesis between economy and morality (civic virtue) seems to be a main theme in their pursuit of careers. A couple of informants could easily live on their inheritances, but they are actively engaged in charitable activities and volunteer work. To some extent, that is a "rational" action aimed at gaining exemption from taxation. However, a sense of *noblesse oblige* is deeply grounded in their cultural ethic, and "doing (giving) nothing" is severely despised as being "irresponsible," "idle," "mean," and "selfish." "Work" is irreducible to "job" among these upper-middle-class informants.

Even as far as jobs are concerned, morality (or "civic virtue" in the form of "duty," "fairness," "faithfulness," and "honesty") occupies a central dimension of their pride and "honor." One informant in the investment business remarks:

> It is certainly a very tough and competitive world. But, as long as you deal with the "human being," that's all right. When you began chasing "numbers," that becomes a problem. Well, my father was a lawyer and my grandfather was a banker, so I know how to deal with this world. I suspect this is a very unnatural and difficult world for new money.

Boston society is still perceived to be small enough for bad rumors to spread quickly, and these informants are careful not to appear anti-social in the handling of their business because "old names still tend to be recognized in Boston." Those engaged in more intellectual professions seem to feel privileged at being rewarded for pursuing their curiosity. "I am extraordinarily satisfied. Work is a medium for my self-actualization, self-expression, and social contribution. It is just like religion!" "I receive a number of Christmas cards from my former students who are now teaching across the world. It makes your heart full when you see your subject is now taught by younger scholars."

Elderly informants affirm that they felt less pressure from their parents in selecting their jobs than they did in choosing their college. "My father used to say, 'You can go to whichever college you like. But if you go to Harvard, I will pay the tuition.'" "In my family, Harvard was *the* college, and all the other places like Yale or Princeton were considered to be secondary. I applied only to Harvard." Such pressure on the selection of a college and job is almost nonexistent among the younger generations. However, I heard about a couple of cases in which family pressure for success was too strong for the children to bear. In the case of a prominent Brahmin family, a son, now around 30, entered Harvard but majored in the fine arts despite his authoritarian father's expectation that he would become either a lawyer, a doctor, or a businessman. The son receives about $100,000 each year from his trust and other venture capital. Even though he is engaged in farming and environmental activities in New Jersey, he appears to my informants to be "wandering" and "aimless," unable to find a serious drive for a deeper commitment to society. Having defied his father, he continues a disenchanted relationship with him. He occasionally returns to his home using his own helicopter, but he cannot stop his body and voice from trembling. In the old Boston, at least one son was expected, explicitly or implicitly, to "make money," but the above case is regarded as "very extreme" or "too bad," even in the eyes of my informants.

I will describe the situation of female informants later on, but in general terms, women of the older generations were expected to coordinate human relationships in the family, oversee the maids and other home employees, and to become involved in charitable activities. The baby-boomers (those in their mid-thirties to late-forties at the time of the study) and their children (the so-called "MTV generation" or "Generation X") are more geared to business and academia, prolonging the period of their single lives. The women of these generations tend to be engaged in various nonprofit organizations (especially in education and the environment), artistic enterprises, therapeutic care, publishing, and academia (especially in the fields of the fine arts, anthropology, history, and literature).

I did not come across any in the fields of banking, investment, law, marketing, or other types of "high-powered business" that are considered to fall within "men's" or "middle-class women's" domain. Very few wives stay at home, and one informant estimates that nearly half the wives in the baby-boomer's generation in the Somerset Club or Tavern Club have outside jobs, primarily for self-fulfillment or self-growth. This ratio would be much higher among other families, especially among those of the younger generations, who are less wealthy and conservative.

Success

"Being successful" is considered to be a norm rather than an accomplishment, especially among the older generations. My informants have few memories of being praised or rewarded for doing something exceptional in their younger days. "I was punished for having done something mediocre!" "New Englanders are very poor at praising! But I feel we have been more encouraged to praise our kids more as time passes by." "Although WASPs are dying, I think the so-called 'Protestant ethic' of diligence is still persistent." Those who failed to embody that ethic are oftentimes described as "dropouts," "refugees," "wanderers," or "nuts." Even I was admonished at the time of my preliminary fieldwork: "Keep yourself busy! Otherwise, you'll end up just having a tea at Brahmins' summer houses!" Evans-Pritchard was fortunate.

A sense of pressure did accompany the successful pursuit of a career among my informants, however. A former college professor testifies that "I certainly felt the pressure of 'publish or perish' until 50 or 55 years old. I had to push myself hard to save my face. Sometimes it was difficult." Others said: "My business is going well, but I would have done better if I had graduated from law school. In this society, it is very difficult to become a prominent social figure without having a law degree." "I didn't get my Ph.D., and I feel a little bit ashamed of it."

However, "being successful" is becoming more demanding and can hardly be taken for granted for the younger generations. A top Harvard official, who is also a descendant of an old Yankee family in New England, testifies:

> As Vice President Gore mentioned the other day [at Harvard's Commencement in 1994], there is a very strong sense of cynicism towards the compact among people, businesses, and government. Our students know that the company will not keep you forever. The company knows that you will not stay for long. There is a mutual mistrust between them. Our students know that the world is beyond their knowledge and abilities. They are in despair. But, at the same time, they are very desperate to program themselves for the golden path to success. Most students tailor their college years so that they can get into business school, medical school, or law school, instead of government. They know that a Bachelor's degree is not enough to make it in our society. This tendency became intensified around the time of the Vietnam War and the students' movement in the late 1960s.

Another informant told me:

> I feel business is getting more and more aggressive without asking how! ... The Americans are quite notorious for being unkind. But I feel there is more lying and bad manners, and more consciousness of power in our society. I can understand why young people are emphasizing self-growth. After all, nobody is looking after you!

How to look after oneself? Her son, who was of my age, answered:

> I don't know. I will just keep pushing myself. ... I don't think I will be as famous as my father was. I am totally unknown and poor. So is my brother! He feels kind of

ashamed of it, but I don't. I feel I have more freedom than my father did.

"Defeat" in my life means to lose the passion for life. I don't care about how much money I earn or how others think of me. I like to be full of spirit and to explore the knowledge of myself and life. So, it's no a big deal even if my project goes bankrupt. It is a "mistake," not "defeat." You see what I mean?

Success is thus construed by the younger generations more in an existential and self-expressive sense than in terms of income and status. There seems to be an element of reaction, in this phenomenon, to the social despotism of the old Boston. However, it seems to me also that they are struggling to make sense of the process of cultural dilution and downward mobility that they are experiencing.

Tastes

Shifting the locus of investigation towards the more cultural domain of family life, Aldrich's (1988) analysis seems to be relevant in illuminating the basic ethos of my informants. He argues:

> In order to survive in this New World, the Old Rich (and the New Rich seeking to become Old) have had to grab on every old work of art, every piece of music, every old book, every old chair and table, every old style and fashion, and set them as props, in every sense of the word, of their historical legitimacy (p. 63).

Antiquity here connotes not only the temporal dimension but also a sense of the so-called Puritan ethics of frugality, moderation, and simplicity. Conspicuous consumption, as symbolized by Hollywood and New York City, is derided and abhorred as bad taste, materialistic, or superficial. Similarly, shining cleanliness and perfect tidiness is deemed to be more "new money" or middle-class taste. When I interviewed one informant at an old pub in Harvard Square, he jokingly complained to a waitress, "This table is too clean! I liked the little dust which used to darken my fingers slightly!"

As far as the sizes and exteriors of my informants' houses are concerned, I cannot conceive any striking features that distinguish them from those of other houses in their vicinity. The Victorian style was certainly the norm until the turn of this century, but today a great deal seems to depend on personal preferences and financial conditions. Some members of the younger generations reside in condominiums in urban areas and tend to move relatively frequently. Those in the suburbs are a little more conspicuous, in that their houses are prone to be located in the vast plots of land (50–100 acres) that accommodated their ancestors. Distinctiveness can be identified more in the decor of their houses: high ceilings, old Persian carpets, mantelpieces, leather chairs, Victorian dishes and tables, antique lamps and ornaments, seascapes, and portraits of ancestors on the walls, collections of rare hardcover books, high-culture magazines (like the *New Yorker*, *Harpers*, and *Atlantic*), and thoroughbred dogs (such as Labrador retrievers). It is not rare to find a house decorated with more than 100 paintings. There are television sets, but only small ones, normally placed somewhere away from the living and dining room.

None of the informants drives a Ferrari, Jaguar, or Cadillac. They seem to prefer simpler designs such as the Mercedes-Benz, Volkswagen, and BMW, or more practical types such as mini-vans and jeeps for driving through open country. My informants have summer houses and some favorite vacation spots throughout New England. Among the most popular are Northeast Harbor, Southwest Harbor, Mount Desert, Cranberry Island, Kennebunkport, Somes Sound, Cape Cod, Watch Hill, Groton, Madison, Brattleboro, Manchester, and Bretton Woods; spending vacations at the same place over and over is very much the custom. A branch of the Forbes family owns an entire island off the Cape Cod coast. The houses in such areas are much simpler in terms of decor, but often have more than 20 bedrooms and five bathrooms to accommodate friends and guests. A couple of informants have third houses on Manhattan's Upper East Side, where they occasionally stay after visiting museums and theaters.

An esthetic of sobriety is observed in terms of clothes and foods. Contrary to the stereotype among people in the street, there is nothing "flashy" about the way members of the old families dress for either formal or informal occasions. I probably would not recognize them by what they wear in the street, and actors in soap operas are far better dressed. The combination of wrinkled shirt (or polo shirt) and jeans (or casual skirt or trousers) is fairly common, and few male informants wear ties with their jackets in informal settings. They certainly have formal clothes of good quality, tailored in England or at J. Press, Brooks Brothers, Burberry's, and so on. Unlike social celebrities in the entertainment world, however, my informants are rarely preoccupied with upgrading their clothes. "I have been wearing a suit since the 1960s and a pair of shoes since the 1970s. They were custom-made in London and actually very good quality." "You can see that the emblem on this blazer is worn out, can't you? That's why I love it! I bought it 30 years ago when I was a college student." "My wedding dress was the one both my grandmother and mother wore. You can always buy a new one, but you cannot buy the sense of history." I seldom saw gold accessories or heavy make-up.

Meals were usually prepared by maids in the past, and they still are in some families even today. Recipes vary significantly in different families, but I found them fairly conservative, even abstemious, although I am far from being a gourmet. Breakfast is either a cup of coffee (or tea, or juice) or simple continental style. Lunch tends to vary according to who is at home, although sandwiches or pasta seem to be the most standard dishes. One family always has the same kind of pasta (Genovese) for lunch. Dinner normally consists of meat (or fish), salad, beans (or potatoes), and cooked vegetables, accompanied by wine, dessert, and coffee (or tea). The most elaborate dish that I was offered was a pate made from a duck which my informant had shot in his field. The size of the portions is quite moderate and self-restrained, which might explain why I did not come across any corpulent informants. Inviting guests and friends for dinner is fairly common. Dinner also takes place at social clubs, at friends' houses, and, much less frequently, at restaurants. All members of the family who are at home are expected to dine together; and as far as my research families are concerned, they do so.

The culture of the upper-middle class is embedded in, and expressed through, the kind of sport and recreational activities they engage in. Polo, tennis, golf, fishing, sailing, canoeing, hunting, and skiing have wide popularity, although some individuals prefer to engage in these activities only at country clubs or in Europe.[13] Many informants also identify chatting, reading, playing cards, visiting museums and theaters, and taking walks together as an integral part of family recreation. Jogging, aerobics, yoga, bowling, and Nintendo are rarely practiced.

In the past, the church provided a communal space and time for the family and the community, but fewer informants, especially the younger ones, take religion seriously. "I am supposed to be an Episcopalian, but I never considered myself as such. Watching sea and mountain makes me more religious." "We baptized our kids at an Episcopal church. That's it! Our duty is done! We don't go to church at all." In contrast to their low interest in religion, they have a keen awareness of politics. Nearly all the informants vote in elections. I had speculated that politics might be an almost taboo topic, but my informants were quite straightforward. A couple of informants started our first meeting by asking me, "What do you think about political correctness in our society? I think it is sheer nonsense!" or "Do you understand why the Americans picked such an idiot as Reagan? I still don't get it!" Those in academic/intellectual circles have a propensity to vote for Democrats, while others are "moderate" or "old-style liberal" Republicans who nonetheless voted for Lyndon Johnson and Bill Clinton. I did not encounter a far-right Republican who favored Pat Buchanan, or a far-left Democrat who supported Jerry Brown. "I usually don't trust people who look too sure that they are correct!"

A tradition of "liberalism" (not necessarily in recent political terms) is highly cherished among these informants as symbolizing the virtues of the upper-middle class and is closely related to the ideas of *noblesse oblige* and civic commitment. Negative images of Yankee culture once propagated by Marquand's 1937 novel *The Late George Apley* are still prevalent, but many informants and their ancestors have expressed their liberal tendencies in activities like building a Catholic church for Irish maids, raising funds to establish public schools in South Boston, paying for an Irish maid's eye surgery, providing financial assistance to Jewish immigrants, or coordinating a summer camp for youth, as mentioned earlier.

Simultaneously, liberalism has a close affinity to such notions as eccentricity, iconoclasm, and snobbery. Collecting Oriental arts, traveling to India, studying "primitive" peoples, collecting specimens of rare insects – all these activities are well received and are seen as representing individuals' distinct identities.[14] As Samuel Adams and Francis Hancock postulate, even defying Yankee culture itself can be regarded as a way of defining themselves on a deeper level.

However, what is indeed distinctive in their cultural domains might be that the constellation of qualities they use to represent their identity as distinct is gradually being fragmented and enfeebled as time passes by. Even if a preference for antiques among their possessions still persists, it is becoming more difficult to objectify and perpetuate it. Antiques tend to be scattered among offspring, sold off, or donated to museums for tax deductions. A house with high ceilings and elegant mantelpieces is hard for the younger generations to afford. Purebred pets and high-value paintings may seem out of place in their houses and, as one informant claims, "You shouldn't keep a pet if nobody can stay at home during the day."

Mark Gelfand (1998), in his biography of Ralph Lowell (1909–1978), widely known as "Mr. Boston" for his service as a trustee of almost every notable charitable, civic and cultural institution in the city, illustrates:

> While he took pleasure in seeing children continue the tradition [of the Lowells], Ralph realized that he was, in fact, the last of a line. A minor provision in his will reflected that reality. Portraits of seven generations of Lowells, stretching from Ralph back to the Reverend John Lowell of colonial Newbury, had long graced the walls of his Westwood home. Aware that subsequent generations might be unable to provide appropriate residential settings for this collection, he charged the executors of his estate with finding a suitable site. They chose Lowell House at Harvard so that every year a new class of undergraduates could draw inspiration from the family's example (p. 279).

Waves of mass production and mass media have made obsolete the distinction and privilege of aristocracy, and accelerated the merging of tastes with the "mass." "I personally don't like TV programs because their quality is so bad. But my kids need to know what is going on there to keep up a conversation with their friends at school." Tennis and golf can be played even by middle-class and working-class Americans today. Ethnic foods are much sought after. Summer houses are being sold, often emasculating both family cohesion and the implicit socialization artery of the clan. Being an Episcopalian or Unitarian matters little. Exaggerated Yankee accents are becoming obsolete, and the distinction between upper-class and working-class accents, which was very evident in the past, has become less clear cut. Having a suit tailored in England, driving a Volvo, and subscribing to the *New Yorker* are not so difficult, but the mere acquisition of these commodities is either "shabby-genteel" or a distinction without a difference. The boundaries between dignified sobriety and shabbiness, as well as those between eccentricity and weirdness, are thus becoming more and more ambiguous.[15]

Love and marriage

Love

Love is strongly idealized as the primary drive for marriage that should transcend sociocultural categories such as race, nationality, or class, and it is left to children to decide how they form affective relationships.

> I was not interfered with by my parents concerning my girlfriends. My parents put hands off – perhaps too much!

> My wife and I didn't like our daughter's boyfriend. But, of course, we couldn't say "no" to her. ... So, we just prayed for their breakup. And, actually they did! She soon met a very nice Jewish man, who became her husband later on. He was from a blue-collar "steel worker" family in Chicago, but I have no problem about that kind of class stuff. My wife and I visited his family last week and had a

great time. His father told me that he would beat me at bowling. So, I replied to him, "All right. Then I will beat you at tennis!'"

I don't want my daughter to marry a "lad" [a punk with tattoos and piercings] in Harvard Square. If he has a medical degree from B.U. (Boston University) or a Ph.D. from Harvard, I would feel very comfortable with him. But, more than anything, I will look at his personality and integrity.

A daughter of a prominent Brahmin family recently became engaged to her dark-skinned, Catholic college classmate in Cleveland, who was once imprisoned by a foreign government for activist conduct, but it hardly seemed to upset her family. Other informants remarked:

Our family's genealogy has incorporated many Jewish people. I'm sure my grandparents would have been astonished if they were alive today. I certainly don't want an extremist, but as far as he or she doesn't fanatically stick to Judaism, that will work well. Actually, I feel Unitarianism and Judaism have much in common in terms of their liberal tradition.

I would caution my son if he got married to a Black, but I wouldn't be able to say more than that.

These cases clearly indicate that the importance of class, race, and religion is changing. The younger generations are, in an elderly informant's words, "mixed up with all sorts of people." Yet a closer investigation reveals that more than 90 percent of "all sorts of people" fall into the category of White, middle or upper-middle-class, college graduates, and that love was usually generated within such institutional frameworks as schools, workplaces, and social parties which accommodated only limited numbers and types of people. Also, as well manifested in the harassment letter that my informant received for having married a woman of working-class background, there still exists a strong antipathy to the actual practice of the love-conquers-all motif – at least among some "stuffy" people who cherish their group's "grand past." In a similar fashion, no informants oppose homosexuality, but they tend to hesitate to admit (even to their kinsfolk or intimate friends) if a child or sibling is homosexual. "I would be upset if my daughter turned out to be lesbian, but I would have to accept it."

> Actually my brother is gay. We found it out a couple of years ago, and he half admitted it. My parents didn't flip him out, but we really had a difficult time to accept it. We thought it was a shame. ... Now we feel much better, but we still keep it confidential even from our grandparents.

Cohabitation

Cohabitation is certainly prevalent in this segment of American society as well. "All of my three kids did it. The times are changed." None of my informants object to the concept, and some actually elaborate on its merit. "'Love' depends so much on sexual drive. If you live together for a while, you can be more realistic about it." "If my kids ask me for a tip for a successful marriage, I would tell them to cohabit for a certain period of time. A good marriage involves good chemistry." A male informant in his late sixties attests:

> [Cohabitation] was quite unthinkable when I was younger, but it became gradually acceptable since the 1960s. I had two divorces, and have been living with a woman, a very intelligent woman, for more than ten years. She is just wonderful. I feel I am awakening to the broader world. She is more liberated and more society-conscious. I feel I am growing into a more independent personality with an ability to do good for others. Marriage? If it is legally advantageous, we'll do it. But, I don't think it is so important after doing it twice!

His will defines the woman he lives with as one of his inheritors. "There is a fear of commitment to long-term relationships. But also there is a fear of solitude. People are shying away from marriage and heading toward cohabitation." Love is very much sought after, but my informants are not blind to the harsh reality that in the United States half the marriages end in divorce. Cohabitation is taken as a rational, realistic and strategic improvisation.

Weddings

Among very old-fashioned Brahmins, a bridegroom-to-be is expected to visit his father-in-law and discuss his financial situation before the engagement. If necessary, and if the parents are well off, they might provide some support for the new couple. However, in most cases, the bridegroom is financially independent, and the meeting is quite informal, although he will be dressed formally. A typical wedding is attended by 200–400 friends and relatives and held at a church, to be followed by a reception at the bride's home, social club, or summer house. The wedding party and reception are organized by the new couple and hosted by the bride's parents.

My informants have little knowledge about how much was spent on their own weddings, but they testify that it cost them $5–15,000 to host the functions for their daughters. Invitations are mailed to uncles, aunts, and first cousins, but ultimately the selection rests on how close these relatives are in both a geographical and an emotional sense. Attendance by the spouses and children of these guests is optional. It is common for the bridegroom's parents to host the rehearsal dinner, which is much smaller in size, normally attended by 50–100 intimate relatives and friends of the couple. Sometimes ex-lovers are invited to these ceremonies. Although I did not come across any cases in which an ex-spouse was invited, I witnessed a couple of occasions where the ex-spouse's siblings and parents attended.

There is a great deal of flexibility in these general schemes. When the parents of the bride are deceased, the bridegroom's parents host the ceremonies. Sometimes the new couple opt to marry overseas and hold just a reception or cocktail party in the United States. In cases of remarriage, the ceremonies and receptions tend to be much smaller, usually with 20–50 intimate relatives and friends. Usually, children from earlier marriages attend. Guests are dressed properly but by no means in a rigidly formal fashion. Jazz music, dancing, balloon decorations, clam-bakes (if close to the seashore), and bridegrooms' humorous speeches characterize the receptions, which may last well past midnight. It can be observed that these projects are infused with more personal preferences among the younger couples, who aspire to express their own selves in a less formalized and ritualistic manner. In addition, the size of these ceremonies is shrinking because the younger couples favor a more relaxed and cozy ambiance with less financial burden. They are more involved in financing their own projects, and many opt for saving more for honeymoons, furniture, and mortgages. In short, their celebrations look more and more like ordinary, middle-class weddings.

Division of labor

The downsizing of the family, along with the rising costs of wages and the development of service industries, reduced the number of servants from "several" to "a few," or "a few to none" in the post-war era. Today, a part-time maid who does cleaning (and occasionally cooking as well) once a week or so seems to be the most prevalent form of outside support in the baby-boomer generation. The younger generations are without help (or are what they call "self-reliant" and "self-sufficient"). The division of labor between husband and wife is set very differently by each family. According to a couple of lawyers, 60 to 70 percent of couples in old families have a "pre-nuptial contract," but a "marriage contract" (about who takes out the garbage and who does dishes, etc.) is rare.

This gendering of domesticity is believed to be natural among the parents of the baby-boomer generation. In one case, the husband "knows nothing" about housekeeping matters, and the wife is in charge of almost all the domestic business. "We are very much departmentalized. I tend to do these [domestic] matters because it takes too long to teach my husband!" The husband is able to put up bookshelves, make coffee, and make the bed. The problem is that "he does it just for himself." However, the husband helps her when needed, and the wife does not feel that the status quo is unfair.

> My mother was always well dressed at home. She kept a lovely home. A nice entertainer, she taught me how

important and difficult it is to run a house. She considered it very seriously as a full-time job. I don't think of it as a secondary job as many other Americans tend to. I feel I am very fortunate.

I investigated how miscellaneous tasks are allocated between couples – cooking, putting away the dishes, picking up the mail, shining shoes, making repairs, vacuuming, shopping, ironing, carpentry, gardening, decorating, childrearing, and so on – only to recognize the high degree of variability and flexibility.[16] In the case of one elderly couple, for instance, the husband cuts the meat while the wife cuts the vegetables. She vacuums the first floor, and her husband the second and third floors. He polishes the antiques on the first floor because he is particular about them. The wife makes a shopping list, the husband does the shopping, and then the wife sorts out the purchases at home. She loves repairing. Although the ideology of female domesticity is still generally held in this generation, there is a range of improvisations and exceptions.

Subsequent generations have experienced a transitional period in which more wives are incorporated into the public sphere for economic reasons or for personal growth (or both). As befits a time of transition, there was some confusion and conflict. A female informant in her early fifties comments:

When my kids were still small – I mean in the early 1980s – I was teaching evening classes at college. But I was preparing dinner as well. I felt oppressed and frustrated. Now it is more shared and fair. My husband has improved a lot. He is good at making pie!

Another female informant reports:

When our small kid got sick, I was always expected to stay home by taking a day off from work. I thought it understandable but also anachronistic and unrealistic. I had a career as he did, but it was always I who was made to feel guilty! I suspect that it is still the case among many families in our country.

A male informant attests:

> In my first marriage, I was in charge of turning the heater on and off, doing repairs, and polishing my own shoes. My wife considered the home essentially her territory. Compared with my friends' homes, ours was too traditional. I didn't feel it was my home. I was afraid to touch even a cup! My second wife is working as a journalist. She does the vacuuming and laundry, and I send off my kid, do the cooking, and wash dishes. The rest is all shared. I feel more comfortable and equal today.

This transformation is well reflected in the way my informants treat guests. I witnessed several cases in which wives took the guests' coats and served cocktails while their husbands sat nearer to the kitchen at dinner and even served their special dishes. One's identity, once predicated on the gendering of the domestic sphere, is thus becoming more contingent and flexible. Many young fathers today carry their babies on their backs and change their diapers. This phenomenon is a response to the changing social environment as well as to the idealism of "intimacy" that many informants missed in their own upbringing in the past.

Divorce

Conflict

Conflicts in married life are mostly precipitated by such small things as forgetting to turn off the lights, leaving things messy, being indecisive, spending too much on clothes, treating antiques improperly, and so on. These issues disrupt the conjugal relationship, but mostly only temporarily. My informants know how to solve these sometimes critical, even though small, issues. "We discuss how to clarify the mutual responsibility." "Time solves." "It is a kind of rule that we compromise with each other on the next day."

> When we get into a serious fight, my wife cooks something she knows I don't like so much. I retaliate by going out for

a drink just with my friends. At this stage, she begins referring to me as Mr. XXX. There we stop it.

Sexual intercourse is experienced also as transcending the frustrations which occurred during the day, although none of the informants accord it a special status. Fidelity is highly valued, but a couple of informants, male and female, openly admit that they have ventured into secret extramarital relationships. Some informants visit their therapists on a regular basis. "I want to know about myself and our relations more objectively, I mean scientifically." "It always helps to get advice from the outside. Therapy has superseded kinship in this capacity." "I can get the ethos for improving myself and searching for happiness and success." They all acknowledge the positive effects of therapy in their search for a stable self and relationship, but there are increasing numbers of cases that can be solved only by dissolving their marital bond.

Divorce

The principle of "serial monogamy" is well embraced even by the relatively conservative members of social clubs. Many informants know that Ernest Fenollosa (1853–1908), a "proper" Bostonian whose expertise was in Japanese arts, was fired from the position of Director of the Peabody-Essex Museum because of his divorce. This kind of stigmatization is felt to be "utterly unthinkable and nonexistent" today, and only one of the 13 informant families has no record of divorces among its parents, siblings, and children. Nearly half the informants (and their siblings and first cousins) in the baby-boomer generation have terminated their marriages, and so have about one-fourth of their parents. The duration of marriage ranges from two to 20 years.

The timing of divorce differs significantly, just as the age of marriage varies greatly. However, many informants testify that the 1960s was a "confused and confusing" era in which "self-actualization" movements gained ground, and the conventional notion of marriage as a structured social institution began to be openly contested. As a consequence, the sentimental/sexual dimension of marriage ("feeling good") became more emphasized. However, it is rare to come across anyone who has been married three times, and the interval between marriages normally lasts from six months to five years.

Process

The process of marital dissolution is usually predicated on the perceived unfairness and imbalance of power relations, but a marriage crisis is occasionally induced when high expectations are not fulfilled.

> In the past, divorce was caused by sickness and fickleness, right? In my case, I had no serious complaints about him. I just wondered "Is marriage so important?" I didn't feel abused or oppressed at all. I just didn't feel marriage was the quintessence of my life. So, I proposed divorce to him. It was almost 20 years ago. Divorce itself was certainly painful ... a tremendous pain ... but much better than being unsatisfied or hurting him by staying married. ... There was stigmatism, but my impression was that it largely came from married couples. They needed to defend themselves and their marriages, I guess. Our daughter visited each of us every other day. Of course, we both showed up on parents' day at her school. Even today, we sometimes spend weekends together, spend summer together, have dinner together. We meet at least once in a couple of months. We got separated not because we couldn't tolerate each other. ... I once complained to my lawyer who spoke so badly of him! He agreed to pay $450 monthly for the upbringing of our daughter, but I declined it when she was ten because he is not so well off. He now pays only for our medical insurance. He told me that he cannot pay for her college expenses. I said, "O.K. Let's split." My name? I still maintain his (non-Brahmin) name simply because I want to have the same last name as my daughter. I have actually been proposed to by a man, although I am not inclined to get married again.

For people like this respondent, divorce is not seen as evidence of the "moral decadence" of contemporary society. Divorce is, in a sense, a defense mechanism against possible manipulation and abuse in married life, and simultaneously a revelation of the high standard of "self-fulfillment" or "love" demanded in marriage today.

> Sure, I was terribly shocked when my parents got divorced. I cried a lot in bed. It was awfully painful. But, my parents explained to me why they had to be separated. It took me a while to accept it. But, as time passed by, I began thinking that I might have felt more pain and been more miserable if they stayed married just for the sake of marriage. My parents are now good friends, both remarried, and both happy. I am glad to see that. I don't consider my parents as my role models, but I feel I am lucky anyway.

This young informant may indeed be "lucky," because there are many cases in the United States in which children are indoctrinated by one parent to avoid (or even resent) the other, and children in low-income families are impoverished by their fathers' negligence of custodianship (Brannen and Wilson 1987; Delphy 1984; Goldin 1990). My informants' financial conditions still seem able to ensure economic security, but declining fortunes might exacerbate the consequences of marital dissolution for future generations.

My informants tend to feel restrained and awkward at the thought of imposing their opinions on the education of their stepchildren, although this is very contingent upon the age of the child. The issue of step-parenting becomes more complicated when a divorcee who has a child produces another with her new husband. While her first child retains the surname of her ex-husband, her new child assumes that of her new husband. These children are domestically united by maternal care and residence but publicly divided by the patronymics that come from their respective fathers. Whether the first child spends such family gatherings as Thanksgiving or Christmas with his/her new father is normally specified in the custody agreements, but the actual arrangement seems to be more contingent on the child's age, emotional and geographical proximity to both old and new fathers, and so on.

Childrearing

Birth control

Some elderly informants appear dismayed by what they consider the sexual immorality that they associate with birth control pills, whereas the younger ones tend to take a favorable view of the broadened freedom and choice. Artificial abortion is unanimously perceived to be "sad but better than unwanted pregnancy." The average number of children in a family has decreased from "several" to "a few" in the postwar era, which might reflect the consolidation of the idealism of childrearing saturated with "parental love" as parents can give more care and attention to each child in smaller families (Kett 1977; Zelizer 1985).

Democratization

"Young couples carry babies on their backs!" That is how one elderly informant portrays "postwar upbringing," and other informants echo this characterization. What is implied in this statement is the increased informality of parenting styles and the reduction of emotional distance between parents and children. "As far as I observe my own family and other families in the Somerset Club, there is less discipline but more communication." Even those who regret the social transformation in the postwar era seem to take a favorable view of this phenomenon.

> Even before I was put into a boarding school, I had been mostly taken care of by nannies. My mother was very self-centered. She was busy serving as the chairperson of the board of Radcliffe College. All she did for me was to rub my back for ten minutes or so before my going to sleep. My first father was serving in the military when I was small. My stepfather was not interested even in his own children. I suspect my parents were just concerned about my social status. I never revealed my emotional pains to them. We never talked about the content of books. ... So, now I'm making a conscious effort not to become like them. I want to interact more – be more friendly – with

Fred [his 13-month-old son]. You know what? I'm telling him, "Fred, I put my hands away from you, not on you!" We always eat together, which is becoming rare in American families, and Fred is always seated between my wife and me.

My field notes recorded numerous narratives of this kind.

My sister entered a boarding school at the age of eight, and so did I when I was 14. There was little sense of family unity per se. I have two children now, and I really think we have a very strong unity today.

I feel much closer to my daughter than my mother was to me. Sometimes we are just like friends. Why? I don't have any maids, so it is impossible for me to create such distance. Also, my access to various resources that produce an "elite social life," like joining social clubs and so on, is limited. ... We often share clothes, which was unbelievable when I was a kid! But, more than anything, I just want to be close to my daughter. My mother knew little about me. ... I want to understand my daughter as much as I can.

The parent–child relationship is thus democratized and childrearing is sentimentalized, becoming a more intimate experience that is meant to be emotionally satisfying for both parents and children.

"Be assertive." "Decide what you want." "Do what you want to." These phrases, which struck me when I first came to the United States, are well demonstrated in my informants' discourse. Nearly all the informants in the baby-boomer generation regard it as their responsibility to choose schools and sponsor college education for their children. However, the selection of college, major, and occupation are marked off as the "children's business." "Don't say 'Don't' – this is the basic principle of postwar upbringing."

In the past, Harvard was *the* college, and the rest were all second players. We only asked "what year?" Now it's not easy to get in there. So, I don't want to put any pressure on my son, although I'm asking him not to wear a stupid Harvard shirt sold at the Coop!

Liberal arts were considered "proper" when I was a college student. I mean the subjects not for living but for making living more enjoyable. But I am going to approve whatever subjects my daughter wants to major in.

[A] blue-collar job is usually not so interesting ... so I don't recommend it to my kids. But, if they really like it, that's fine. It is very eccentric, isn't it?

There is a scene that is deeply ingrained in the memories of my fieldwork. A son of a prominent family was driven to a train station by his mother to make a trip to Washington, D.C. In those days, he was at a loss whether he should go to college or not, while his parents strongly wished for him to do so. To this family, a college degree is taken for granted, and it would have been rather a shame if he had opted not to pursue it. However, the parents did not voice their preference at all during their daily conversations. While waiting for the train, the mother spoke little, only smiling at him gently. She might have been inclined to say something about college to him on that occasion, but she did not. She wanted him to decide what he wanted to do by himself without being bothered by other people's opinions. Being moved by the depth of her affection, I was impressed by the thoroughness with which individualism was fostered in this family's childrearing.

Overprotection

As the parent–child relation becomes more democratized and childrearing more sentimentalized, the definition of "true" parental love becomes more problematic. A middle-aged informant on Beacon Hill comments on Bostonian parents:

I often find my friends are extremely protective of their children. They drive their kids back and forth between the North Shore and Boston. I admit that Boston is not necessarily a safe place, but it is by no means a dangerous place.

> I let my kids go to South Boston or Dorchester by them-selves. In my days, kids were all more adventurous and streetwise. I understand that my friends are doing that because they love their kids very much ... but perhaps too much. I don't think it is good for kids in the long run.

Another informant, who taught at a prestigious private school for more than 20 years, expounds on the phenomenon of "overprotec-tion" among young parents, who even do their children's home-work. A child who is helped in this way may receive better grades and gain entry to a better college. Parents will be proud of the accomplishment that is embodied in the child's success. Still, this act can be interpreted not only as "unfair" but also as "impeding kids' self-growth."

At this school, the Christmas celebration was suspended because some parents thought it unfair to Jewish students. The school then planned a Hanukkah celebration, but it too was suspended because it was considered as segregating non-Jewish students.

> So, we canceled both. Yes, we were "politically correct," but children lost an opportunity to celebrate their own cultural heritage and appreciate the different traditions of their friends. I think it was a stupid judgment, made only from the parents' points of view or purely on political grounds. I saw many students disappointed.

This incident entailed a series of long discussions about the rela-tionship between home (parents) and school (teachers).

> Both parents and teachers are confused. I think schools are trying to communicate with parents more. My own parents used to come to my school only once or twice a year. Now parents have to attend P.T.A. meetings at their kids' school 15 to 20 times!

Nobody repudiates the virtue of parental love, but my informants are struggling over how best to express their love without spoiling their children or suppressing their growth.

Family life

Continuity

Historical continuity is strongly perpetuated in the given names in these old Yankee families. In the lineage of Theodore Lowell Appleton, "Theodore" has been used since Theodore Eliot in the eighteenth century, inherited by Theodore Lowell, Theodore Lowell Eliot, and three Theodore Lowell Appletons before him. There have been eight Francis Hancocks. William Lyman Saltonstall testifies that his father and his son both have "William Lyman" in their names. He is referred to as "William," and his son is distinguished as "Bill."

A sense of continuity is also inscribed in such prestigious graveyards as the Mt. Auburn Cemetery and the Forest Hill Cemetery. However, geographic mobility means that family members may be buried at cemeteries scattered almost across the country. Furthermore, people seemed to me more flexible about graveyards than over naming. For instance, Thomas Dudley Cabot (1897–1995), who passed his first name on to one of his sons, wished to be cremated, and his ashes were scattered on a hill in the wilds of Butter Island overlooking Penobscot Bay in 1995. Interestingly enough, nearly half the informants in the pre-baby-boomer generation expressed a preference for cremation and having their ashes scattered in places they were attached to, rather than attending the "ultimate family gathering" in graveyards.

The sense of place is nurtured through various customs and rituals in everyday life. All of my informants take meals very seriously in this respect, and they testify that they actually shared the time and space of breakfast and dinner with the rest of the family until they (or their children) left home.

> My kids were all attending boarding schools. But on weekends and during vacation we always ate together. Their grandfather joined us for Sunday brunch. So, I was still eating with my parents!

> Sometimes meals are very tense. ... I feel reluctant to eat with my parents. ... In that case, I would call up my friends

and eat out. But it is just once or twice a month. I think meals are really important for the family, and it is actually fun most of the time.

Most Americans don't eat together. Kids heat up pizza and drink coke. They eat while watching TV in their own rooms. I wonder what the family does mean to those kids.

These voices capture common feelings among my informants.

In one family, mother would cook, young daughters prepare the table, father would serve dessert and tea (or coffee), and young sons wash dishes. Dinners were filled with laughter and lively discussions. There were several moments when nobody could utter a word without a roar of laughter at the funny anecdotes of grandparents, friends, and each other. I first suspected that this might be a kind of "performance" in front of an outside investigator, but I became more and more convinced that these were authentic moments. For these parents, who both grew up with maids and cooks, this must once have been an unimaginable situation. "Yes indeed. But we love it! I feel my family is very much united!"

However, for young professional couples with small children, preparing meals (and in some cases even dining together) is by no means an easy task.

We don't cook complicated stuff. Sometimes we have so-called "microwave foods." On weekends, we like to relax. So we tend to eat out. ... But I don't think microwave foods or restaurant foods have weakened our bond. Instead we can have quality time.

Communication

Greater informality and the reduction of age-related divisions in family relationships has made it less taboo to talk about sex, illness, or money at home – although over-realistic descriptions that might offend others tend to be avoided. In earlier generations, fathers had a propensity to be rigid and authoritarian, preferring to lay down the law rather than engage in discussion, although mothers were more flexible. Today, the atmosphere is more friendly and casual, and children can freely disagree with their fathers. Some elderly informants feel uncomfortable with this transformation:

> My daughters began "debating" with my wife at the dinner table when they were teens. I was appalled to see that. I thought a child's respect for parents was gone!

Rituals are also performed in a less formal atmosphere.

> In the past, my grandfather always read the Thanksgiving prayer, and I ate a slice of turkey of the same thickness every year. Today, it doesn't matter who reads the prayer, and you can eat as much as, or as little as, you want.

One informant notes:

> When I was a kid, we spent weekends together. We were very self-contained. I didn't socialize with my friends on weekends. But my son might spend more time with other kids by belonging to the Boy Scouts or Little League. It's inevitable since the number of kids is small today. Things will get much less formal. We might be skiing on Christmas in ten years, but this is still quite unthinkable.

His wife adds:

> We hope to instill in our son confidence without a sense of entitlement ... well, I mean the place in the family. My parents both divorced and unsuccessfully remarried. I didn't have the sense of place in family and in history ... and I remember wondering "who am I?" and "Where am I from?"

But how can they inculcate that feeling when symbols and rituals are more and more informal and fragmented? Can "love" alone assume that transcending power? Her husband adds, expounding on the predicament of its implementation:

You know, a man is a pilgrim who searches for meaning –
who you are and what is important to you. But, today,
people don't seek, nor do they struggle. ... Everything is
easy to obtain or too difficult to obtain.

The elderly

Parents are disposed to respect a child's freedom and preserve
their own self-reliance even in their old age. In the past, their children would be living nearby and could keep an eye on the welfare
of their independent parents. However, high mobility among the
younger generations has made this arrangement difficult. Many
elderly informants live by themselves as long as they feel comfortable with daily activities, and when they do not, a maid is hired on
either a part-time or full-time basis. Some older people miss their
distant children, but they do not regard it a child's obligation to
look after them. "My daughter sometimes sends me presents and
cards, which is very nice. But I don't have any desire for her to live
near us." "If I wanted to live near my child, then I would move
near to her place. She has her own family and her own career." All
the informants share this reasoning and feel that occasional
communication in the form of cards, presents, telephone calls, and
visits are sufficient to please them.

Several of my informants' parents suffer from Alzheimer's
disease. All these patients seem to express their resistance to being
institutionalized, and their children feel "guilty." These patients
are mostly looked after by their partners and/or by professional
caregivers. One woman declined to participate in my interview
because she knew that her life would be extraordinarily hectic
caring for her father with Alzheimer's as well as bringing up her
young children, and so she would have very little extra time. In
the case of this informant, the situation is slightly alleviated by the
fact that she lives in the same area, she is primarily a housewife,
and her father gets on well with his part-time caretaker. Another
case is more problematic:

> The other day, my sister and I went to see a couple of nurs-
> ing homes around this area for our father who has
> Alzheimer's. Actually, we found those homes much better

than I thought, excellent medical services, much freedom, and more communal atmosphere. ... But my father wouldn't listen to our suggestions and hates even home nurses. So my mother is taking care of my father by herself for the most part. I think the work is too much for her at her age.

This informant occasionally visits his father, but it is impossible for him to move to the father's house or bring the father to his home because his wife is working full-time and they have a small child. His sister's situation is more or less the same. Although cases of Alzheimer's disease might be extreme (though by no means unusual) scenarios, these examples suggest that structural reshuffling is needed to cope effectively with a highly mobile social context so that both care of the elderly and the children's freedom are ensured without entailing any severe strain.

Finances and inheritance

Finances

The monthly expenses of each family vary significantly, depending on the number and ages of the children, income level, residential area, status in society, mortgages, maintenance cost of summer house(s), insurance, and other miscellaneous and incidental factors. None of my informants, young or elderly, applies any formal program of home economics, but they do have a rough budget scheme in their minds. The average monthly expenditure per couple ranges from $3,000 to $12,000.

In the case mentioned earlier of the family that received letters from the "Frustrated Four," the husband earns $35,000 from his investment job and receives $35,000 from bonds and $30,000 from trusts each year; the total of $100,000 more or less corresponds to the family's annual expenses. His wife is entitled to $25,000 from her husband's resources, and she is responsible for the food, half the cost of maids, insurance of her engagement ring and car, and the son's clothes. They have already opened accounts for their one-year-old son at a local bank and with Merrill Lynch and have begun to deposit $10,000 annually (the amount that can legally be distributed from the trust before the demise of the grandparents).

Another informant, a retired college professor, annually receives a total of $60,000 from Social Security, a retirement fund, and family trusts, and spends approximately the same amount. However, this figure does not cover the property tax ($12,000 per year) in his wealthy neighborhood. Also, the house is somewhat too big for his wife and himself, so they are planning to move to a suburb in the very near future. Both of these informants have donated a substantial portion of their assets (e.g. money, art works, historical documents, and real estate) to "all sorts of charitable organizations" for tax incentives after careful consultation with their trust lawyers.

The type and arrangement of bank accounts vary tremendously. Some informants do not favor joint accounts because of the trouble involved in updating the balance and because they want a certain financial autonomy. Some prefer joint accounts because these are more efficient in an emergency. "It's totally up to each couple." Some know their partner's password although they have separate accounts. The decision-making process over the financial disposition is basically egalitarian, although the final decision and responsibility (for things such as tax returns and high bills) tend to be taken by the partner whose contribution is disproportionately high or who is more detail-oriented. Most informants opened their own accounts when they were around 12 to 15 years old. No informants know the bank passwords of their parents or adult children. However, they seem to have a "rough" estimate of each other's savings. While major local banks such as the BayBank, Shawmut, and Cambridge Trust, and Bank of Boston are well utilized, the selection is a matter of personal choice and convenience. "I used to use BayBank, but after retirement I changed to Shawmut simply because it is closer to my home. It's not a big deal."

Family trusts

Inheritance, in contrast, is a big deal, as it is the means of perpetuating historical continuity and financial security for offspring. According to a couple of lawyers advising some of the old families, the total amount of assets (inclusive of house, property, and stock) among these families falls within the range of $2–8 million. The allocation of an inheritance depends on prescriptions in the will that normally take into consideration miscellaneous factors such as the inheritors' ages, financial conditions, characters, and so on. Massachusetts has long been known as a state with a high inheritance tax. A legatee can receive $600,000 as a tax-free inheritance, but any amount beyond this is subject to a 50–60 percent state tax. This being so, many families have opted to relocate their residential registration outside of Massachusetts and to incorporate their grandchildren as heirs to alleviate taxation. Yet, these strategies play only a passive role in slowing the process of declining fortunes over time, especially in the face of the geometrical proliferation of inheritors.[17]

All of my research families take advantage of further incentives to "play a game" (Bourdieu 1977) with the state by setting up family trusts and foundations, by investing in the stock market, and by donating or loaning their money, art works, antiques, and real estate to various charitable organizations, museums, schools, hospitals, and so on. Some elderly informants were engaged in the process of establishing trusts for their grandchildren and great-grandchildren during the time of my fieldwork in order to minimize taxation and to ensure the upper-middle-class lifestyle of their offspring. "My lawyer is telling me that the income would allow them to pursue college degrees."

According to the lawyers that I interviewed, the concept of "trusts" was first implemented in Boston in the mid-eighteenth century (the first such development in the nation), for the protection of minors, widows, the elderly, priests, and sailors who were in a financially disadvantageous position in society.[18] People in the heyday of Brahmin hegemony between the 1830s and 1860s pursued a high-risk, speculative investment strategy to keep their fortunes intact and avoid fragmentation across generations. A web of elaborate legal arrangements prohibited the whimsical and extravagant use of inheritances by spendthrift descendants: "They didn't trust their children!"

This legal and financial security, however, led to a decline of the entrepreneurial spirit among the inheritors, especially before the 1930s, except for such owners of family corporations as Charles Francis Adams (1886–1954) and Thomas Dudley Cabot (1897–1995). "Even the Lowells have done nothing ever since they made big 'mine' money in 1807!" This tendency was exacerbated by the fact that trust officers, being concerned with the protection and preservation of their money, were prone to making conservative and safe investments that produce only marginal profits.[19] According to the lawyers, the growth of divorce and remarriage in the postwar era has also accelerated the erosion of family assets. "Since 1970 or so, people have begun making a conscious effort to make money, but just for their survival!"

Today, most of my informants receive $10,000 to $30,000 as their annual trust income, depending on the size of the capital. Specific terms (eligibility, duration, methods of payment, restrictions, and the like) are legally prescribed, with enormous variations from one trust to another and from one family to another. Some middle-aged informants are surprised to receive a sudden notice from a relative's trust that they are named as a beneficiary.

> I didn't know that my aunt included me in her trust. I am very grateful to her for that. But it is a great pity that she is no longer alive. I wish I could have thanked her face to face. Also, I wish she had informed me of this long before. ... Then, I would have been able to plan my life a bit differently. But perhaps my aunt didn't want to spoil me by telling me that.

This example is indicative of an opacity of trust mechanisms that was often admitted to freely during the course of my research. "I know how much I can receive, but I have little knowledge about how it works. It is so technical and complicated. You may call up my lawyer, if you wish." As Marcus (1983), Aldrich (1988), and Marcus and Hall (1992) suggest, the complication of legal codes has a tendency to gradually shift the command of trust management from the hands of family members to those of legal experts. In some (usually wealthier) families, formal lessons are provided for children on what trusts mean, how they function, and how to utilize them. However, except for those who become lawyers themselves, their knowledge tends to be, according to a lawyer, "very superficial, premature, and inapplicable" in the context of the highly intricate and competitive real world. The invisibility and intangibility of the whole mechanism seem to be making some informants very suspicious and cautious:

> I am thinking about establishing a trust for my children. But I am afraid to lose control over my own money. Some lawyers are too businesslike and sometimes make completely bad investments. I know many families that were devastatingly hit by those blunders.

The web of complex legal and financial terms certainly fosters family identity, but it is a kind of identity over which they have little control. It is also an identity which is essentially predicated on a "businesslike," utilitarian rationality. "If trust lawyers were gone, our family would also be gone." This is perhaps an exaggeration, but might be capturing a certain truth.

Trust lawyers have conventionally been selected among (or through) one's classmates, friends, and relatives. The "age" of the lawyer is a significant factor to some informants:

> I got my lawyer through my friend, but I consciously selected a man much younger than I am. There are two reasons for that. The first reason is that I thought things would get a bit complicated if my lawyer retires when, or soon after, I retire. Another reason is that I wanted him [the lawyer] to pass down my memories to my great-grandchildren.

Sometimes, a trust lawyer, well acquainted with the family, happens to marry one of its members. I wondered if that causes any conflict of interests and sentiments among its members. "That's unheard of. You know, if the lawyer ever does anything tricky or unfair to his own advantage, he would not only lose his job but also his trustability in the Boston society. There is still such social pressure." Hiring "from within" is certainly based on a suspicion of "outsiders," but the ties among the "old-boys' network" are loosening as the members' backgrounds are diversified.

Inheritance

Although the content of a will falls within the discretion of the testator, the state law normally recommends that the surviving partner inherit two-thirds of an estate and the children the remaining third.

If this ratio is significantly modified, the testator needs to submit a justification for it. Among the children, inheritance is divided more or less equally in terms of monetary value, whether the heirs are male or female, young or elderly. The testator often takes into account each prospective heir's preference for particular objects. Otherwise, the division of various objects will be determined by the heirs. A lottery seems to a popular method of ensuring the principle of fair play. "If you don't like what you got, you can, of course, make a deal with others!" Although the heirs' preferences are valued, the testator often prescribes the patrimonial objects to male heirs (or those who have a male child) to ensure the continuity of family identity.

When all the inheritors are female, objects are destined to be transferred out of the family. In most case, this fact presents no problems in the mind of the testator. "That's perfectly all right. Actually, we have a silver spoon that has been passed down from our family to the Thayers, then to the Coolidges, and finally to us. Do you call it 'kula' in anthropology?" However, I heard of a couple of rare cases in which someone married an heiress in order to preserve a family's ownership of certain properties and houses.

Works of art and historical documents are, if not wanted by prospective heirs, sold off or, in most cases, donated to museums to ensure they will be preserved and to reduce taxes. Some informants have listed the estimated prices of almost every single piece in their collections on their computers so that their children will not be cheated by market dealers or professional retailers. Although the disposition of inherited objects is basically left to the discretion of each heir, the exodus of art objects, antiques, houses, and properties could promote the fragmentation of family identity and historical continuity embedded in those objects and symbols.

> I have no problem if my art is eventually passed down to my daughter's illegitimate child. Blood is important. To homosexual partners or cohabitant partners? It depends on how serious she is and how stable the relationship is. I hesitate to say "no," but I don't feel so comfortable about those cases.

Most of my informants know one or two homosexuals among their relatives, but have little information about how their inheritance has actually been disposed.

There are some subtle politics of inheritance taking place in the domestic sphere. In one family, there is a "baby bed" that has been traditionally passed on only to male infants. This bed has been acquired by a daughter who does not have a male baby. My informant has heard some discordant voices from her siblings, but is trying to ensure the situation does not cause problems. "Well, I am her stepmother, and I don't want to jeopardize the relationship that I have built with her. Also, I think it might be an anachronism to stick to lineage." In another family, an informant complains that his sister is assuming that their parental house in Beverly Farms is hers. "The house is now owned by a trust, but still there seems to be a sphere where we might battle!"

There are more serious cases. According to an informant who once served a notable Brahmin family as a maid, the elderly widow of the family did not want to be transferred to a nursing home.

> But the kids finally put her in one – almost forcibly. Why? The kids wanted to sell her $5-million house to obtain their inheritance as soon as possible. The nursing home cost $350 a day! They also sold a picture that she loved very much for $400,000. She became so furious with them. She was always crying in front of me ... and she passed away alone. I think that family is just crazy! They were so rich, but they were also very mean. They even took the batteries out of the clock when they traveled. They bought little food. So the refrigerator was always empty even when they had helpers to feed. On the other hand, they took everything that the government provided, I mean, even cheese and milk, for their elderly mother. They were too preoccupied with money. After her death, I had to dispose of her personal correspondence. But I was appalled to find that almost all the letters from her husband and children were just about money! Her child still lives nearby. But her husband spends only 15 minutes a day socializing with their kid. She is also busy playing golf during the daytime. Actually, her husband is involved in the investment business. Before the mother's

death, the couple slightly changed her will. The mother told me that she didn't want to see them at all. I feel how fortunate I am not to have been born into a rich family. Too much money sometimes makes you unhappy. After all, there was no sense of love in that family.

There are other cases. The father-in-law of one informant was excluded from an inheritance because he married the daughter of a local fisherman. In another instance the father sued his children who attempted to invalidate his will because they claimed he was mentally ill. My informants view these cases as rather exceptional, "not to say too exceptional." "It is that kind of damn ugly world that we are trying to transcend." The apotheosis of "love" in the familial sphere can be seen as a poetics of such sentiments.

* * *

Thus far, I have scrutinized the process of how the transfigurations of social environments and family backgrounds have both sensitized and reflected the "politics of culture" in such specific facets of my informants' actual social lives and relationships as neighborhood, philanthropy, social clubs, kinship, friendship, work, cultural taste, love and marriage, divorce, childrearing, care for the elderly, family life, finance, and inheritance. While the new family pluralism, the democratization of social relationships, and the expansion of personal freedom and choice are widely celebrated, there are sentiments, interpretations, and attempts which strain to reify and restore the cultural traditions of people who regret and fear the fragmentation and dilution of their niches. In actual field situations, these interpretations and sentiments are more mixed, ambivalent, subtle, and contingent even in the mind of each informant. Yet to accommodate this "politics of culture" in any balanced fashion poses challenges both epistemologically and practically to all the informants.

To avoid essentialization and to illuminate their experiences further, I would like, in the next chapter, to explore how the Irish Catholics of Boston have appropriated this "politics of culture" in the vicissitudes of their lives. As was explained in Chapter 1, Irish Catholic cultural histories and social realities contrast sharply with those of the old Yankee families. The relationships between the Brahmins and the Irish are perceived to have been worst at the time of Mayor Curley before and during the Second World War. Curley was provocative enough when he denounced the Yankees' political organization, the Good Government Association, as "that select and exclusive body of social bounders in the Back Bay" (Eisinger 1980, p. 38). Since the dissolution of the Association in 1933 after three decades' of activity, no Yankee has ever aspired to contest the Irish rule over the city.

The tension has eased in the postwar era, and many Yankee informants perceive no serious conflicts between the two groups today. However, stereotyping ("Yankee domination" and "Irish insularity") still persists, and my informants, while declining to identify themselves as Boston Brahmins, strongly deny that the Kennedys have any affinity with them. As a matter of fact, few informants have close associations with the Irish in their private lives. Some have never even been to such blue-collar neighborhoods as South Boston, Dorchester, and Charlestown in their entire lives, although these are all located less than an hour's drive from "proper" Bostonian areas. The distance is observed by the Irish as well. It takes less than 20 minutes to travel from Beacon Hill to South Boston by car. However, many skyscrapers in the downtown area look as if they are segregating these two neighborhoods both physically and emotionally.

Now I will move to South Boston and then look back at Beacon Hill from there. In Chapter 4, I will view both Beacon Hill and South Boston from the sky and contemplate the implications of my observations in relation to the wider sociocultural and historical context of the United States in the late modern era.

3 The Irish family

A changing society

Testimonies

Joseph Doyle views the postwar era as a major turning point for his fellow Irish Catholics in the Boston area: "We finally became first-class citizens." He perceives this "upgrading" to have been facilitated by various factors: "Strange people flocked to Boston, seeking any kind of job to make a living;" "We spoke English, unlike many other immigrants;" "The Irish are affable, loving to tell stories;" and "The G.I. bill made it possible for us to have a college education and own houses." The Great Depression occurred when he was nine years old. "It was the time when there was no social welfare. My father lost his job, and we were indeed impoverished."

After graduating from South Boston High School, he joined the military and served in Japan. In 1947, he married a South Boston "native" and worked for the Coast Guard and as a fireman, bus driver, and taxi driver until retiring in 1994 at the age of 75. "I realized that my response time became a little longer." He defines himself as "middle-class," on the grounds that "I have never had my paycheck stopped and I have my own home." His house is one of the "model houses" in North Weymouth, a Boston suburb located within a 30-minute drive from South Boston, built by local high school students as a part of their vocational curriculum, and he purchased it in 1950 for $10,000. "We wanted to live in Southie (South Boston), but it became so crowded after young people came back [from the war]."

His mother, one of 14 children, immigrated to Boston in 1904 and raised eight children. She temporarily served in the home of a Boston Brahmin family, which was generous enough to pay for her to have eye surgery. She met her husband at a dance in South Boston. Joseph's paternal family crossed the Atlantic in 1910, and his father, one of eleven children, was engaged in farming in Beverly.

Joseph and his wife raised six children who are now in their forties and are engaged in military services, fisheries, receptionist work, and the foreign service.

His daughter, a diplomat stationed in South Asia, has a college degree. "You can see the difference. My wife and I first opened an account in 1972 when I was 50 years old. Our grandchildren already have their own accounts even though they are still in their early teens!" The upward mobility of the Boston Irish is thus a lived experience to Mr. Doyle in light of the upgrading of jobs undertaken by his family. Interestingly enough, he relates this shift to the "middle class" not only to employment opportunity but also to the perceived decrease of liquor consumption among his fellow Irishmen over the past several decades.

> The Irish used to drink a lot. Actually my father made beer and whiskey at home, although he didn't sell them. Alcohol was a part of our culture, but not just for socializing. They wanted to escape from, and forget about, their stressful and tough lives. They sipped a bottle of whiskey and just went to sleep before going to work several hours later. There isn't so much necessity to drink today because life is not so bad. I know how to make beer but drink much less.

However, Mr. Doyle pinpoints some negative aspects of the transition and the subsequent success story.

> Young people were supposed to be seen but not heard. Today, they are very self-centered and materialistic, getting more degrees and moving around for more high-paying jobs. I believe that everybody has "something" that he can offer to society, but there is too much emphasis on becoming lawyers, doctors, and company executives. Well, they are perhaps disillusioned about society after seeing that Americans interfered in others' lives and were defeated in Vietnam. But, there is too much loss of authority and morality in society. Freedom is O.K., but you can't be totally free! If you become too free, you can't appreciate freedom. Now, I feel authority is encroached on by the dollar: I mean Hollywood, Nintendo, violent scenes on TV.

You know, a TV program one day tells you that coffee works good for you, but next day that it doesn't. How can we believe science? After all, even science is too much commercialized today. Yah, I think people are feeling uncertain about the future and unclear about the overall picture of society. In the past, South Boston was one of such overall pictures. Now, TV gives you so many pictures from such distant places, I mean, like Bosnia and Somalia. It is just impossible to imagine the big picture of society! Young people might call me too narrow and outdated, but this is the way I used to be and I am too old to change!

... I think that such a sense of uncertainty for the future makes it difficult to feel tied to history as well. Both parents and children don't know, and don't care, about the continuity of history. Why? Well, because the USA itself is a young country, because there are too many different histories for different ethnic groups, and because the speed of industrial life itself is so fast. I mean, in the countryside, you can still take the time to walk along the seashore and reflect on yourself and your father, but it's just impossible in the urban area. People tend to focus just on "now." Well, my kids know much about our family history because I like talking about it, but I don't think that they care about it so much. I have visited Ireland twelve times since 1976, and actually I can identify all the names and faces of my 42 first cousins there! Anyway, in Ireland, when someone dies, all the people in his community attend the funeral, sharing his memory and mourning his passing. It is quite rare in the United States. This society loves "individual-ism" and the "self-made man." But I think the "self-made man" is nonsense. I know that one seldom looks back at others once he gets money and status. Even Einstein was not a self-made man. He had his teacher and his mother, didn't he? Nobody can live alone. Well, in the past, we used to have six to eight kids in one family, but now it fell down to two or three. Perhaps it is making individuals more nuclearized, I feel.

Edward Murphy is a contemporary of Joseph Doyle, but he still resides in South Boston. He once served as Chief Marshal at the St. Patrick's Day celebration, and showed me a couple of certificates of commendation that he received from the city. His grandfather immigrated to Boston in the 1840s, around the time of the Great Famine in Ireland, and worked as a boilermaker in Boston. His maternal grandfather was a Protestant who, as was often the case with other non-Catholics, converted to Catholicism. Edward's father was a customs officer, and his brother worked in the post office. His sister is, as was usual in those days, a housewife, although she now works part time in a local municipal office.

Edward himself served as a postal worker for 35 years, retiring twelve years ago at the age of 60. He now lives in the house where his wife was born and raised. There was no college graduate in his family until his children's generation. His eldest son graduated from Boston College and now works as the director of public relations in a local municipal office. Three other sons graduated from the University of Massachusetts in Boston or Northeastern University, and are now making their livings in the Greater Boston area, one as an engineer, one as the prosecutor in a local court, and the other as a chief clerk in another local court. His only daughter graduated from Boston College and now lives in Virginia, where she works as the head nurse at one of the state's biggest hospitals. One of his nephews graduated from Harvard and one of his nieces from Tufts.

All of his children except the youngest son are married, and three of them married spouses from South Boston. Although most married "Irish Catholics," the children's spouses include a Jew, a Lithuanian, and an Italian. As with the Doyles, there has been no divorce in Edward Murphy's family, and upward mobility is a tangible experience for them as well. He has been back to Ireland four times, and his relatives there regard him as a rich man who has achieved the American dream.

Even after retirement, Edward Murphy leads a very busy life, being involved in veteran's organizations, church activities, and so on. At the time of my interview, he was writing a letter to the City of Boston, communicating his neighbors' frustration with the parking conditions around a nearby tavern.

Living in Southie keeps you busy. Why? Because people outside of this community keep criticizing us for having opposed busing, the [racial] mixing of tenants, the gay participation in the St. Patrick's Day parade, and so on. Both the [Boston] *Herald* and the [Boston] *Globe* write so badly of us. I don't want them to tell us what to do! I was interviewed by those news reporters when I was the Chief Marshal, but they didn't quote me correctly. I could see their clear intentions to change us. They report only bad news about South Boston. There are lots of good deeds, good people, and good help in the community. You know, we have many people who volunteer to coach children's hockey teams.

While thus endeavoring to protect his community from outside interests and prejudices, Mr. Murphy acknowledges the fragmentation of what Joseph Doyle called the "overall picture" of South Boston that has provided a sense of security and historical continuity.

I think I would move out of Southie if I were younger. Although Southie has a beautiful beach and is located in close proximity to Boston, it no longer has a good social atmosphere. Only a few families in my neighborhood have lived [here] as long as 40 years, as we have. Many families have left for the suburbs as they got more money, and they are renting their old houses to outsiders, especially to college students. Those kids can share three or four bedrooms for $800–900 per month. Considering this location, I think it is a fairly good deal. But that has deprived us of a sense of community that I strongly felt until the late 1960s. These days, I am a bit scared of walking alone at night. There used to be more policemen, teachers, and municipal officers living in this neighborhood. ... You know, one of our sons still lives with us. It's just because he is still single. I am sure that he will move out of Southie after getting married, and I think he should do so for his children.

This is indeed a radical statement because children are still expected to stay close to their parents.

Edward Murphy echoes Joseph Doyle in deploring and impugning the fracture of authority and morality in society.

> I think the American society is in crisis. Parents have no time for their kids. I don't mind if women work or not, but each couple should work out how to rotate their job shift, as my wife and I did, so that at least one parent can always stay with the child. Young couples are too liberal and irresponsible. Well, many Americans insist on freedom and choice, but they are taking these concepts for granted. Some people are even burning our national flag, saying that they have the right to do so. It is just too much! It's just impossible! What happens to our social symbols? Many friends of mine died to protect this country! Also, in the past, we played sports just for enjoying teamwork and doing our best, but now people are aiming at getting titles and becoming superstars. They have become too selfish and greedy. Partly, schools are responsible for this moral decay. When we were at school, our teachers taught faith, values, and heart to us. Now, our kids are encouraged to be innovative, independent, and ambitious.

Cynthia Sullivan O'Leary and her husband, Patrick, are both babyboomers, one generation younger than Joseph Doyle and Edward Murphy. Their grandparents immigrated to Boston at the turn of the twentieth century, and such jobs as waitress, bartender, secretary, receptionist, truck driver, postal worker, meter reader, and fireman was a part of the family tradition and identity for their parents and grandparents. "Everybody" married Irish Catholics from South Boston and never divorced. In Cynthia and Patrick's generation, however, this social picture has incorporated several divorces; a few college degrees; a few managers; spouses of Lithuanian, Polish, and Greek backgrounds; and homes in such Boston suburbs as Framingham, Medfield, Melrose, Quincy, and Tewksbury. Their only child, Peter, is majoring in computer science at the University of Massachusetts in Boston, and hoping to work in a challenging environment such as that of Silicon Valley. In Peter's generation, more people are attending college, working in other locations, and married to outsiders. "As far as you are happy, that's fine. The family is becoming like the United Nations!"

Cynthia and Patrick, now both in their forties, have no college degrees and rent the first floor (two bedrooms) of a three-storey house. Patrick has been working for Boston Edison for the past 25 years, including 14 years spent reading meters. Cynthia has been working as a secretary at a university medical center in downtown Boston for six years on a full-time basis. She works as a volunteer on Saturday evenings. Both Cynthia and Patrick, whose fathers had little time at home because they were holding down three jobs, see their present life as "very secure and comfortable." Especially for Cynthia, who grew up in a "project" (a housing welfare program where the monthly rent was only $25 when she was in her teens in the late 1960s), her current $800-a-month apartment, which is well maintained and furnished with a large TV, VCR, couch, and computer, betokens the upward road that she has moved along over the past decades. Cynthia remarks:

> The Irish were discriminated against until the 1930s and 1940s, but after the war, we gradually controlled the Fire Department, Police Department, and City Hall. Our socioeconomic status has improved a lot. We are now living a much better life than our parents did, and we owe this to those of the previous generations. Pat's father, for instance, was extraordinarily dedicated to the Union. Pat's mother saved $5 for her children every day. ... [Cynthia spoke tearfully]. Actually, she passed away quite recently. ... Pat is now doing research on his family history and will present the result on his father's 75th birthday in October.

Patrick interposes:

> Well, we all grew up by observing how hard our parents were struggling, and we are all grateful to them. Many young Americans take their parents' efforts for granted. I don't mean to say that the American family is so corrupted as the media report, but there are some serious problems. You know the so-called "latchkey kids," right? I feel very sorry for them.

They have nobody to speak with, and share their ideas with, when they come home. Parents just shouldn't leave their kids alone, no matter what they are doing! When Peter was five or six years old, my wife was working full time, and therefore I decided to change my shift from the nine-to-five shift to the seven-to-two. It meant losing $100 each week. It also meant to abandon my promotion in Boston Edison. But, in my philosophy, childrearing and family are more important than promotion.

Some people call us "poor." That's fine. We have chosen not to have money. We are not rich, but we are happy. Some people call us "bigots." That's also fine. The mass media always delivers prejudiced images of us. You know, even a small fist-fight can appear on the front page of the *Globe* if it happens in Southie. People are afraid of us, and don't move in here. That's just fine. We can maintain our community. This is a wonderful neighborhood. You can walk at night. You don't have to lock the door at night. My neighbors have been living here for more than 100 years. You know, an old lady lives upstairs. In fact, she has Parkinson's disease. We are very concerned about her. You see there, we have an intercom. We can go up there if she suffers a stroke. Have you ever visited the Vietnam War Memorial on Broadway Street? It was built for those killed in Vietnam. Everybody in this neighborhood knows about it. Whenever they go nearby, they drop by to salute those soldiers. Although many people moved out of Southie at the time of busing, many people are actually coming back because this is a real community. We'll keep living here no matter how badly we are spoken of. Southie is just like a big family.

The above three testimonials well epitomize the first-hand witnessing and experience of, and sentiment towards, the social transformation in the postwar era among the Boston Irish inform-ants. On the one hand, their upward mobility into middle-class, "lace-curtain" status seems to be a source of pride in themselves and in their heritage.[1] On the other hand, however, they are disheartened by the perceived fragmentation and debilitation of authority and morality precipitated by the American pursuit of freedom and choice that are, according to them, often informed by materialism and egoism. As we will see in the following sections, this ambivalent sentiment towards the changing society is reflected in the politics of culture in their everyday lives. Their observations and sentiments are certainly articulated, as is the case with my Yankee families, by predicating family life as the matrix of their explanatory scheme and the center of their cognitive map of society.

South Boston

However, of analytical interest here is the fact that these Irish informants, compared with their Yankee counterparts, seem to be weaving their family discourse more tightly in the web of the neighborhood. *Southie Is My Home Town* was a vaudeville folk song composed by Bennie Drohan in the 1910s. Some of my informants sang this "South Boston anthem" as a metaphor for their attachment to their neighborhood. On one occasion, Joseph Doyle and I met an old lady who immigrated to Boston more than 80 years ago. She began singing and weeping to this upbeat tune as Mr. Doyle played it on his harmonica. It was difficult to interview her because of her weak voice, but her tears were convincing enough for me to appreciate the vicissitudes of her life, which have been interlaced in the microcosm of South Boston.

Southie Is My Hometown

I had an argument the other day
With a guy from Oskaloo,
He was braggin' bout his old hometown;
Says I to him, "What to do."
I got hot right under the collar,
To that scholar I did holler,

"I was born down on A Street
Raised up on B Street,
SOUTHIE IS MY HOMETOWN.
There's something about it, permit me to shout it;

They're the tops for miles around.
We have doctors and scrappers, preachers and flappers,
Men from the old County Down.
Say, they'll take you and break you, but they'll never
    forsake you
In Southie my hometown!"

In a similar fashion, many informants proudly recommended two books on South Boston written by "native" authors for my reference: *South Boston: My Home Town* (1988) by Thomas O'Connor (a professor of history at Boston College) and *That Old Gang of Mine: A History of South Boston* (1991) by Patrick Loftus, Jr. It came home to me that any analysis of their lives and families first requires scrutiny of the history and culture of Southie, their hometown.

After my fieldwork was completed, such films as *Good Will Hunting* (1997), *Southie* (1998), and *Mystic River* (2003) were set in South Boston, to evident local excitement. *Good Will Hunting* is based around the life of Will Hunting (Matt Damon), a troubled orphan who grew up in the slums of South Boston but was found to be a math genius by a MIT professor. In *Southie*, Donnie Wahlberg portrays a young man who tests his recovery from alcoholism by returning to South Boston – "the toughest neighborhood in America" or "a city within a city" – and deciding whether to walk away from his roots or make a stand for his family. *Mystic River*, Clint Eastwood's latest movie as a director, is a story about three small boys of a South Boston neighborhood reunited after the daughter of Jimmy (Sean Penn) is found murdered.

A changing South Boston

The Lower End and the Upper End

South Boston lies on a peninsula of 3.75 square miles of land (annexed to Boston in 1804), with Fort Point Channel to the north, Dorchester Bay to the south, Boston Harbor to the east, and the Southeast Expressway and Penn Central railroad yards to the west. The city's financial district is less than two miles away, across two bridges. With Logan Airport just across the harbor, the sound of jets making their approaches and departures is a part of the district's everyday life. While Broadway runs from a subway station to City Point on the seashore, Dorchester Street, which intersects the main thoroughfare approximately at its mid-point, demarcates the peninsula's two socially distinctive landscapes.

The area west of Dorchester Street (the "Lower End") is a somewhat run-down, working-class area with many fast-food restaurants, auto shops, taverns, and housing projects. The eastern section of Dorchester Street (the "Upper End") is populated largely by Irish Catholics who work as policemen, firemen, clerical and service workers, nurses, social service workers, teachers, and government workers and in similar jobs. The Upper End has a more residential ambiance, with interspersed multiple-family homes (two- and three-storey blocks), single-family dwellings, and newer brick apartment buildings. All of my informants live in this area, though some have moved "up the hill" from, or are working in, the Lower End.

The distinction between Lower End and Upper End is sharply drawn and articulated by all the informants.

> What I mean by "community" is the area from G Street to City Point where people are very homogeneous, and women can walk alone at night. The Lower End is inhabited by many Asians and Hispanics. Some of them don't know even how to use a toilet. It is very noisy and very dangerous.

> The Lower End is poorer. There are many single parents living in housing projects. They have immigrated from other neighborhoods in Boston because the rent is very cheap. Also, there are many immigrants from Puerto Rico, Cuba, Cambodia, Vietnam, and so on. Those people have no attachment to Southie, so they don't vote. As a consequence, local politicians tend to pay more attention only to the Upper End, and the Lower End becomes more neglected and deteriorated. It is completely a vicious cycle.

> Basically, you have more wealthy people as you move up to the beaches. You know Marine Road and Columbia Road, right? We call those streets "millionaires' streets."

[116]

My sister lives there, and her house costs about $250,000! Can you believe it? It is just incredible! The Lower End is inhabited by welfare people and immigrants who don't understand English.

There are still Irish Catholics living in the Lower End, especially around B Street, but essentially the Lower End is more "colored" whereas the Upper End is much "Whiter" with many Irish, Germans, Italians, Poles, Lithuanians, Czechs, Armenians, Albanians, and so on. Of course, the White people can speak English.

These cognitive maps demarcating the Lower End and the Upper End, though somewhat exaggerated, capture the perceptions of social life, and have been fabricated in the historical process of South Boston.

The Great Depression

The employment created by the Civil War increased the population of the peninsula by 50 percent to above 30,000, and the prosperity based on such heavy industries as iron foundries, locomotive factories, glassworks, machine shops, and shipyards ultimately led to the establishment of the South Boston Savings Bank in 1863. At the same time, the number of Protestant churches in South Boston declined sharply, in contrast to the remarkable increase in Catholic churches and their members, which symbolizes the consolidation of the Irish-Catholic flavor in the area in the period after the Civil War (Satkewich 1979). More immigrants settled down in South Boston, and found employment in such new manufacturing plants as the Standard Sugar Refinery and the Walworth Manufacturing Company, in new public-utility companies like the New England Telephone and Telegraph Company, the Boston Edison Electric Company, the Massachusetts Electric Company, and the Boston Gas Company, and in such transportation companies as the Dorchester Avenue Railroad Company and the Broadway Railroad Company. Broadway had become the main thoroughfare of South Boston by the 1890s.

With its economy becoming more independent and its infra-structure more solidified, South Boston transformed itself from a refuge for "other Bostonians" (Thernstrom 1973) into an integrated neighborhood of its own where residents lived and worked. Many statues and monuments honoring the heroes of the Civil War were erected, most notably the Faragut statue in South Boston's Marine Park and the Dorchester Heights monument. In 1901, the first St. Patrick's Day parade took place, and South Boston High School was established. The L Street Bathhouse, originally built in 1865 as a sanitary facility for the impoverished immigrants, gradually became a major center of sports and recreation. Thomas O'Connor (1994), a historian from South Boston, describes the phenomenon:

> Organized sport significantly intensified the feelings of unity and solidarity that had become a distinctive part of the spirit of the neighborhood. With their own beaches and bathhouses, playgrounds and parks, football and baseball teams, a roster of legendary sports heroes, the people of South Boston could feel proud and comfortable in the insularity of their district and the fitness of their institutions (p. 117).

As Horgan (1988) understands it, the "coalescence of residence, church, and parochial school (or public elementary school) within a small geographically closed area was a feature of the Catholic parish that the church administrators wisely fostered in the first half of the twentieth century" (p. 56).[2] The parochial school system was expanded to provide a Catholic education and instill the patri-otic spirit of "For God and Country" in as many children as possi-ble. Church and state thus became inseparable in South Boston (Horgan 1988; O'Connor 1994; Ryan 1979). By the early 1900s, there were eleven divisions of the Ancient Order of Hibernians as well as such social clubs as the Irish-American Club, the Wolf Tone Club, the Celtic Association, and the Clan-na-Gael in South Boston (Canavan 1979). Those clubs served as "social centers where friends and neighbors could relax among their own people, talk over old times, and exchange the latest news and gossip" (O'Con-nor 1994, pp. 122–3). O'Connor expounds on the relationship between the Irish-Catholic ethic and the spirit of capitalism:

By the turn of the century, although there were some doctors, dentists, pharmacists, lawyers and real estate agents in the City Point area, most people in South Boston could be classified as "working-class" people, and a definite class consciousness contributed to their perception of themselves. The lower end had many day laborers, longshoremen, tavern-keepers, grocers, industrial workers and bricklayers, while east of Dorchester Street lived carpenters, plumbers, electricians, streetcar conductors, policemen, firemen and letter carriers. Whatever their occupation, parents worked hard, took pride in their jobs and raised their children to admire the working-class value of hard work and determination despite their modest homes and meager incomes. School teachers commonly reminded children that while it was acceptable to come to class wearing clothing that was sewn or patched, it was expected the garments would be washed and ironed (1994, pp. 124–5).

The Great Depression was an unprecedented disaster for the working-class neighborhood. The loss of jobs, the disappearance of small savings, the foreclosure of mortgages on homes and small rental properties, the surrender of insurance policies, and the sluggishness of stores and theaters – all broke the social compact they had lived by (Thernstrom 1973). According to O'Connor's (1994) reminiscence, South Boston just survived these devastating effects of the Depression:

> to a great degree because of the interconnected family network that was still the hallmark of the community. Those who still had jobs parceled out their meager incomes to friends and neighbors who were out of work. Families shared their butter, eggs and sugar with one another, exchanged shoes and clothing for the children and opened their homes to relatives who needed a place to live. In the closely knit parish system of the day, officers and members of the various St. Vincent de Paul societies worked overtime helping the needy in days when there were no public social or economic benefits available to ease their plight (p. 185).

The fact that the residents of South Boston could withstand the demoralizing ordeals of the Depression consolidated their pride in the virtue of their "working-class" neighborhood – a community that was determined to hold onto its own distinctive values and styles by encapsulating the ethos of the Boston Irish.

The postwar era, however, posed a series of challenges to this working-class spirit in South Boston. Many young soldiers came back and often found their homes too small. The development of highways and the popularization of automobiles provided an incentive for them to drive to the suburbs. At the same time, the Boston banks' policy of "red-lining" categorized South Boston as a blighted or depressed area where banks refused to grant mortgages or assign home-improvement loans, and this exacerbated the predicament of the neighborhood and promoted the exodus of the population to suburban areas. The population of South Boston decreased by 50 percent, to 40,000, by the late 1950s, dispersing and emasculating the web of social relations that was tightly interlaced in the neighborhood (O'Connor 1994).[3]

> Young people tried to get away from the traditional culture. Young men's world-view was broadened after serving in the military for several years. Also, televisions and cars broadened the view of both men and women. They became more liberated and independent, and the so-called "me-generation" was born. They led a better life in the suburbs.

> People became no longer interested in local athletes, singers, and actors. Their stars became all high professionals who appear on national broadcasting programs.

The implementation of a social welfare system advanced upward mobility, but at the sacrifice of social connectedness.

> Yes, we got social welfare. So we didn't have to help each other as we had to during the Depression.

> The G.I. bill made it possible for young people to attend college, but college graduates became not interested in

playing cards or drinking beer with old men at the taverns. They don't sing *Southie Is My Home Town* anymore.

During the Depression, we used to exchange sugar, salt, and the like. But it became increasingly rare. The other day, my neighbor came to borrow sugar, and I got very surprised!

Scolding others' children has become less common. "Mind your own business" is the motto nowadays.

Projects

The other major challenge was the so-called "project": public housing for lower-income working families. While the first two projects – the Old Harbor Village (later renamed the Mary Ellen McCormack Project) in 1935 and the Old Colony Project in 1939, both on the outskirts of the district – maintained neighborhood homogeneity and therefore won local residents' acceptance, the D Street Project in 1949 resulted in the deterioration of entire blocks in the heart of the Lower End after accommodating thousands of displaced residents from other neighborhoods in Boston. O'Connor (1994) elaborates on its transformation into the "permanent homes for the poor, disadvantaged and dispossessed":

> With the courts imposing stricter limits on the power of project managers to screen out potential troublemakers or to evict those classified as undesirable, many managers and their staff simply gave up. Supervision and mainte-nance in projects across the city fell off sharply. Trees and shrubs were uprooted, benches and playground equip-ment destroyed, door locks broken, windows smashed, hallways unlighted, basements scarred by vandals and walls defaced by spray-paint and graffiti. The population of the projects changed markedly, too. An increasing percentage of the new families were without fathers, and an even larger percentage was on some form of public welfare (pp. 199–200).

According to a local social worker, the percentage of single parents in South Boston has increased from 17 percent to 40 percent over the past two decades as the Lower End has rapidly become inhabited ("intruded on," in one informant's words) by newcomers who live on welfare with little attachment to "Southie."[4]

> The project area in the Lower End, I mean, along Dorchester Street except for the new apartments on B Street and C Street, is a big shame. You know, most of them are high-school dropouts and they are sucking our taxes. Since their houses are subsidized by the government, they can live for $100 instead of paying $700. They have no self-esteem, no role models, and no morals. At the very beginning, that area was sort of a good starting point for veterans who just came back from the war, but now the entire blocks are inhabited by parasites. I don't think it is a good idea for those poor people themselves. In terms of income level, it is the most impoverished area in Boston.

> I grew up in the project there around the 1950s. In those days, there was an unwritten code that you leave the place to other poor families once you become better off. Everybody cared for his house very much. We mowed the weeds and cleaned the hallways. Oh, yah, we sometimes had cookouts with other families. People today don't care about the place at all. The weeds are left untouched, and the building is very dirty. Some people live as long as 30–40 years with the "I owe nothing to the government" mentality. They take all the services for granted – heating, lights, food stamps, and medical attention. ... They are all paid by our taxes. How ridiculous!

Michael Patrick MacDonald (1999) recalls his boyhood in a project:

> I found out in City Point (the Upper End) that we were "project rats" and "white niggers." The Point kids chased us back down the hill to the Lower End, "where you belong!" they yelled from the Heights, standing ground at the invisible line they too didn't dare cross (p. 61).

A *US News & World Report* (October 17, 1994) article, "The White Underclass," cited census data to show that the Lower End had the highest concentration of poor Whites in the US and called it the "White underclass capital of America." In 1997, an epidemic of teenage suicides, suicide attempts, and drug overdoses spread in South Boston, especially in the projects. Ten young people hanged themselves and 200 more, most of whom were male, allegedly attempted suicide. Noting that hanging is relatively uncommon among teenagers, MacDonald comments, "Who hangs themselves? People in prison hang themselves" (*International Herald Tribune*, August 18, 1997). "Prison" here is connoted to mean an enclave trapped in despair, isolated in poverty, and plagued by alcohol and drugs (heroin in particular). One informant in her late sixties residing in the Upper End sent a letter to me in England (where I was doing my postdoctoral research), noting:

> I understand there have been 75 overdoses from So. Boston admitted to local hospitals this year. Yes, these are lower-end youths, White, from the projects. Remember I told you that the projects aren't really part of So. Boston!! They are warehouses of single mothers who don't work, don't vote and don't have a strong role model for the sons especially. To me we have despair, depression and depressive drugs. Nobody in Southie will say it just like that, but that wall of silence isn't helping our neighborhood. When I finish this letter I'm going to write to a friend in City Hall to volunteer some time. I may well be rebuffed, like sticking my nose where it doesn't belong (personal correspondence, August 28, 1997).[5]

My informants' demarcation between the Lower End and the Upper End is thus founded on their antagonism and frustration over the perceived "unfair" game that those "parasites" are playing and their disinclination to espouse the working-class virtues that saved Southie even from the most catastrophic plight during the Depression. The problem, they say, is not that the Lower End is inhabited by many newcomers who are poor and colored by different linguistic backgrounds: "It is a question of values." The sharp demarcation that my informants make between the Lower End and the Upper End is thus a socio-historical artifact.

Busing

Closely related to this distinction is skepticism towards the outside bureaucrats, politicians, journalists, and liberal intellectuals who attempt to "moralize" Southie by applying their "rational" vision of society to the neighborhood. The D Street Project is viewed as one of the most conspicuous cases demonstrating the failure of the mentality of the so-called "best and brightest" (Halberstam 1972). The fear among local residents that "outside interests" might eradicate the communal atmosphere of the peninsula district were shown to be more than mere paranoia when a series of urban renewal projects were announced (and partly implemented) from the late 1960s to the early 1970s.[6] The "saddest moment" came in 1974 in the form of the busing of schoolchildren that the federal government ordered so as to achieve the goal of racial desegregation. As is well known, the busing aggravated, rather than alleviated, the confrontation between "Black power" and "Green power" that sometimes resulted even in the loss of young lives. If that was the time when African-Americans rediscovered their roots, it was also the time when the Boston Irish accentuated their ethnic pride inside and outside of South Boston, among friends, at churches, at homes, in local newspapers, on T-shirts, on bumper stickers, and on street signs.

The logic of their opposition is probably best summarized in the speech that William Bulger, a South Boston native who grew up in the Old Harbor Village and was then serving as a state legislator,[7] delivered on Dorchester Hill on the eve of a national anti-busing rally in Washington D.C. in March 1975:

> Opposing busing does not mean that we bear any ill will to Black children or children of other racial strains. It does not mean that we oppose the ideal of integrated education. It does not mean that we are unwilling to share our educational facilities with children from other neighborhoods who may wish to use them. ... It does mean that we are unwilling to yield to the demands of a judicial fiat that

strips away the parents' natural rights (quoted in Brookhiser 1991, p. 74).

Bulger's resistance to the state's intrusion into, or interference with, "parents' natural rights" in selecting their children's schools is acknowledged even by those of my informants who do not concur with him on other political issues. Despite the legend of the Kennedy family, Senator Edward Kennedy is still unpopular in South Boston for having supported busing during this period. "No politician can make it here in South Boston if he or she stood for busing. It is just impossible. No way."

Since busing was a red-hot national issue, the mass media paid close attention to its development in Boston and frequently condemned South Boston residents for their localism, parochialism, and provincialism. O'Connor (1994) maintains:

> [Busing] marked the community indelibly in the minds of people throughout the nation as a depressed and depraved area where beer-bellied men and foul-mouthed women made war on defenseless children simply because they were Black. It was a terrible stereotype, reinforced in all the national media, from which it was difficult if not impossible for the community to recover. ... They refused to have it changed by outsiders who looked upon their morals as medieval and who regarded their lifestyles as barbaric. They might well go down – but they might go down fighting! That was the South Boston way (pp. 229–30).

Busing was thus not only a matter of the state's intrusion into the private sphere but also the contestation of community identity against outside stereotypes. At the same time, as Lukas (1985) and Dezell (2000) argue, the busing crisis was not only a racial conflict but was also a class struggle, as well as a "family feud" between the Irish who had "made it" (like Judge Arthur Garrity, who graduated from Harvard Law School and resided in an affluent suburb) and the Irish who had not (like those in such urban neighborhoods as South Boston and Charlestown).

During my stay in the United States, this "no-nonsense" mentality was strongly in evidence in the opposition to another federal stipulation: that the districts' housing projects should accommodate more minority residents in order to comply with the principle of fair distribution of spaces. "If you can't force on us how to run a school, then you can't force us on where to live." However, former Mayor Raymond Flynn, a vocal opponent of the busing and the first mayor (1983–93) from South Boston, under a series of financial and legal pressures from both state and federal agencies, complied with their demands. Although he gained a landslide victory in the election of 1988, even obtaining a mandate from the Black sections of the city, in 1992, he lost both of his hometown wards in South Boston because of his succumbing to the "outside" forces. "Ray Flynn simply forgot where he came from." Many informants, while being conscious of the distance between the Lower End and the Upper End and, to some extent, among the various White ethnic groups inside the Upper End itself, feel that South Boston as a whole can bind together in a common effort to protect its "natural rights." If "insular South Boston" is an invention of downtown Boston, South Boston responds to the external imposition of identity by actually employing this stereotype to unite the community and legitimize their solidarity. Patrick O'Leary's remark should be recalled: "Some people call us 'bigots.' That's just fine. We can maintain our community."

Gentrification

As in the case of Beacon Hill, the principle of economic Darwinism – survival of the richest – is encroaching on this community that adjoins downtown Boston. Many young urban professionals ("Yuppies") who can afford the costs of luxury townhouses and expensive condominiums are increasing the gentrification of a once working-class neighborhood. Bars and hardware stores have become boutiques, spas, and cafes. According to local real estate agencies, it is not at all rare to find a property whose market value has skyrocketed by a multiple of ten over the past decade, and there are few vacancies in South Boston.[8]

> They are nice people, but have nothing in common with us. They don't participate in local functions at all. They

might move to Los Angeles if they find a better job and sell their home to another rich man who has no link to this neighborhood. Real estate prices have gone up too high. That's one of the reasons why many young Boston Irish have left Southie.

There is a strong apprehension that South Boston's proximity to the central city, the airport, highways, and seaports might intensify the utilitarian calculation of public planners and private developers and stimulate the process of gentrification at the sacrifice of the local ethos. "There are a couple of new projects going up in the waterfront area. I suspect that those outsiders are sticking their noses – again – into our community!"

As a matter of fact, the city's plans for a $700 million convention center (originally a megaplex with an attached football stadium for the New England Patriots and a nearby baseball park for Boston Red Sox) to be located in the waterfront area of South Boston became one of the hottest issues at the State House in the latter half of the 1990s. Genuinely angry that South Boston was chosen without being asked first, the neighborhood opposed the "forced stadium" and "forced ballpark" as fiercely and successfully as it had opposed "forced busing." South Boston politicians won, with their elaborate maneuverings, a dramatic concession: 51 percent of the linkage money that commercial developers were required to pay into a fund for housing and job training in the area – a sum amounting to $65–75 million over the next two decades – was reserved exclusively for the working-class, blue-collar neighborhood of South Boston. (This deal was heavily criticized by other neighborhoods and the mass media as ignoring the needs of the rest of the city.)

The Lower End and Downtown Boston

These social realities and cultural histories constitute a sharply contrasting self-definition with that of the old families on Beacon Hill, in West Cambridge, and on the North Shore. Many Boston Brahmin informants defined themselves as belonging to the upper-middle strata that is, in their opinion, distinguishable from those below them (the "middle class," "ordinary people,"

[127]

or "mob") and those above (the "new money" or "newcomers") who are "functioning without contexts." Most of the Boston Irish informants, on the other hand, identified themselves as either "middle class" or "working class." This ambiguity and flexibility connote the perceived distance between downtown Boston ("rich," "liberal," or "outsider") and the Lower End ("poor" and "parasite"). On the one hand, being "working class" is different from being "poor" in a subtle but significant way. Many informants often underlined their "middle-class" status to avoid the possible conflation of this important and subtle distinction between the two. On the other hand, "working-class" is, as indicated before, given a more positive meaning and was often underscored as an antithesis to those in Cambridge (especially the "ultra-liberals in Harvard Square") and downtown Boston.

> Yasushi, you know what? Hearing that you are from Harvard, I was very suspicious that you might be one of those people who would deride us as "shanty Irish" or "Irish bigots" living in "slums" in the "rough" neighborhood in South Boston.

If the name of Harvard opened the opportunity for approaching "proper Bostonians," as mentioned in Chapter 1, it sometimes worked to the contrary for these "other Bostonians."

These findings resonate with those of Lamont (2000) in her comparative study of the culture of French and (Black and White) American working-class men:

> The White American workers I interviewed primarily use moral standards ("the disciplined self") to distinguish between "people like us" and others: they distance themselves from the upper half, who lack integrity and straightforwardness, and Blacks and "people below," who are lazy and hold wrong values. ... [W]hile White American workers view socioeconomic status as an indication of moral worth when evaluating the poor and Blacks, many abandon this standard when evaluating the upper half (pp. 241–2).[9]

Like their Anglo-Saxon Protestant counterparts, these Irish Catholic informants are highly conscious of the stereotype about themselves, and they invent their self-definition by internalizing such an externally ascribed identity. Some people strive to construct a new identity by breaking out of the stereotypical images and absorbing new modes of thinking and behavior. Others use such stereotypes to legitimize their being and status quo. Each informant's social action, while being informed by various forces in the larger society, is also contingent on how the person's agency is exerted in internalizing the externally imposed identity (category), as Giddens (1979, 1984) and Bourdieu (1977) elaborate in their theoretical schemes.

Having thus sketched some of the central themes around which these Irish-Catholic informants' social realities and cultural histories are woven, I would like to examine how the perceived social transformations in the postwar period – the upward mobility, the fragmentation of the "overall picture," and the consolidation of the we–they (both "downtown Boston" and the "Lower End") distinction – are interlaced with the politics of culture in such crucial facets of my informants' actual social lives and relationships as neighborhood, work, kinship, friendship, cultural taste, love and marriage, conjugal segregation, divorce, and childrearing.

Neighborhood

Continuity

Compared with the neighborhoods on Beacon Hill, in West Cambridge, and on the North Shore, the Upper End in South Boston retains a density of community that can be compared to that of "fictive kinship" in Stack's (1974) metaphor. During the course of my fieldwork, there was a tragedy in a Boston suburb in which an elderly woman locked herself out and froze to death. She sought shelter at several neighbors' homes, but they all refused to open the door after recognizing her merely as a stranger (*Boston Globe*, January 21, 1994). Such indifference is "quite unthinkable" in Southie.

> Southie is still a real community. We know everybody in our neighborhood. We don't lock the doors at night. If our

shower is out of order, then we can ask one of neighbors to let us use theirs. It is no problem at all. Absolutely not. Have you been to the corner store over there? We know them for decades, and we can buy things on credit. Although we go to the Stop and Shop for major shopping, we go to that store for our daily supplies. Things are slightly more expensive there, but we feel that we are sustaining our community by shopping there. After all, we are friends, not customers. You shouldn't be so rational. The store is a sort of community center where we make sure that our kids are doing O.K., and we exchange information about what's going on here and there. There are many Italians in this particular block, but it doesn't mean anything. They are just like us.

On payday, I used to come home with 5–6 pounds of cookies, lots of apples, bananas, and so on. And I just put them on the dining table so that the kids could pick out whichever they wanted. I think 40–50 kids came all the time. A couple days ago, one of those kids surprised me. He dropped by my home and greeted my wife and me by saying, "I just want to say hello." He moved out of the neighborhood almost 15 years ago. You can imagine how delighted we were, right?

We have five hockey teams here. Each team has more than 100 boys. Also, we have many girls' dancing teams. At the soccer tournament in the fall, nearly one-third of the population, which means about 10,000, showed up in Columbus Park, including thousands of parents, grandparents, and relatives. There are hundreds of volunteers who work for the special dinners and functions for senior citizens. Many parents make the extra effort to get the kids to the library on rainy days, or to hockey games at 6:00 in the morning, or to Irish step practices, or Little League, or chess club, or swim team, and so on. Many nurses volunteer their time for blood pressure checks, and many homeowners take the time to shovel an elderly neighbor's walk. We won't allow any one of us to go down. We are clannish and proud of it.

What Bellah et al. (1985) call the "community of memory" is still preserved through the stories of such epoch-making events as the Great Depression, the Second World War, the Korean War, and busing as well as the anecdotes of neighbors and their parents. As Bellah et al. point out, all these stories of suffering, success, and failure comprise "conceptions of character, of what a good person is like, and of the virtues that define such character" (p. 153). The *South Boston Tribune* is to Southie what the *Transcript* was to Beacon Hill. The *Tribune* is a community paper that features local events and services, politicians' opinions, and commercial advertisements, along with pictures of bake sales, church bazaars, and midget-league ballgames, on a weekly basis. While this paper has no "reporters" per se, local residents submit enough articles and pictures to fill 20–25 pages. With its first issue published back in 1964 and a weekly official circulation of 8,500 copies throughout South Boston, this community paper certainly contributes to arousing people's "imagination" (Anderson 1983) about the past, the present, and the future.[10] A sense of continuity seems to be an integral part of residents' pride in the neighborhood.

> Well, many friends left Southie after the war, especially at the time of busing because they wanted to protect their children. But some of them are coming back to Southie after finishing up educating their children. They no longer need to live in a big house in the suburbs. Back in South Boston, you have many friends and streets that you are all familiar with. Actually, their adult kids are returning to Southie because it is convenient to commute to Boston and it is a very safe neighborhood.[11]

> You know the L Street Beach? That's a beautiful beach. Many of us had our own particular spots there, and we used to hang around there with our families and friends. And now our grandchildren are exactly at the same spot with their parents and friends. That's the Southie culture.

However, the three local institutions that have secured the sense of continuity and kept the "Southie culture" alive are being confronted with a series of disruptive forces from the outside.

Politics

Compared with their Yankee counterparts on Beacon Hill, in West Cambridge, and on the North Shore, these informants' commitments are more geared towards the immediate concerns in their neighborhood, and they have a definite recognition of who the guiding figures in their community are. As a matter of fact, all the informants instantly named some of the local politicians as their community leaders. For my Yankee informants, city politics stimulates little interest because their lives exist outside of the miscellaneous social issues that local politics problematize and address. While well acquainted with the names of politicians in Washington D.C., those informants, like many of my colleagues at Harvard, have little, if any, knowledge about who represents their local districts. Their counterparts in South Boston, however, are quite knowledgeable about each politician's personality, background, social engagements, moral convictions, and political position, which they all take into account in deciding whom to endorse.

> I think that most Americans have been quite disillusioned and distrustful about politicians, especially since the Watergate scandal in the 1970s. I agree that many politicians are not moral figures. But I think that politicians are still taken seriously in South Boston.

> Curley was *the* man. We owe so much to him.

> I know Jim Kelly (then President of Boston's City Council from South Boston) well. We once belonged to the same gang, the Mullins. He was a tough guy. I basically like him, but what he said about the housing stuff disappointed me a lot.

> Bill Bulger is *the* guy for us!

> We don't need a limousine liberal who talks nonsense. We need someone who can fix the streetlights so that children can cross the streets safely. There are lots of trucks running there. Hometown loyalty is the most important thing.

Thus, local politics constitutes an integral dimension in my informants' social universe, whereas politics on both the national and international level is more an abstraction to them as long as "those outsiders don't stick their noses into our community."

> I once drove J. F. Kennedy from South Boston to Governor Bradford's house on Brattle Street in Cambridge. Later on, I was asked if I was interested in serving as his driver in Washington D.C. But I declined the offer because I wasn't interested in such an elite society.

According to this informant's friend who resides on Marine Road ("millionaire's street" in the Upper End), such a response represents a typical "working-class" mentality.

These Irish-Catholic informants are mostly "conservative Democrats" (or "blue-collar Democrats" or "Reagan Democrats") who have endorsed Reagan's patriotism and Clinton's populism. "Well, the 1992 election was tough. Bush is a war hero whereas Clinton evaded the draft. Clinton is for the ordinary people whereas Bush is for the rich people." Among my informants the poll was split. They have a common political ground in repudiating anti-Vietnam activism, school busing, affirmative action, racial integration in the city's public housing, and homosexuality. I again recall my meeting with the near-centenarian lady whom I introduced earlier. She showed me a letter that she received from President Clinton that solaces her and acknowledges her accomplishment as a first-generation Irish immigrant.

> You know, this is the country where its President gives a letter to a person like me. This is the country that repelled the United Kingdom. My children served in the Second World War and the Korean War, and my grandchildren served in the Gulf War.

To her, her offspring, and other informants, burning the national flag indicates the denial of this honorable essence of the United States.

Similarly, affirmative action (and its cousins multilingualism and multiculturalism) are perceived as a kind of "overprotection" that pampers new immigrants, preventing them from emulating the Irish efforts to melt into the American pot and from upholding the social ethos of what Abraham Lincoln called "the last, best hope on earth." "We have all suffered from poverty and discrimination, but we all tried hard to overcome them. Why do we have to allow them [new immigrants, homosexuals and other minorities] to go to the head of the waiting line? It's outrageously unfair and un-American." "After all, I often wonder, 'For what did we fight? What did we get by helping Japan and Germany?'" This informant, like most in his neighborhood, was quite disenchanted with the 1996 US presidential elections, claiming to be an "independent voter" who finally endorsed Clinton with reluctance and reservations.[12]

These shared sentiments and opinions facilitate the organization of political groups and events; there is a strong belief, almost an "unwritten law," in South Boston that voting should be used as a strategy to take control of city politics.[13] The depth of commitment to the neighborhood and the width of the local network are the litmus tests for leading figures in South Boston, and as such many prominent political figures have served as union leaders and the heads of community clubs at a younger age.[14] Some of my informants who were assiduously involved in community activities were referred to as "powerful guys," "big names," or "key people." While those activists are predominantly male, there are a couple of women who emulate Louisa Day Hicks (1916–2003), the "first lady" of South Boston and the soul of the anti-busing crusade in the 1970s. "Do you want to meet Jim [Kelly]? I can call him up if you want to speak with him": this kind of casual reference to local politicians was not something that I encountered among my Yankee informants – although one proper Bostonian asked me if I wished to be introduced to former President Bush at his summer house in Kennebunkport, Maine.

O'Connor (1994) maintains that the neighborhood style of politics was altered by the emergence of the welfare state in the early 1930s:

> Roosevelt's New Deal program had produced a vast network of federal agencies that replaced neighborhood politicians and big-city bosses. ... With the passage of such

New Deal legislation as social security, unemployment insurance and workmen's compensation, followed after the Second World War by the wide-ranging veterans' benefits contained in the G.I. Bill of Rights covering housing loans, professional training and college education, there was much less reason for anyone to go to the local ward boss for help when Uncle Sam could provide bigger and better benefits. And with more federal offices, court houses, post offices, banks and veteran's bureaus appearing on the scene, civil-service appointments provided numerous jobs far beyond the jurisdiction of local politicians (pp. 200–1).

While benefiting the upward mobility of the Irish in South Boston, these developments made ambiguous the role of the neighborhood and its politicians. In a broader perspective, the landslide victory of John Hynes over James Curley in the mayoral election of 1949 was symbolic of this transformation to a more bureaucratic and progressive politics. As noted in Chapter 1, the financial hegemony of the Brahmins and the political power of the Irish could find a common ground after the mutual antipathy of almost half a century, and a series of urban renewal projects were launched in the interest of rationalizing and modernizing society.

Having said this, however, a couple of local politicians that I interviewed strongly hold that people in South Boston are still "very demanding," and they are energetically engaged in cleaning parks, fixing street lights, zoning parking places, listening to school dropouts, and dashing off to fires. What they feel really is at stake is how to reconcile the local and insular viewpoint in South Boston with the larger Commonwealth or with American society. Richard Brookhiser, in his essay on William Bulger in the *New Yorker* (October 28, 1991), extracts Bulger's intrinsic principle – "I dance with the girl that brung me" – which connotes his faithfulness to his constituents and his social origins even at the risk of confronting such rationalizing and moralizing forces in society as the federal government, liberal intellectuals, and the mass media (most notably the *Boston Globe* for its liberal flavor). Brookhiser witnessed a very Bulgerian spirit when walking with him after his interview:

By the time we reached the State House, with its bloated golden dome, Bulger's step was brisk. A young guard seated at a desk was looking over the *Globe* without verbs [*sic*]. "Don't believe what you read," Bulger told him brightly. "I only read the sports and *The Far Side*," the guard answered. "That's the spirit," the Senate President said (p. 77).

This contrasts sharply with Raymond Flynn's accommodation of outsider pressures from both the federal and state governments on the issue of racial integration in public housing, which won him major support from the Black community but resulted in his losing all of his home wards in South Boston. Flynn's political choices were progressive and pragmatic, aligning him with a wider constituency and Boston politics with the interests of the larger society. Yet they also signified a detachment from "the girl that brung him" and the heartland of South Boston.

Bulger is still in Southie, hosting his famous St. Patrick's Day breakfast at the Bayside Club down there and opening his house for his neighbors and guests in the afternoon. All the important people, like Governor Weld and Senator Kerry, came to the breakfast, and even President Clinton called there from the White House. Isn't it impressive that a small neighborhood like Southie can get that much attention? Flynn left us. He has flown to the Vatican as the US Ambassador [in 1993]. You see the difference, right?

Being able to manage the tension between local and national values is a requirement for political life, and such current issues as homosexuality, the mixed housing, the waterfront developments, abortion, affirmative action, and multilingualism have enormous political implications in this context.

The annual St. Patrick's Day parade on March 17 well exemplifies the tension between local (or localizing) forces and rational (rationalizing) forces. In 1994 the parade was canceled because its organizers, the Allied War Veterans Council of South Boston, withdrew their support after an unsuccessful effort to prevent an Irish-American gay group from marching. After the cancellation, they finally won the right to march without the gay group's presence, but city officials (including Mayor Thomas Menino) shied away from participating.

> The US Supreme Court (in June 1995) voted 9–0 in favor of a view that the parade is not an official event. You know, we are not discriminating against gay people. We simply don't want outside liberals to moralize us. They should mind their own business. We mind our own, and we have the right to do so.

Local newspapers report that the 1995 parade attracted more than 800,000 onlookers all across Greater Boston, and many of them wore something green and carried American flags and Irish tri-colors. Plaques were placed on street poles, commemorating those South Boston soldiers who fought for the country at the sacrifice of their own lives. While everybody along the streets rejoiced at the resumption of the parade, some of the informants seemed somewhat bewildered at the commercialization, politicization, and trivialization of the event.

> The parade once was *the* family gathering day. It was taken more seriously than Thanksgiving and Christmas. Today, it is just a fun day. Everybody wears green and makes everything green. I am not sure how many young people down there know about the history of this neigh-borhood. Also, I think that the parade has become too political. Mass media features just the gay issue and Bulger's breakfast.

In 2003, a group of veterans opposed to the Iraq War, along with an Irish-American gay and lesbian group, was accorded permis-sion from Boston Police to march "behind" the parade (at the end of the procession); the group's members were barraged with both cheering and booing from onlookers. In December 2003, a Federal Magistrate ruled that allowing such unauthorized groups to march so close to the actual parade was a violation of the organiz-ers' free-speech rights, and decreed that those groups must march at least a mile behind the parade.

The Catholic Church

The tension between local and outside values is also manifested in the locus of the Catholic Church in South Boston. The development of a "rational" society in the postwar era is perceived to have undermined the position of religion as the explanatory scheme of a changing world.

> Before the war, priests and politicians were the leaders in this neighborhood.[15] But it [the Church] is not taken so seriously today, especially among the young people. After all, it has become less and less useful to solve immediate social issues here.

> Compared with those who moved out of South Boston to the suburbs, we are still religious. Norms are stricter, and the pattern of socializing among clergy and parishioners is more formal. Sure, there are many community activities that are organized by local churches, and many people are somehow involved as volunteers. But family schedules are much less organized by the church, and they have more flexible schedules. I think the church has become very much secularized, and priests are not necessarily our role models as they used to be.[16]

> More people marry non-Catholics, and more people accept divorce. More people have non-biblical names. More people favor abortion, sterilization, and vasectomy. More people think that the celibacy of priests is not necessary. More people understand feminism.

According to several priests that I interviewed in South Boston, the attendance rate at masses by those of Irish descent is approximately 20 percent today. This figure is perceived to have leveled off over the past couple of decades but is significantly lower than that of the prewar era when attendance at Sunday masses and the special holy days was required and nearly half the Irish residents are believed to have actually congregated.[17] Grace is said before meals only by three (out of eleven) informant families.

In March 1995, two armed robbers stormed St. Brigid's in City Point, firing a shot into the doorjamb and demanding money, allegedly to buy drugs. This incident shocked my informants because it occurred in a reputedly safe neighborhood, and particularly in a Catholic Church, and was perpetrated by the Irish residents who went to a Catholic school there. The *Boston Globe* (March 7, 1996) quotes John Ciccone, spokesman for the South Boston Information Center: "We want to send a message: don't do this again. This sort of thing will not be tolerated in this neighborhood. That's what makes South Boston different." The robbers were turned in to the police by their own relatives. Father Culloty of St. Brigid's is cited as stating: "We are not immune to the problems that affect all of society. ... I still feel very safe here. This is a stable, safe community. But communities are changing."

This incident is indeed an exceptional and extreme case, but, as some informants note, it may symbolize the fragmentation of church authority in the neighborhood. As we will see in the following sections, the expansion of personal freedom and choice in the private (domestic) sphere in turn puts spurs to the erosion of church authority and the politics of culture in the neighborhood.

SS. Peter and Paul's in West Broadway merged with St. Vincent de Paul's in 1995, and five years later a West Roxbury-based developer paid the archdiocese $2.4 million for the now-redundant church and its adjoining rectory. When I revisited South Boston in the summer of 2003, it was being turned into a luxury condominium.

Gangs

South Boston is by no means free from crime.[18] Before undertaking my fieldwork, I was cautioned by some friends that South Boston was a "dangerous place" or a "slum" inhabited by lots of "bully-boys." While this is a highly exaggerated and insulting stereotype, the existence of "gangs" is openly acknowledged by my informants. However, "gang fights" are viewed as a kind of "social sport" through which teenagers acquire some interpersonal skills and social norms.

Both my son and I became active on the streets and belonged to local gangs. It is a sort of rite of passage. We don't want kids to fight, but we also don't want our sons to be beaten up or not to stand up for their rights. Girls know which boys would stand up on their behalf!

When other groups crossed the line, we went into fights. But, we didn't use guns as the real gangs in Los Angeles do. We used only fists for actual fights. Weapons were hardly used because only cowards and sneaks were supposed to use them. It was very interesting that several rival groups suddenly formed an alliance when similar gangs from other neighborhoods intruded into our territory. Many of those kids entered the United States Marine Corps.

O'Connor (1994) illuminates the social dimension of the gangland culture:

Members of these youthful gangs often maintained close association with one another over the years, like the members of an alumni association or veterans of a combat regiment. Dr. William J. Reid, former headmaster of South Boston High School, recalls a man who donated a large sum of money for a new scholarship. When asked in whose name the scholarship was to be established, the man thought for a moment and said: "Make it the gang on the corner of Old Harbor and Eighth Street" (p. 177).

All of my informants who once were active on the streets confess that they decided to "graduate" from the gangland culture when they completed high school or when they started a family. James Kelly was a leading figure in a gang before establishing himself as the President of Boston's City Council, and Michael Rezendes of the *Boston Globe* reported on Kelly's slightly belated transformation at the age of 30:

Kelly traces his metamorphosis from barroom brawler to community leader to March 24, 1971, the day he took his last drink. "I could see the heartbreak I was causing in the people who were near and dear to me," he (Kelly) explains. "My mother, my sisters, my ex-wife, my friends, were all ... very fond of me. And my children were getting older. I didn't want them to see that their father was a crazy guy who did crazy kinds of things. So I just woke up and said, 'That's it. I'm done'" (*Boston Globe Magazine*, March 5, 1995, pp. 23–7).

Although occasionally engaging in real organized crimes, these adult gangs are considered to play an important social role in overseeing the "rules of the town" against the encroachment of outside values. The most conspicuous leader of organized crime in South Boston, William Bulger's brother ("Whitey"), went on the lam in 1995 when the State Police and the FBI were about to arrest him for racketeering. However, not a few of my informants, while condemning Whitey's criminal acts, voiced their view of him as the salvation of the "irrational" men and the guardian of the neighborhood against the "moralizing" forces from outside. MacDonald (1999), a South Boston native, recollects his boyhood in the 1970s:

> Visible or not, we all had a hero, a powerful champion, in the midst of all the troubles that enemy forces were heaving on us since the busing. Whitey was even more powerful than our politicians. They worked for him, that's what Ma [mother] always said. I wanted to see the face of Whitey Bulger, so that I too could feel that power that everyone else bragged they were so connected to (p. 112).

A policeman commented anonymously on the robbery case at St. Brigid's: "If Whitey was still around, this wouldn't have happened" (*Boston Globe*, March 7, 1996).[19] What bothers my informants seems to be the fact that weapons are gradually superseding fists, which results in undermining the spirit of "social sport" and leads to the intervention of "outside" authorities.

Thus, the evolution of "rational" society has gradually challenged the authority of local institutions that had assumed a central role in ensuring a safety net and ethical standards on the local level. While local institutions still preserve and exemplify the Southie spirit, their hegemony and legitimacy in the overall picture of my informants' neighborhood life has been relativized by a series of new pictures of the larger society with which residents have been confronted in the postwar era. The principle of "dancing with the girl that brung you" is still cherished and strongly sought after, but it becomes less imperative to abide by it when new opportunities knock and new rules prevail.

The unwillingness to compromise

This having been said, however, this is by no means a unilateral process. There are conscious efforts to reify the sense of continuity and restore the overall picture of society. The tradition of "Southie Day" was first invented in the early 1970s: it is an occasion for families who have left the community to be reunited with their relatives and friends on the South Boston beach every summer. On this annual "homecoming" day, foods, beverages, games, songs, and memories are shared with the families still "in exile" in the suburbs. The "Broadway Bazaar," a three-day sidewalk sale and community event, was co-sponsored in 1996 by the South Boston Chamber of Commerce and South Boston Main Streets, a program to revive small family businesses that have lost their competitive edge in the postwar era due to the emergence of shopping malls and supermarkets. In 2000, the "Great Southie Reunion" was sponsored by South Boston Pop Warner and the South Boston Claddagh Society, and attended by about 3,000 people who may live in the suburbs but still feel that South Boston is where they come from.

As a matter of fact, all the informants in this study are involved in social organizations that have close ties with the neighborhood: the South Boston Citizens Association, the South Boston Residents' Group, the South Boston Information Center, the South Boston Branch Library, the South Boston Neighborhood House, the South Boston Irish American Society, the South Boston Yacht Club, the South Boston Theater Group, the Allied War Veterans Council of South Boston, the Boys and Girls Clubs, SoBAD (anti-drug/alcohol organization), Kit Clark Senior House, the Castle Island Association, the Gold Star Mothers, the Mattapannock

Woman's Club, the Ancient Order of Hibernians, the Laboure Center, and many other religious, political, sports, health, and educational volunteer groups in South Boston. "We don't have money, but we have time. So we can help other people out."

The Laboure Center, for instance, is a community service center of Catholic Charities that provides services for children and the elderly. Its annual Christmas House Tour, a fund-raiser for the Center, involves more than 300 local volunteers. The South Boston Neighborhood House offers various forms of child care, sports lessons, study halls, tutoring, financial aid, vocational counseling, computer training, drug counseling, and shopping trips for the elderly. Many of those organizations and activities are assisted by the Catholic Church and subsidized by the donations of such South Boston/Irish-related corporations as the Gillette Company and Boston Edison. "Helping" is highly valued, and those who do not make a commitment to others and society are condemned as "selfish," "spoiled," or "immature." What is at stake is their pride in the working-class virtues and neighborhood that safeguarded their lives even in the midst of the Depression and distinguished them from the "parasites" in the Lower End. "We can't compromise it!"

Their unwillingness to compromise is often viewed as insular and exclusive – not only by outsiders but also by some native residents. One Italian coffee shop recently had a difficult time opening a branch of its chain on West Broadway. "Why do we have to help a shop from the North End? That was the reason." "Unless you are born in South Boston, people will consider you as an outsider – even if you live in South Boston for 40 years." When a new pub opened recently, a false rumor spread that customers from outside South Boston were receiving discounts. Such graffiti as "Yuppies, Go Home!" and "No Liberals!" were painted on walls near the pub.

I was told that anti-Black and anti-Asian feeling is still strong in South Boston. As Dan Pearson reports in *Boston Magazine* (October 8, 2000), for instance, Jim Kelly "refused to approve a resolution honoring the work of Thurgood Marshall, the nation's first African-American member of the US Supreme Court" in 1992, and later "blocked a resolution condemning a series of Black church burnings and then lashed out at councilors seeking a tribute to the life of

Jackie Robinson," and "opposed a permit for an all-Black circus to perform in South Boston" in 1999. "[E]ven right-wing zealot Patrick Buchanan, a man Kelly professes to admire, once said at the annual St. Patrick's Day roast that he would be considered a moderate in Southie."

Work

Ambition and competition

The wave of new opportunities and principles has had its ramifications also in the sphere of work, attracting young people to the white-collar jobs that reward bureaucratic and instrumental rationality as well as an enterprising mind.[20] One informant, now in his early forties, was once a college dropout, "hanging around in an island off South Carolina, drinking all day, inhaling cocaine."

> I was rejected by my girlfriend, defeated in a college election, and my grades were very bad. ... Also, I was already 21 years old then, and wanted to have a more independent life away from my parents. I was paying my college education by loan. So my parents accepted my decision.

However, he came to himself when he bumped into a man on the island who was only in his early thirties, but whose teeth were completely decayed because of drugs. "That guy looked almost 50 years old. I was just horrified to see him, and decided to go back to school. Thereafter, I studied very hard and behaved more rationally." After graduating from the University of Massachusetts in Boston, he worked at City Hall and the State House before launching his own organization geared towards the wellbeing of South Boston, especially of the Lower End.

> We have less volunteers who can make themselves available for the benefit of the disadvantaged in this area. So I found it imperative to create a solid organization like this to advance various social programs here. I don't want to see those teeth in this neighborhood!

His everyday life is highly routinized and deeply embedded in the middle-class, white-collar time frame.

> I am a typical American, working from Monday to Friday, from eight to five, and taking a two-week vacation in summer. I spend time with my family after dinner. On weekends, I take my kids to hockey games or to movies. My parents live nearby, which is sort of un-American today, and we sometimes visit them.

While feeling proud of his past accomplishments, he is ambitious enough to consider upgrading his career "a couple of more times" in order to reach out to the wider population. "I like my current job, but it is getting less challenging. I'm actually interested in Washington D.C. now, but my disadvantage is that I don't have a professional degree for selling myself better there."

The importance of a degree is strongly recognized by all my informants as the key to maintaining the status quo and the momentum of upward mobility.[21] The lack of a college degree seems to be a source of inferiority complexes among those whose highest qualification remains a high school diploma. In one family, there was apparent tension over a child's recent withdrawal from college. The parents incessantly reminded the child of the significance of college education, even at the dinner table, in the living room, and during an outing in the car. The parents themselves do not have college degrees. "That's why we can understand how vital it is!" The job market is perceived to have become more competitive and the educational requirements more demanding.

> I was the first high school graduate in my family, and a high school diploma was enough to find a good job. All of my kids graduated from college because it is vital to get a well-paying job. But I read somewhere that many kids go on to graduate school to get a job! I think this is a bit too much.

One female informant obtained a nursing certificate in her teens right after the war, and began working at a local hospital on a part-time basis while raising five children.

I worked only on weekends because I had to take care of my kids during the week. On weekends, my husband stayed home instead. He was very cooperative. I worked about twelve hours a day. Of course, the income was supplemented by my husband's income. There was no vacation, and the only recreation in those days was to go to the beach down the street. But as time went by, I felt it both necessary and pressing to recharge my batteries so that I could function more effectively as a professional nurse. So I enrolled at Emmanuel College in my forties and got both a Bachelor's degree and a Master's degree there. My kids were all grown up by that time, but I was still working at the hospital, and I paid all the tuition by myself.

She retired from the hospital in 1992 at the age of 63, but is still active as an independent therapist in the community – a vocation that she has been engaged in since 1978 both for economic security and for personal satisfaction.

While her circumstances enabled this informant to recharge her batteries, her progress is difficult to emulate for those who assume the primary role of breadwinner by working full-time outside the home.

I know that a graduate degree will boost my career, but once you have a family, it gets incredibly difficult to go back to school. The tuition is high, and I have very little time and energy left after working eight hours and playing with my kids. This is a dilemma.

While the G.I. generation benefited from a series of government incentives, the baby-boomer generation has been living an age of diminishing expectations that is characterized by soaring inflation and corporate downsizing. Many aspire to increase their competitive edge by obtaining advanced degrees, but when the acquisition of such qualifications is difficult, people have to lower their expectations of life, and compromise their American dreams, as is often the case with many middle-class Americans today (Ehrenreich 1983; Krugman 1994; Newman 1988, 1993).

The human touch

The jobs held by the two informants quoted above – the neighbor-hood development and the therapeutic business – are closely related to the community and its people, and some of the young adults opt to remain in the neighborhood, despite their educa-tional advantages and career potential, because they do not want to forsake their hometown. Yet the majority of the younger gener-ation are employed in a more bureaucratic environment outside of South Boston.[22] A working mother who is doing secretarial work in downtown Boston openly admits: "My plan is to reduce my workload when my son enters college and to quit the job when he graduates. I am working just for his education and for our Social Security." Her husband, an employee at a utility company, states: "I am working just to pay the bills. After retirement? I don't know. I might be cutting wood."

In a sense, members of the preceding generations were more pressured and desperate for economic security. Many elderly informants reminisce about the hardest times, when husbands had to take on two or three jobs for the sake of their family's survival. A male informant, in his early seventies, recollects: "I used to go to work before our kids woke up and come home after the kids went to bed. Sometimes I came home only two days a week. My kids have more freedom and family time, which I think is good." This kind of story constitutes a common discourse among members of the G.I. generation.

Yet these informants also point to a more personal and communal atmosphere at workplaces in the past.

> It was the time of the Great Depression, and jobs were very precious for all of us. I used to work about 100 hours a week. Sometimes I had to sleep in the truck three nights in a row. That was really tough! But it was fun to work there. Our boss brought turkey and cake to our homes on Thanksgiving and Christmas. We could confirm our loyalty and solidarity there. Now, your boss knows that you will quit the job tomorrow, and you know that you can be fired quite easily. Nobody trusts anybody. Also, our work ethic was "You wouldn't leave the job if happy." In

my case, I had no non-sick absences and I was very honest with my boss. Now, young people move around and change their jobs tomorrow. They are too short-sighted.

I have been a construction worker, a paper deliverer, and a letter carrier. I enjoyed all the jobs. Particularly I loved to work with my colleagues – chatting with them, listening to the radio with them, and so on. Nobody cared about your degree. There was no competition. Well, there were several kinds of exams that gave you a promotion. But I didn't take any sort of such tests. We trusted our bosses, and they protected us. I felt no insecurity with my jobs. Nowadays, everything is too businesslike. If you make a mistake, you are fired. That's it.

Upward mobility has carried the younger generation to middle-class, white-collar jobs that are physically less challenging and economically more competitive. Their everyday lives are more liberated and affluent. However, this mobility at the same time emphasizes and rewards objectivity, efficiency, competitiveness, and functionality – all the qualities demanded for the successful completion of middle-class, white-collar jobs. Mistakes and failures are feared, responsibility avoided, and human capacity trivialized. The sense of deep human connectedness might be hard to nurture in a "too businesslike" ambiance in a workplace where social relationships are translated into a series of abstractions, especially when people's jobs have little direct relevance to their local lives.

What also distinguishes the baby-boomers from their parents' generation might be the meaning of work in their lives. An elderly informant who was driving the shuttle van of an eye hospital proudly contends:

Well, most of the patients were quite a lot older than I am. But I loved the job so much. I like to help old men and women and to see their happy faces. I don't know why. Any good society must have respect for the elderly, but American society is losing it – because they are considered to be useless unless they are connected to status and money. I respect them, and I like to be liked by them. Their smiles make me extraordinarily happy. I was once working as a government officer. It was extremely inhuman and bureaucratic. I felt the loss of the human touch – so I quit it after six months. It paid better, but I thought it was a silly job.

Another G.I. who served as a postal worker comments:

I have lived without having any ambitions about my life. In other words, I didn't opt to live by setting any goal and striving for it. When you don't have an ambition, you don't have a defeat. I didn't pursue a "career" as such. I didn't need it. Money is important, but it is a means to an end, not an end in itself. You see, I had a good job with nice colleagues and bosses. I could have a three-week vacation and travel to Ireland. I am healthy. My wife and kids are all kind to me. I have a house and a car. What else should I expect? I am very satisfied. I'm often wondering why I was, and am, so happy and so lucky. I don't worry so much about the world. My biggest worry is my wife's health and my daughter's health.

Dilemma

This lifestyle contrasts with that of the baby-boomers, which entails "pushing" oneself harder, "selling" oneself better, and "upgrading" oneself further in more "challenging" settings. Another informant of the G.I. generation, then in his early seventies, comments:

Being ambitious is not necessarily a bad thing. It makes your life more exciting. So I don't want to impose my philosophy on my kids. But I don't want my kids to believe that it is the only way of living.

This informant's son, a bank clerk in his late thirties, replies:

I know that. And perhaps I will be saying the same thing to my kids 20 years later. But society has changed, and society tells you to become more ambitious. Society favors more ambitious people.

Another son, a computer engineer in his early forties, adds:

It is a kind of shame to go back to a blue-collar job. It's just impossible. It means a defeat of my life. And if you're going to get ahead, you'll have to do it [by] yourself. You have to keep pushing your own. I don't know how far I can go, but the important thing is to try my best.

The father fell silent, not knowing how to respond.

It is indeed hard to foresee how their best efforts and honesty will reward a sense of self-worth for these respondents – especially at a time when their jobs are "too businesslike," their credentials are not highly competitive, and the economy is in recession on both local and national levels. They are desperate not to fall into a "parasite" status by losing such middle-class symbols as house, car, and vacation. Life is more challenging and exciting, with a higher degree of freedom and choice, and self-fulfillment can be vigorously pursued even to the point where the self is exaggerated or burned out. Yet this lifestyle potentially threatens other sources of their pride: the working-class virtues and the values of the neighborhood. While feeling guilty for being unable to make enough commitment to their families and community, some informants also fear that they might be distanced from others by their competitiveness.

This tension between working-class virtues and middle-class value thus poses a dilemma and causes strain. There is a conflict of values (politics of culture) over the meaning of work, and how best to accommodate this conflict and resolve the dilemmas is becoming a personal question. As a matter of fact, the computer engineer quoted above was once invited to join a software company in Silicon Valley, but declined the offer because he did not wish to "desert" his aging parents, nor did he want to be seen as a selfish person by doing such a thing. "I fell into a big dilemma. It was a very difficult decision." An elderly woman comments on her children and their generation at large:

They are leading a better life in the suburbs, but sometimes they appear to be just "wandering," I mean, still searching for something. ... I feel that they are missing "relationships." ... Well, I don't know. I don't know what they are thinking about.

The question of how to foster good relationships with society through work seems to be becoming all the more important as more young people are employed outside of the context of life in Southie, the hometown that would "never forsake you."

Kinship and friendship

Kin network

The neighborhood's two- and three-storey houses are widely construed as a symbol of the "diffuse, enduring solidarity" of kinship. According to O'Connor (1994), those houses were

> not only an efficient form of immigrant architecture, allowing a maximum amount of living space on a minimum amount of land, but they also brought three or four families together into one extended household. These families exchanged clothes, shared food, loaned each other money, cared for each other's children, nursed the sick and buried the dead in a pattern of communal life that could be found all through the district (p. 125).

Most of my informants of the G.I. generation – the second and third-generation Irish Americans, born in the late 1910s and in the early 1920s – used to share those houses with their parents and grandparents. O'Connor continues:

> At a time before social security, unemployment insurance, retirement benefits, or old-age homes, it was also customary for young couples to take in grandfathers, grandmothers, maiden aunts, spinster sisters, widowed sister-in-law and separated brother-in-law. ... [R]esidents could usually name the families on a street-by-street basis (pp. 174–5).

While this residential pattern itself is somewhat marginalized and out-dated in South Boston today, my informants are acquainted with several families that still live with their own kin in those multi-storey houses, and two of my eleven informant families have actually inherited this residential arrangement. Meanwhile, it is fairly common for my informants to live in the houses that have been passed down by their parents or kinsfolk.

> We used to rent a house, but decided to buy my aunt's house a couple of years ago because it became too big for her. The house cost $120,000. She made a special agreement with me that I would pay $5,000 every year for ten years with no interest and pay the rest using a credit union loan program. This kind of transaction was very common in South Boston and is still the norm if your relatives live here.

However, high mobility in both socioeconomic and geographical terms has made reciprocity and interdependence among kinsfolk less integral or feasible.[23] Brian Dooher's family is a typical example. In his grandparents' generation, no one completed high school; jobs such as waitress, school staff, repairman, and physical laborer were standard; all married Irish Catholics from South Boston; and all the relatives resided within a radius of 70–100 yards in South Boston. Although his grandparents were the first owners of a telephone in the neighborhood, Brian situates them in the "lower" stratum in the Boston society of those days.

His parents' generation, according to Brian, made a "big leap." Most graduated from high school and worked at the Boston Edison Company, in public high schools (as teaching assistants), at the post office, and for the City of Boston. Most married South Boston Irish Catholics, but several relatives married people of more or less the same socioeconomic level but of different ethnic and geographical backgrounds whom they met at work.

Several relatives moved to such Boston suburbs as Arlington, Lynn, Dorchester, and the South Shore (mainly in order to secure enough living space and to avoid the busing of their children) or to other states such as Florida and California (usually in search of work). Those of this generation belonged, in Brian's view, to the "lower-middle class" in that they appropriated such "middle-class" characteristics as high mobility, suburban residence, inter-marriage, and ownership of house and car. Brian defines his generation as "middle-middle class," in having risen above the previous generation in "every respect." Brian's 30 first cousins have college degrees (and some have masters' degrees), white-collar jobs, and spouses of various White ethnic backgrounds from different locations. Brian's immediate siblings still dwell mostly in South Boston and Dorchester, but his cousins are dispersed "all across the nation."

Brian, like most other informants, can name his grandparents' siblings (and even those siblings' spouses in a more sporadic fashion) along with their occupations, and can tell anecdotes about them. He reciprocates greeting cards, telephone calls, and visits with his relatives as actively as his Yankee counterparts on Beacon Hill, in West Cambridge, and on the North Shore. On average, he sends 20 Christmas cards, primarily to the kinfolk who rarely meet, and telephones a couple of relatives each week "just for chatting." He dines with 10–15 relatives on Thanksgiving, and greets about 80 at Christmas. He attends one funeral and three or four weddings a year.

> On Christmas, we first visit my wife's parents' place, spend a couple of hours there, then move on to my parents' place, and eat there. We meet more than 100 people in one day! You know what? We begin our Christmas shopping in July because we can get the leftovers from the previous year at the lowest price.

Other informants echo Brian in talking about enduring kin relations that are predicated on mutual care and obligation.

> My kids are out of touch because they are either in California or in Wisconsin. But I am very close to my niece and nephew living a couple of blocks down there. We have each other's keys, and I can be her custodian in case of emergency. Actually I am going to baby-sit for my niece this afternoon.

> We don't visit all of the first cousins even in case of hospi-
> talization, but we feel it an obligation to visit a cousin if his
> hospital is located in Greater Boston, and if he is well
> enough to see us.

> Do we help our relatives' move? Of course! At least, as far
> as they move within our proximity. We store up claims for
> the future in that way!

While these testimonies convey the sense of durable involve-
ments and obligations in their kin world, Brian points to some
subtle yet significant transformations in kin relations that
capture his attention.

> There is little that we can do for our children's job hunting
> anymore because they tend to have a better network
> through their colleges.
> … Well, we used to loan money to each other with our
> kin. But, now we are financially more or less stabilized,
> and borrowing money tends to be seen as an evidence of
> the lack of self-management or independence. It's a bit
> shameful. We will go to the bank first.

Although family is still perceived to be the "most reliable" institution in times of trouble, the majority of its functions can be now
carried out independently or by outside agencies, and geographical
distance has become greater, eroding the centrality of kinship and
confining it more within the sphere of personal preference and
choice.

The children of the baby-boomer generation (the so-called
"MTV generation" or "Generation X") recognize their kin to the
extent that they can identify most of their first cousins, but the
relationships seem to be genealogical rather than substantial.
Brian's daughter, now in her second year at high school, remarks:

> We tend to meet each other at weddings and funerals. Of
> course, we say "Hi" to each other. But, the conversation itself
> remains kind of superficial, not to say phoney. You know
> what I mean? I have two close first cousins, and we are sort

of good friends. It's just because they used to come to our place often, and our chemistry fits well. But, otherwise, I don't socialize with other cousins.

Family events enhance kin interaction, and none of my informants denies the importance of kinship. However, they seem to lack the incentives to substantiate their relationships further, especially with those in the suburbs who are remote and self-dependent. This phenomenon is certainly also observed among their Boston Brahmin counterparts. Yet if family trusts and summer houses mitigate the dilution and dislocation of Yankee kin relations, my Irish-Catholic informants have little means to cope with this process but to resort to each individual's "common sense" – the sense of shame, guilt, and obligation.

Indeed, such notions are the cornerstone of the working-class virtues that were nurtured in the multiple-storey houses and took them through the Depression. Such pride, tradition, and common sense are, however, becoming all the more difficult to pass down and be perpetuated by the younger generations who have grown up with new rules and opportunities. This leaves more room for confusions, misunderstanding, and conflicts concerning the meaning of kinship and ultimately of society. Brian relates his bewilderment and frustration:

After we became more independent, some relatives began turning away from their kin. I can name a couple of those uncaring relatives. Most of them live in the suburbs, and by not caring for their relatives they are isolating themselves from the world. Even in South Boston some prefer paying more than $5,000 each year for childcare when their relatives are living close enough. I know that people seldom look back at their family and relatives once they get money and status, but ...

Intimate friendship

Compared with their Yankee counterparts, these Irish informants seem to have a higher degree of association with the White Americans in their vicinity – mostly Irish Catholics of similar age and

[155]

the same sex who went to the same school or worked together over the years. "I haven't socialized with anyone who graduated from Harvard or who earns as much as $100,000!" However, reflecting the high mobility of the postwar era, my informants' friendships are gradually overreaching the ethnic boundaries of South Boston.

> My closest friends are not only Irish but also Albanian, Lithuanian, and Polish. Before the war, each ethnic group stayed with their own kind. Sure, we met at work, at political events, and at community activities, and we got along very well. But we never visited each other's homes or went out drinking together. At night, everybody returned to his own enclave. The Polish lived in Andrew Square, and the Lithuanians lived around D Street on the west side of Dorchester Street. Many Jewish merchants had their clothing shops in South Boston, but they lived in Mattapan. Mattapan has become a Black community since the late 1960s. We had little contact with Blacks until busing took place. Because of busing, I still don't have a good impression about them. I don't like to shake hands with them. But my children are more open-minded. They have a lot of friends among WASPs, Asians, Hispanics, and Blacks, and it doesn't bother me at all. More and more people are doing the so-called "inter-racial marriage." My kids are married to an Anglo-Saxon, an Italian, a German, and a Lithuanian. It was just unthinkable before the war.

In the case of one elderly informant, his six close friends (Scottish, Polish, German, English, French Canadian, and Irish) of similar age hang around in a local deli "just for chatting" around 3 o'clock in the afternoon. "We greet each other by saying 'Oh, you are still alive today!' and spend an hour to gossip." This is a very familiar routine to this informant, who, like many of his contemporaries, used to drop by the same pub each night for one or two beers with his friends before going home to a hot supper. Men often socialize with their friends over a couple of beers, or by playing cards on weekends. Women tend to meet their friends for lunch.

However, a sense of intimacy is becoming more difficult to perpetuate in a tangible way, especially among members of the younger generations. "More women are working outside the home today, and the pace of life has become so fast, so it has been becoming very difficult to visit [friends at] home even for tea and coffee." With their school friends and former colleagues more dispersed across the country, it becomes much harder to keep in close touch with each other. The Southie culture, however, still retains its centripetal force.

> A little while ago, I bumped into one of my high school classmates for the first time after 30 years. We talked in the street a while and decided to organize a reunion. It was on extremely short notice, just one month before the date. But only one person out of 30 classmates couldn't make it. Others just replied, "We'll be there!" Can you believe it? Some came all the way from New York, Chicago, and Atlanta. Even if you haven't seen each other for several years, you can go back to the past quite easily!

This informant proudly introduced one of his favorite school songs to me:

> Remember the times you've had here
> Remember, when you're away.
> Remember the friends you've made here
> And don't forget to come back someday.
> Remember the Heights and Strandway,
> The High School on the hill –
> For you belong to Southie
> And Southie belongs to you.

Taste

My Yankee informants, I reflect, had an acute consciousness of being subdued and restrictive. I was entertained by their wit and by their deep knowledge about Harvard, world history, foreign cultures, and classical arts, among other things. If they were curious about the academic side of my research, their Irish counterparts in South

Boston seemed more concerned to know whether I was not getting cold or I was writing to my parents regularly. In most cases, I was treated to lunch or dinner at the very first meeting (meals were basically standard menus consisting of oatmeal at breakfast, chicken soup, spaghetti with meatballs, and pizza at lunch or supper), whereas it took me a little while to reach that level of socialization with the Yankee families.

They were quite proficient in entertaining their guests. A young couple demonstrated, with exaggerated gestures, how they fight at the dinner table in their everyday life. (The wife shouted at him while throwing green beans, and the husband got up from the table and stormed off.) During a meal another, older couple began performing some Irish dances to acquaint a foreign fieldworker with their cultural heritage. Many generously took time out to show me various historic sites within, and even outside of, the neighborhood. I received occasional letters containing newspaper clippings which informants thought would be relevant and helpful to my research. Some were so concerned about my flu as to present me with fresh vegetables from their backyards. (I found them at my house door with a get-well card when I woke up from my sickbed.) Such qualities as intimacy, personal touches and hospitality were identified as important virtues of "Irishness."

I witnessed many families congregating on their front steps and chatting with friends and acquaintances who passed by on summer nights. On such occasions people call their male friends by nicknames (e.g. "Basher," "Big Mouth," "Bugs," "Onions," "Wacko," "Dumbo," and "Crazy"). Nicknaming is considered one of the domains in which Irishness is well exemplified and distinguished from the "impersonal" human characteristics and relationships outside of their community. O'Connor (1994) notes:

> Tagged with a nickname at an early age, a youngster carried it with him to his grave. One observer suggested that the practice stemmed, at least in part, from the common Irish use of nicknames not only as an outlet for their irrepressible humor, but also as a practical means of identification. Parishes in Ireland usually had many families with the same surname – Ryan, Flaherty, Kelly, Sullivan, Murphy and so on. As a practical means of

distinguishing between the individuals, the Irish became adept at supplying nicknames that described the person and suggested some measure of local opinion. ... [N]icknames served as a permanent bond among young men of the district and helped to solidify further the feeling of comradeship over the years (pp. 177–8).

According to my informants, male members of other ethnic groups are sometimes given nicknames as well as "Irishized" surnames in token of their good friendship.

Upward mobility into the middle-class can easily be identified in the realm of material culture. Such modern artifacts as air-conditioners, VCRs, CD players, personal computers, and answering machines are widely possessed. Popular magazines featuring fashion, homemaking, automobiles, gardening, entertainment, and sports are occasionally found in the living room, together with a nice TV set. Brooks Brothers and Saab may be still beyond their reach, but L. L. Bean, Lacoste, the Gap, Chevrolet ("Chevys"), Ford, Plymouth, and Honda products are widely embraced by the younger generations. All these items clearly show that their taste is highly informed by the scheme of consumer culture of the larger, middle-class society. However, it is interesting to note that they take pride in the upgrading of their material culture (particularly in comparison with the "uncivilized" living conditions of "parasites") while mocking consumerism and materialism, especially among the rich. These reactions are apparently contradictory, but can be seen as reflecting ambivalent sentiments towards others – resistance to the rich (or downtown Boston) and contempt of the poor (or Lower End) – that define and represent the Irish identity as distinct.

Baseball, football, basketball, hockey, golf, tennis, and swimming are popular, and the names of favorite sport teams (the Boston Bruins, Boston Celtics, New England Patriots, and Boston Red Sox in particular) often appear on windbreakers, trainers, caps, and bumper stickers, which I do not recall among my Boston Brahmin informants. Forms of recreation reflect upward mobility into middle-class status. In the past, folding chairs on the beaches and one- or two-day trips within New England for sightseeing, picnicking, or skiing were the most common. Today, sailing in the

Boston Harbor, vacationing in Florida for a couple of weeks around Easter, and traveling abroad are gaining ground:

> Because I am a veteran, you can stay at nice hotels for $60 per night for two people when they normally cost you somewhere between $100 and $150. Since I retired, my wife and I have traveled to Ireland, Israel, Australia, Europe, and various places in the United States. In most cases, $1,500 per person is sufficient. When we traveled to Australia, it cost around $10,000 for the two of us, and it was the most luxurious trip in our lives.

All my informants of the G.I. generation and the baby-boomer generation have visited Ireland and met their distant relatives there. Books on Ireland, pictures of those relatives, and small Irish flags are found in their homes. While such trips, often locally organized, were made to assure themselves of their ethnic roots, a couple of my younger informants admit that their trips were in a sense "obligatory" in order to demonstrate loyalty to their ethnic heritage and facilitate conversation with neighbors and club members.

Most informants are quick to mention that drunkenness was one of the Irish characteristics of the past:

> Holding a drink was very important to be macho, and drunkenness was acceptable unless [you were] getting violent or rude. Insulting women or forcing women to drink was prohibited. Usually men drank at bar-rooms. Four of my six brothers were alcoholic. ... So I hate alcohol very much. Until recently men couldn't refuse to join in drinking when your friends call you up. Nowadays, you can instead have tea or ginger ale on such occasions. Alcoholism is very problematized in our society, and it is getting stigmatized in South Boston as well.[24] The socializing method is changing.

Minstrel shows, once a fixture of Boston's Irish neighborhoods, ceased to be a tradition with the prevalence of television, and because of political pressure since the 1960s. The "twilight of White ethnicity" that Richard Alba (1985) observed among Italian immigrants seems highly applicable to the case of my Irish informants, as they keep "crashing the gates" (Christopher 1989) into a mainstream, middle-class American status. "We are losing our color" – this feeling is congruous with that of White ethnic groups in the process of cultural assimilation (Alba 1990; Lieberson and Waters 1988; Shannon 1989).

Yet it should be underscored that this process is informed, mitigated, and resisted by their uncompromising pride in the working-class virtues that are anchored in the notions of intimacy, personal touch, and hospitality; in the practice of nicknaming; in the derogation of excessive consumerism; and in the display of Irish heritage. Nicknaming is their strong criticism of anonymity in the middle-class culture.

Love and marriage

Weddings

Before the war, parents were deeply involved in decisions about children's marriages (Horgan 1988). Today, decisions about marriage are left to the children themselves, and mixed marriage is becoming more common among Irish Americans in South Boston. "As long as you are happy, that's fine. The family is becoming like the United Nations!" However, so far as my primary informants (though not necessarily their children, siblings, relatives, and friends) are concerned, this "United Nations" is constituted predominantly by their fellow Irish Catholics from the same neighborhood. Thomas Keefe, a civil servant in his early forties, remembers:

> I first met my wife in my fourth grade when we were both active in the St. Peter's band. Later on, we met again at a boat club at the Charles River and at U Mass Boston. After a couple of years, we met again. It was 1980, and I was 25 years old. She was working at the Defense Department, and I was working in a local restaurant. We both had lovers at that time, but we got passionately attracted by each other. We decided to marry fairly quickly and began saving for marriage for two years. We had our wedding at

St. Augustine's in 1982. It cost about $500, and was paid for by her parents. After the wedding, everybody moved to downtown Boston, and we had a reception at a hotel in the Back Bay. My parents contributed $1,000 as a gift. That was enough to cover drinks. My parents-in-law paid for the food. About 50 relatives and 75 friends came from each side. The relatives included uncles, aunts, and their spouses. Some of my first cousins and their families also came, as long as they were close both physically and emotionally. Guests brought various gifts like china, lamps, blankets, and so on. But the most typical gift was cash, say, $50 to $100. We had our honeymoon in Florida for ten days.

Some informants met their spouses at beaches, at volunteer activities, or at dance clubs, all in South Boston. Some had their receptions at the bride's home or at social clubs in the neighborhood. Some made a partial contribution to the reception out of their own savings. Some preferred a smaller wedding with a larger proportion of kin. Some traveled to New York or the West Coast on their honeymoons. Yet the above testimony well represents the common pattern of marriage and weddings among other informants. Even those of "Generation X," who are disenchanted with the ceremonial side of social life, nevertheless dream of having their marriages sanctioned by the Catholic Church – the place from which they admit they have been "away a little while."

My Yankee informants might view it as a perfect manifestation of Catholic conservatism that few of their Irish contemporaries relied on contraceptive technology for family planning, allegedly until the 1970s. "We were told that you would die quickly if you used it!" – this remark by a man in his mid-seventies made his children (and myself) burst into laughter. However, the tension between religious doctrine and scientific rationality still makes my informants feel awkward when discussing the issues of abortion, homosexuality, and contraception in public:

Those topics are highly politicized, and you've gotta be very careful not to speak to the wrong persons. There are people who are still very sensitive about those issues.[25]

Premarital relationships were prohibited and possible only at the risk of having a baby. I know several friends who married because they had a baby. There was a sense of guilt for using condoms even in the early 1970s, and abortion was considered to be a sin. Even today abortion is frowned upon as murder. Most people in this neighborhood are "conservative Democrats" and "pro-life."

Although sexual conservatism in "the old days" is acknowledged by my Yankee informants, they testify that contraceptive technologies were practiced in their circles as early as the 1920s. Male Yankee informants now in their mid-seventies confessed that premarital virginity was exceptional among their friends, whereas the great majority of their contemporaries in South Boston affirmed – proudly – that they had no sexual experience before marriage. Chastity is strongly emphasized, and no informants admitted extramarital affairs as some of their Yankee counterparts had openly done.

Birth control

My informants' annual incomes range from $15,000 to $40,000. In the case of Thomas Keefe's family, both he and his wife have full-time jobs, and their combined annual income amounts to roughly $65,000.[26] This figure falls to around $42–44,000 after taxes. The family's average annual expenditure (with two teenage children both attending a parochial school) is approximately $40,000. They embrace the so-called "middle-class" lifestyle by owning their own house and car, spending a two-week vacation in Florida every winter, wearing neat clothes, and so on. "I don't complain about the way we live, but it's still difficult to save money against a rainy day."[27]

Many families attribute the diminution of the number of children partly to rising educational costs. Thomas Keefe comments:

Granted that you attend a parochial school, your parents have to pay $2–3,000 a year. It was free when I was a kid. That's why many parents cannot have five or six kids anymore. I have only two kids now, and we have no plan to have more. We want to concentrate on these two lovely kids and to send them to the Boston Latin School. That's the best public school, giving you higher chances of getting scholarships for college. The [private] Boston College High School poses too much strain on our finances.

Mr. Keefe understands the Catholic prohibition of birth control but finds it "unrealistic" in financial terms.

In the case of his family, medical insurance is almost entirely subsidized by their employers, and no interest is applied to half the mortgage because of a special agreement with the previous owner of their house, who is a relative. "We are very fortunate." Feeling "marginally well-off," Thomas Keefe joins many other informants in pinpointing high tax rates and expensive medical insurance as "pressing" issues among their neighbors.

Conjugal segregation

Polarity

The division of labor in the home between husband and wife has been undergoing a major transformation over the past 50 years. It was common for the men of the G.I. generation to hold a couple of jobs to support the family, and almost all the domestic work was undertaken by the wives. A female informant, now in her late sixties, remarks: "I was a telephone operator, and I quit it when I got married in 1947. It was a kind of custom to do so. Home-making was considered to be a woman's 'real' job." While such jobs as repairing and major physical labor fell within the man's sphere, the husband had little knowledge or skill to perform other types of housework.

My husband knew how to drive a truck. I knew how to run a home. We knew that both jobs were tough. I felt quite fair about it. After retirement, he learned some cooking. He does shopping because I don't have a driver's license.

It was quite simple. The wife set the tone of the home. She was the giver. Irish women were very powerful!

[164]

The male was the provider. He worked outside. The Irish husband was generally kind to his wife. Everything was so clear that there was no confusion about it. In our case, my husband was kind enough to do cooking on weekends when I was working as a part-time nurse.

This distinction becomes more negotiable and flexible among the baby-boomer generation, as most wives are employed outside and husbands are engaged in only one full-time job. In the case of one couple, the wife does 10 percent of the cooking, clearing the table, and cleaning, 40 percent of the laundry, ironing, gardening, and decorating, and the husband does 90 percent of the cooking, 60 percent of the shopping and laundry, shoe-polishing, and repairing. Washing the dishes, tidying, and 40 percent of the shopping are shared. "Of course, when I ask for his help, he always helps me." In another case, the wife testifies: "I felt kind of scared when I got married because I had never done cooking or laundry! It was 1974, and I was just 20 years old." Her husband smiled at me and added:

> I was 26 years old, and I had a debt of about $15,000. But money didn't matter. We were in love, after all. You know what really mattered? She knew *nothing* about cooking! So I became a cook. That was fine, and instead, we made a rule that a cook doesn't clean. But, but, but ... as soon as she started working full-time, the rule was totally abolished! So I am cooking madly and washing madly every day!

Both his wife and child roared with laughter. In the case of this couple, the wife does the vacuuming, ironing, and decorating whereas the husband does the cooking, clearing the table, washing dishes, tidying, shopping, laundry, shoe polishing, repairing, and gardening. "When she seeks my help, I do help her. But the opposite isn't necessarily true!" His wife tried to excuse herself, and her face turned red. These boundaries are not rigidly delineated. I saw, for instance, that the wife handed eggs and cabbage to her husband who cooked them. Although tidying is perceived as her husband's sphere, the wife picked up a cushion that had fallen from the sofa as her husband stood up to go to wash his hands. "After all, we have lots of flexibility in our roles. Home is not a company or a factory."

All my informants seemed to have the impression that the decision-making process has become more democratized.[28] A wife of the G.I. generation attests:

> Until our parents' generation, it was basically patriarchal. The male of my generation is more liberal and open-minded to the wife's voice. Why? Perhaps men lost their power when they were away from home during the war, and women became more confident about themselves after working for several years outside of their homes. ... Well, I don't know. Today, I feel it is more equal. We discuss all sorts of matters.

Her husband elaborates:

> Neither my wife nor I have the right to make the final say. My wife and I decided to send our kids to parochial school. In the case of high school, we decided to send them to public school after hearing their preferences. The choice of college was completely made by the kids. My wife and I like the same kinds of foods, so we have no problem. Of course, we always travel together. Usually I do the research, and my wife picks up the best destination among a couple of places that I find interesting.

This perceived sense of equity is generally acknowledged by the children. "It's not perfectly equal in all sorts of decisions. But I don't have a feeling that one side has been dominating the other." The principle of mutual decision-making is inherited by those of the baby-boomer generation, and I did not encounter any serious claims about a perpetuated imbalance of power in their everyday lives.[29]

Veeder's (1992) comparative study of the decision-making process among Irish couples in Ireland and the United States suggests that it can be misleading to assume a sharp polarity between the public, external, and mind-oriented "man's" sphere and the private, domestic, and heart-oriented "woman's" domain. Such an assumption, according to Veeder, tends to ignore the way Irish women's agency is exerted in the "instrumental" domains (e.g. rules, responsibility, and justice) as well as in the "expressive" dimension (e.g. relationship, emotion, and belonging). However, this polarity was one of the main principles by which my informants' parents and grandparents organized and practiced their family lives. My informants attest that the dichotomy between men's and women's roles was "naturalized" and lived out in a more rigid fashion before the war. Younger informants tend to view this distinction as "arbitrary," "discriminatory," "unrealistic," or "anachronistic," and, as indicated above, they approach this dichotomy with a high degree of flexibility and improvisation in their everyday lives.

Deviation or liberation?

The process of "de-naturalizing" the role dichotomy, however, means contradicting the traditional doctrine of the Catholic Church. Although none of my informants defined themselves as feminist (some even being derogatory to radical feminism), I found such concepts as "equality," "right," "choice," and "freedom" for women deeply ingrained in their discourse on family life:

> You can live with your boyfriend without getting married. You can marry whomever you want. You can decide how many children to have and when. You can choose not to have children at all. You can ask your husband to cook.

Is this deviation or liberation? Reactions are mixed, even in the minds of my informants; according to Daly (1978) and Horgan (1988), reactions on this issue are mixed in all American Irish-Catholic communities. Horgan maintains:

> [T]hese issues are intertwined with concepts of sin and with calls to become or remain traditional wives and mothers, it is difficult for women to differentiate their roles as women, Catholics, workers, wives, mothers, citizens, and quite fallible people. ... At issue for Catholic Irish in

this country is the response of those affected by divisive-
ness within the Catholic community, functionaries and lay
people alike, who hold alternate realities to those officially
held by the Catholic Church (1988: pp. 71–2).

This tension between ethno-religious identity and national identity is certainly being felt in South Boston over such issues as abortion, homosexuality, and contraception. As mentioned above,
discussion of these topics is highly sensitized and politicized.
However, as far as the division of labor and the process of decision
making among my informants in South Boston are concerned, the
national identity predicated on the appropriation of such notions
as "equality," "right," "choice," and "freedom" is preponderant,
and the degree of "conjugal segregation" (Bott 1957) diminishes
from one generation to another.

Qualitative dimensions

The sense of equity and fairness about the division of labor and the
decision-making process is not reducible to purely quantitative
terms: it is more contingent upon people's subjective interpretation of the contexts in which a particular domestic task or decision
is executed. "Home is not a company or a factory": this utterance
well expresses the modern ideology of family as a "haven in a
heartless world" (Lasch 1977). At the same time, it also represents
people's bewilderment in organizing the flexibility, contingency,
nuance, improvisation, and indeterminacy of their actual lives into
quantitative pigeonholes.

Ahlander and Bahr (1995), after re-examining the five major
theoretical frameworks of the study of housework (namely, "study
of home management" in the first half of the century, "functionalism" in the 1950s, "resource theories" in the 1960s, the "new home
economics" in the 1970s, and "feminist contributions" in the 1980s
and 1990s), disclose a paradigm inherent and persistent in those
approaches:

All of them are modern, in the sense that they invoke
rationality and technical and technological solutions to
human problems, empirical measurement, and efficiency.

... They are all grounded in a historical period and society that exalted empirical science, industrial production, economic power, and the conversion of all social processes and values to monetary terms. All reflect an underlying economic model that treats families like other social organizations in the sense that what matters is economic production and economic power. ... [M]uch current writing based on economic frameworks suggests that doing housework is inappropriate, a waste of time, and even demeaning for adults (pp. 58 63).

As indicated above, all my female informants of the G.I. generation sounded fairly satisfied, with only some minor complaints, about their commitment to housework, rather than viewing it as "inappropriate, a waste of time, and even demeaning" as the formal (quantitative and economic) approaches in the study of housework tend to premise. Their testimonies provide cases which validate Ahlander and Bahr's call for the analysis of "moral" dimensions of housework: the way in which housework is perceived, internalized, and signified in the actual contexts of social lives. The authors' insistence on a more qualitative approach is congruent with the methodological stance of the meaning-centered approach in the study of family and kinship that was mentioned earlier, along with contributions made by Maybury-Lewis (1979) and Yanagisako and Collier (1987).

Divorce and cohabitation

Divorce and separation

Like many others, my research families are not entirely immune to the collision of interest and emotions.

There was a major conflict last month. I wanted to attend the wedding party of my close friend in Ireland. But I found that our financial situation was not so comfortable as to bring my wife and children. So I bought just my own ticket. My wife lost her temper. She got so furious! I admit that I was a bit too hasty then.

Most conflicts are precipitated by "trivial matters": coming home a bit late, staying on the telephone a bit too long, mixing up cans and bottles in recycling bins, and the like. On average, my informants go through three or four quarrels per month, and, as in the Yankee cases, they have their own channels through which to release their heated tempers. "Yelling. That makes him quiet." Her husband replies: "She yells so loudly. I still get upset!" The wife responds: "I grew up in a family with ten kids. Yelling was quite natural." "When I get angry with my wife? I just go row a boat for a couple of hours. It makes me feel very good. When it's done, I go home. Usually, my wife waits for me – making her delicious dessert." "We kiss each other before going to bed. That's it." It is "very rare" to go to see outside professionals for marriage counseling, partly because it is expensive and partly because they can be counseled by priests and consoled and encouraged by friends (including close neighbors and relatives).

Although no statistical data about the divorce rate in South Boston is available, my informants calculate that it is significantly lower (25–35 percent) than the national average (about 50 percent). No informants have signed prenuptial agreements, and they all speculate that none of their friends in the neighborhood have done so either. "I've never heard of it." "Well, we aren't so rich." Lawyers are hired only by those who are relatively better off, and the process of judicial intermediation goes smoothly in most cases. As a matter of fact, divorce is still a taboo among the faithful followers of the Catholic Church (especially among the older generation), and they have a tendency to opt for "separation" after making a confession. In addition, some people apparently move out of the neighborhood to "save face" after divorce. These two factors make it more difficult to analyze the divorce rate in South Boston accurately. However, as far as my research families are concerned, the combined percentage of both divorce and separation amounts roughly to 10 percent among the G.I. generation and 25 percent among the baby-boomer generation.

In one case, a wife, a faithful Catholic in her mid-sixties, proposed "separation" to her husband about ten years ago:

> I felt sort of "burned out" and wanted to find myself. I mean, I just wanted to enjoy my own life that I had sacri-

ficed by raising five children while working on weekends. I didn't feel resentful of him at all. Actually, we were getting along pretty well. He was very kind. But it was somehow unfulfilling. I still like him, and we meet quite often. But, I have no intention to get re-married again. I had a nice marriage, and that's enough. That's my life.

This couple moved to Needham, a Boston suburb, during the busing crisis to "protect" their children. After separation, she returned to her parents' house in South Boston. She files her tax return jointly with her husband, and meets her children in Needham. "My kids don't want to see us living separately. They haven't visited me here since we got separated. When I become less mobile, I will be living with a couple of my close friends." This woman is still fortunate because she is not financially separated from her husband and the children are all independent. The feminization of poverty after divorce (Brannen and Wilson 1987; Delphy 1984; Ehrenreich 1983; Goldin 1990) often occurs in South Boston as well as elsewhere, resulting in increased dependence on public welfare.[30]

Cohabitation

While hesitant about divorce, the "self-searching" woman quoted above is fairly open-minded about cohabitation, as are most of my other informants. "It's no problem as long as you live together somewhere else. Having sex in this house is not possible. I feel it is a sort of taboo or sin." "There is a romantic side of marriage, but it tends to become less intense than it used to be. After marriage, flowers and chocolates change into laundry. You have to be realistic about what it means to live together." "It's a good way of determining if you really want to live with your partner for the rest of your life. Otherwise, the risk for children is too high. Don't have an illusion of love and marriage." Cohabitation is thus legitimated as a mechanism in which the ideology of romantic love is tested – successfully or not – before the realism of everyday life. However, a priest interprets the situation differently:

Well, we must accept what is happening. But I don't believe in what they are doing. A good society always needs a lifelong commitment, and the family is the most basic unit of society that is sustained by a long-term commitment. But our culture has diminished the role of family and lost the centrality of family. People are afraid of making a long-term commitment. People are shying away from taking on responsibility for family and society.

Are people just cautious about making a commitment, or are they really frightened of taking responsibility? The nuance is slightly different, but its implication is the same: "To keep a relationship is an extraordinary job in our society."

Childrearing

Communication

The boundaries between parents and children are perceived to have become less clear cut in the postwar era, making their relationships more open, more flexible, and thus more negotiable. "Today, children are not only seen but also 'heard.' You could hardly take issue with your parents in the past."[31] "Adult topics" such as sex, money, and divorce have become more permissible at the dinner table. "They are very precocious not only in terms of dressing and make-up. Even kids in their mid-teens know a lot about divorce, child abuse, drugs, and politics. It was unthinkable when I was their age in the mid-1960s."

Relationship building between parents and children has been facilitated by several trends. For one thing, the number of siblings has decreased, from eight to ten among the G.I. generation to five or six among the baby-boomers, and down to two or three among the MTV generation. For another, the process of upward mobility has liberated many families from the chronic economic insecurity that obliged breadwinners to undertake more than one job concurrently, enabling them to spend longer hours at home with children.

> My father is the role model for me. No question about it. But I am trying be much closer to my kids than my dad

was to us. When I was a kid, my father wasn't much around because he had three jobs.

While some elderly informants sounded a little apprehensive about the loss of parental authority and the shrinkage of the child's kin-world that accompany these postwar phenomena, most welcome them as a step forward towards more egalitarian and affectionate family relationships.

None of my research families have hired outside caregivers on a long-term basis, partly because assistance from their adult children and mothers was available, partly because they could not afford it, and partly because a child was believed to do poorly if entrusted to the hands of outsiders. These reasons are interrelated. Moreover, more husbands are involved in childrearing, more visible at home, and more available for domestic affairs. The concept of the "latchkey child" is strongly disapproved of. Either father or mother is expected to stay with children, and all possible adjustments have been made to comply with this ideology of parenthood. Some mothers work only on weekends when their husbands can supervise the children at home. In some cases, husbands concede their work shift to accommodate their wives' jobs so that both a double income and conjugal equality are ensured. Some informants regret this phenomenon as the consequence of woman's "egoistic" pursuit of "self-fulfillment" since the war. Yet such a view may fail to acknowledge that the husband's stronger presence at home and in childrearing is sought after not only by women but also by men.

As more husbands and wives become incorporated into the middle-class, white-collar economy on a full-time basis, there is less flexibility and fewer options are available apart from reliance on expensive childcare, as is often the case with families in South Boston. What the great majority of my informants, especially those in the younger generations, anticipate is structural rearrangements in the work environment (e.g. more flexible hours, longer maternity leave, better child care, and higher wages) as well as changes in governmental policy (e.g. better health care, better schools, affordable housing, a higher minimum wage, and job training), instead of returning to the "family values" of the past that are often lauded on political grounds. This is a reason why the Irish, while conservative in values, still tend to support the Democrats in elections.

Parenthood

As a consequence of the above structural and ideological changes, childrearing is more shared among younger couples, and sex education seems to be the only domain in which the gender factor matters. The shrinking distance between parents and children and the sharing of childrearing, however, do not necessarily make parenthood easier.

> Both of my parents were highly stressed by economic hardship. My father had four part-time jobs, and my mother was a full-time housewife plus a part-timer. But, I think that we are suffering from another kind of stress: I mean, as we become economically more liberated, we have a higher expectation towards personal fulfillment and towards parenthood. I want to read more books for my personal growth, but at the same time I am expected, as their father, to read more books to my kids. I always feel myself running against the clock.

> Streets are no longer as safe as they used to be, and therefore children's activities need to be better organized and better supervised. So, every activity is more structured and scheduled today, and we need to adjust our lives to them.

> There is a sense of uncertainty about the prospects of the economy. In the past, you could buy a house if you worked hard, but it is not the case any more.

These voices reveal that members of the baby-boomer generation feel pressed to run faster to catch up with dreams, as is often the case with middle-class families in the United States (Ehrenreich 1983; Krugman 1994; Newman 1988, 1993).

The difficulty of parenthood is also manifested in the domain of home discipline.

My father cherished honesty and justice. He was quick at knocking down any rogues in town who offended those virtues. Can you imagine how such a man reacted if I skipped a class? It would be a court case today! Young parents are too permissive about children's anti-social behaviors, even if spanking is now prohibited!

There was an unspoken code that father shouldn't beat daughter. So, in my case, I was slapped by my mother. It was damn painful! Nowadays, young mothers scold their kids by saying something like "Do you know what makes your mom sad?" Oh, give me a break! It doesn't matter if you feel sad or not. The most important thing is to make sure that your child becomes a good citizen.

Young parents undoubtedly understand that it is their responsibility to inculcate values in their children. However, the enfeebling of parental authority, while being welcomed as facilitating the communication between parents and children and enhancing the autonomy of the child, makes fulfillment of their parental duties more difficult. "How can we say 'Stop it!' or 'Do this!' to our kids when we are encouraged not to impose our values on others?" The distinction between "discipline" and "imposition" has become more ambiguous and subjective, as neighborhood, religion, and kinship have weakened their role as sources of moral authority and legitimacy. This may be making the issue of home discipline more complicated and problematic. As far as my informant families are concerned, parents are confident enough not to depend on "how-to" books for guidance. I occasionally came across a situation in which parents, grandparents, neighbors, and friends interrupt their relaxed conversations to shout warnings of safety or playful directions to their own and others' children in the streets. Still, being "good" parents seems to be becoming a source of stress not only in a temporal sense but also in epistemological terms.

Parochial school

As far as disciplining is concerned, many elderly informants recollect that teachers at parochial schools were extremely strict and authoritative. "In those days, all the teachers were nuns. We used to be beaten with a yardstick kept in the classroom. No parents complained about it. Actually, both parents and the military thanked teacher for disciplining the kids so well." Reflecting the exodus to the suburbs, the overall decline of church authority, and the soaring cost of education, the size of the parochial school system has diminished in the postwar era after a series of administrative rearrangements. The parochial school population of South Boston consists of approximately 1,500 students attending St. Augustine School, St. Brigid School, the Gate of Heaven School, St. Peter School, and St. Mary School. The financial support of parishioners made the tuition free in the past, but nowadays it costs around $2,000 each year, partly because the decline in religious vocations has made it necessary to hire more lay teachers.

According to some school officials and informants, approximately 70 percent of Irish-Catholic students in South Boston attend a parochial school: the others either have no choice but to go to a (free) public school for financial reasons, are accepted by the (public) Boston Latin School, or can afford the expensive tuition at the private Boston College High School.[32] The traditional segregation of education by gender is said to have loosened in order to cope with the diversification of career tracks among female students. While most parents are satisfied with the parochial schools' religious tenor and strict discipline, they attest that the schools are placing a greater emphasis on educating students to become "innovative," "independent," and "ambitious" today. Some parents regret this.

As the importance of moral education is downplayed and compromised both at home and at school, the sphere of personal freedom and choice expands in children's lives. A local drug counselor diagnoses: "I suspect that the problems of alcoholism and drugs among the youth are caused primarily by having no pressure from moral authority, I mean, both from parents and from teachers. Those kids are pursuing just pleasure and relaxation."

Continuity

Interestingly enough, all my informants agree that one of the most regrettable and ironic consequences of the postwar changes in childrearing and the parent–child relationship is that some children do not have dinner with their parents. My informant families still dine together, but a couple of recent high school graduates testify that some of their friends have their meals in their own rooms while watching the same TV program as their parents do. "I think it is because family size has become smaller. I mean, more privacy is possible, and the family itself becomes kind of suffocating." To those families, home is the place where, when you have to speak to them, they have to speak to you.

What my informants consider important about having meals together is not sharing food per se but sharing a "feeling of unity" and a "vision of the past, the present, and the future." "What I think really important is to tell my kids about the history of suffering that their ancestors have gone through. I'd like to make sure that my kids will not take what they are for granted." "My wife and I have planted a tree for each and every one of our grandchildren so that they will remember us and take pride in their family." "I am producing a family history book for them – just to let my grandchildren know what life was like before they were born!"

Such a sense of place in history is, however, perceived as becoming more difficult to transfer and perpetuate among posterity.

> There are no grandparents in the suburbs. So no history is taught to children, and children tend to be focused only on "now."

> One generation makes a big difference. We cannot impose the values of our generation on those of other generations. I feel that each generation is getting less and less tied to history and more and more interested in his own generation.

> The speed of industrial life itself is so fast. I mean, in the countryside, you can still take a time to walk along the seashore and reflect on yourself and your father, but it's just impossible in the urban area. People tend to focus just on "now."

Indeed, there are expectations and pressures to keep "moving up the hill" for better opportunities and higher accomplishments in the new contexts of life. This is, however, by no means a unilateral process. As we have seen in the above sections, there are a multitude of counter-forces and conscious efforts to reify the sense of continuity and perpetuate the "overall picture" of society. What is at stake is how to accommodate the tensions and confrontations between the working-class (or "traditional," "Southie," and "Irish-Catholic") virtues and the middle-class (or "postwar," "national," and "individualistic") values, without lapsing into a poor or "parasite" status. My informants' social lives and realities are shaped by the struggle to synthesize these contrasting principles through the conflicts of pride, the contestations of identity, and the politics of culture. So are history and tradition. After all, in the process of such endeavor and struggle, history and tradition are also subject to being celebrated, invented, exaggerated, ignored, abandoned, or forgotten.

4 Conclusion

Fieldwork revisited

The influence of the New England region on the formation of American culture is widely noted in both academic and popular discourse, and so is the influence of Boston as the central locus of this northeastern segment of the United States. My fieldwork was aimed at furnishing an ethnographic comparison between two distinctive social groups in the Boston area: the upper to upper-middle-class Anglo-Saxon Protestant family and the lower to lower-middle-class Irish Catholic family. By comparing these two groups in a contrasting sociocultural milieu, I expected to elucidate the diversity of experience and culture within what is generally categorized as White, middle-class America, while at the same time extracting from such diversity some common logic or theme that might be applicable to other Americans in different sociocultural contexts of which the family is a part.

To that end, I was particularly curious about the ways in which these two groups internalize and appropriate the complex, often-times distressing, transfigurations of postwar society in constructing their own cultural histories and social realities and in undertaking the actual practice of everyday life and engagement in social relations.

The construction of cultural histories and social realities

In both groups, the expansion of the national economy, the implementation of social welfare, the development of mass transportation and communication systems, the magnification of legal and bureaucratic structures, the intensification of social mobility, and the transformation of demographic composition are highly significant on the structural level, as is the permeation of meritocracy, rationalism, feminism, and multiculturalism on the ideological level. These structural and ideological metamorphoses in the late-modern (or postmodern) era are perceived to have fragmented and blurred the boundaries of social cosmoses that were once predicated on the homogeneity and functional interrelatedness of residential area, occupation, education, economy, organizational affiliation, ethnicity, religion, and cultural aesthetics.

For instance, in the case of Brahmin families on Beacon Hill, in West Cambridge, and on the North Shore, the absence of primogeniture, the progressive tax system, the geometrical multiplication of inheritors, the impact of inflation, the diffusion of divorce, and conservative financial management, among other factors, accelerated the erosion of material capital and impeded the acquisition of such "symbolic" capital (Bourdieu 1984) as summer houses, aristocratic weddings and decor, and club memberships. The collective memory, sentiment, and identity that were embedded in those symbols have become diluted. The Brahmins' traditional neighborhoods were penetrated by the logic of "economic Darwinism." A web of complex legal and bureaucratic procedures certainly safeguards family assets and identity, but it is a kind of identity over which outside "experts" (the legal system or bureaucracy) have increasing control.

The prevalence of the principle of meritocracy and competition challenged the implementation of the "old money curriculum" (Aldrich 1988) in terms of where to study, where to live, where to belong, and what to do. Political pressure for a more just society forced open the doors of social clubs. A sense of honor and pride that was once grounded in civic commitment became difficult to experience and perpetuate in a highly formalized, competitive, and complex society. The boundaries between dignified sobriety and shabbiness as well as between eccentricity and weirdness are becoming more and more ambiguous.

The overall downward mobility of this social group is well reflected in their perceived notion of the "decentralization of Yankee hegemony," the "endangered WASP species," or the "flattening of the pyramid." Being "upper-middle" has been acutely accentuated in their self-definition, as distinguishable from "others" – especially those below them (the "no money," "middle-class," "ordinary people," or "mob") and those above (the "new money" or "newcomers") who are "functioning in no context or in a context in which they have never been before." At the same time, however, some have found it too difficult to make sense of this emerging reality of life and to create a life of their own.

In the case of Irish families in South Boston, economic prosperity as well as the introduction of the G.I. Bill and social welfare in the postwar period helped them "crash the gates" (Christopher 1989), permitting entry into the "middle-class" strata of society and into the status of "typical" Americans. This upward mobility is a source of pride in their heritage and in the ideal of the American dream. However, it simultaneously entailed the fragmentation of local relationships and institutions that once assumed a central role in ensuring the safety net and ethical standards of the community. Many social functions that kinship once assumed are now performed by outside agencies. With a vast network of federal agencies under the New Deal programs, there was much less reason for anyone to go to the local ward boss for help. Work environments became "too businesslike" and "impersonal" as Irish Bostonians were integrated into the white-collar society. The doctrines of the Catholic Church increasingly became inapplicable to the actual context of lives in which more women work outside the home, more couples practice cohabitation and family planning, and more marriages dissolve.

The fragmentation of South Boston's social picture was further accelerated by the evolution and involution of the logic of utilitarianism, modernization, and capitalism in the larger society. Boston banks' policy of "red-lining" spurred the exodus of the population to suburban areas in the postwar era. The logic of economic Darwinism stimulated the gentrification of the once working-class neighborhood by Yuppies. The potency of mass media invented heroes on a national level, trivializing local talents. The rule of "dancing with the girl that brung you" in local politics was often contrary to the interests of the larger society. Many South Bostonians demonstrated their loyalty to Uncle Sam in wartime, but then felt betrayed by the government over such issues as busing, the mixing of tenants, affirmative action, and the exporting of US jobs overseas. Gang fights have become difficult to justify as a kind of "social sport". Liquor consumption has become highly sensitized.

While "Irish color" is felt to have become diluted and fragmentary, South Bostonians strive to situate themselves in this fluctuating social environment by underscoring their indignation with "others" – especially those in the Lower End (the "poor" and "parasites") who do not emulate their commitment to the neighborhood, and those in downtown Boston (the "rich," "liberals," or "outsiders") who attempt to moralize South Boston. Being "middle-class" is accentuated vis-à-vis the Lower End, and being "working-class" vis-à-vis downtown Boston, in each case enhancing a sense of self-respect.

The loss of a sense of place and the intensification of individualism

Insinuated in these processes of social fragmentation and self-identification in both groups is the enfeeblement and insecurity of a sense of place, in both historical and geographical terms, as a source of moral authority and social legitimacy. The collective memory and tradition that were once woven into the thick web of social relations and symbols lose their centripetal force, reinforcing people's preoccupations with their immediate lives – or, to borrow an informant's expression, "a feel for piety only for one's own interest just ahead." As Frederic Jameson (1987) points out, the loss of historicity means the loss of a sense of the past as well as of the future, "the waning of any sense of that radical difference of the past in terms of which alone we might achieve some sharper sense of the uniqueness of our own present" (p. 554). Individuals are destined to live in a social context without a script, in both temporal and spatial terms. To quote one informant, "We have nothing to hang onto – whether onto history, community, work, or onto family." Morality magnifies its recourse to legal and political procedures, and justice to due process rather than to one of substantive ends. Society is perceived as too multiplex, heterogeneous, and segmented to be "imagined" (Anderson 1983) as a synthetic context or connected whole.

Such individualistic values as "self-help" and "self-dependence" may be virtuous in themselves. Actual circumstances, however, compel individuals to count on themselves as the sole point of reference for moral guidance and social practices. Such concepts as "self-discovery," "self-expression," "self-fulfillment," "self-growth," and "self-actualization" amplify their resonance in everyday discourse. "Feeling good" assumes a kind of transcending power and authority for the existential confirmation of the self. As one informant sees it: "'If you don't like it, just leave it' – there is no limit to such a mentality in our society!" Consumer purchases, credentials, psychotherapy, love relationships, and physical attractiveness, among other elements, become signified as resources for attaining

[182]

such a state of mind and feeling. Legal and bureaucratic authority, as Alasdair MacIntyre (1981) explicates with his concept of "bureaucratic individualism," become an integral means for shielding one's rights and sheltering one's niche. Bellah et al. (1985) observe that "[i]nstead of directing cultural and individual energies toward relating the self to its larger context, the culture of manager and therapist urges a strenuous effort to make of our particular segment of life a small world of its own" (p. 50).

Many of my younger informants feel compelled to "keep pushing" themselves further in the quest for a higher level of "self-fulfillment" and "success" – the satisfaction of their wants and the expression of the fullest range of their impulses – even to the extent of risking nervous breakdown and burnout. Many articulate their indignation over "hyper-individualism" or excessive self-centeredness in society today.

Accordingly, social relationships come to be evaluated by each actor in light of the ideology of the first-person discourse, and hence these relations become more susceptible to negotiation in content and diversification in form. "There is no such thing as an American family." This is a common phrase voiced by many Americans as well as by many non-Americans, with subtle, often intricately mixed, connotations of jest, regret, sarcasm, relief, pride, and envy. Indeed, even a brief observation suffices to show the tremendous variation and complexity in American arrangements of marriage and domestic life. It appears almost as if "the American family" defies any definition except that of being chaotic, and as if such an essentialism as *the* American family can exist only in terms of crude traditionalism or idealism.

In this sense, it can be strongly argued that on one level the popular rhetoric mentioned above reflects and captures a partial reality. However, diversity of social arrangements does not deny but rather reflects the existence of a cultural theme in society. Bourdieu (1977) postulates that social actions that look spontaneous and voluntary are actually informed by wider social forces. In the case of American society, the thematic emphasis on first-person discourse plays a vital role in shaping social practices and relations. At the same time, this logic of individualism has been sharpened and magnified in the course of massive fluctuations in social structures and cultural values that followed the Second World War.

[183]

The family, as we saw in Chapter 1, cannot be analyzed profitably "in its pure form" (Schneider 1968), as it is inseparably interlocked with the historical and ideological matrices in society (Maybury-Lewis 1979; Yanagisako 1985). My informants reveal that the family functions as the matrix of their explanatory scheme as well as the center of their cognitive map of a larger society, and the logic of individualism affects, and is affected by, the process of diversification and transmogrification of family life and relationships. "Love" is strongly idealized as the primary drive for marriage that should transcend any categories of race or religion, and hence marriage can be terminated in the name of "self-growth" without legal attribution of faults.

It is left to individuals to decide with which kin to associate themselves, and so relatives can be either "best friends" or "strangers." Cohabitation is widely accepted as a means of "feeling good" without making a hasty commitment to marriage since half of all marriages today dissolve. Many young couples improvise their weddings so that they can express their individuality in a less formalized and ritualistic manner than is possible through traditional wedding ceremonies. Self-expression and self-assertion continue to be strenuously accentuated in postwar childrearing. Gullestad (1996) expounds on the dilemmas in the transmission of values between the generations in Norway in this late-modern (or postmodern) era; his comments are of great relevance to what I observed among my informants:

> Instead of individuals being resources for families, families are becoming the resources out of which individuals construct their selves. To attain the ideal of being oneself, children must justify their values in terms of their own individual convictions and preferences, not the convictions and preferences of their parents. Parents today should ideally transmit the ability to find oneself and to develop oneself, rather than just specific ideas and specific values (p. 37).

How best to "discipline" children without "imposing" parents' values and judgment? How best to express parental love without suppressing (or being too permissive of) children's autonomy and without being overwhelmed oneself? Childrearing and parenting are as demanding a challenge as marriage, as expectations become higher, going beyond the fulfillment of economic functions, such as providing food and shelter, and embracing requirements for emotional and personal fulfillment.

The evolution of contraceptive and reproductive technology has made possible the separation of sex, marriage, procreation, and childrearing, providing more freedom to individuals and multiplying the logical possibilities of domestic alignments. The spread of adoption has put spurs to this tendency by allowing the family to form "after nature" (Strathern 1992) without a genealogical (biological) grid. More women are being integrated into the public sphere, both for economic reasons and for self-fulfillment, making the traditional gendering of the domestic sphere less reasonable and feasible and the demarcation of family boundaries more ambiguous, contingent, and flexible.

Active agents and social practice

It is important to note that this process of individuation and diversification, while often regretted as demoralizing and alienating, is simultaneously received in a positive fashion as denoting the expanded domain of individual freedom and choice.

Some of my Brahmin informants became highly rebellious against what they saw as the authoritarian and exclusive "elite" culture that their parents and grandparents had embraced, and opted for alternative paths of life which were not covered by the traditional scripts. They chose not to live under their family names, not to belong to social clubs, not to be debutantes, not to marry for status, not to leave babies in the hands of nannies, not to send children to family schools, and not to be patriarchal. Some left Boston, broke away from proper Bostonians in the circle, married outsiders, and socialized with people of different backgrounds but similar convictions. These are the social actors who resisted being trapped by the "Boston Disease." Their determination to transcend the provincialism of Brahmin culture and actualize their new selves was emboldened by encountering "others" at college, at work, and in the neighborhood; by learning about alternative ways of life; and by witnessing the relativizing of their socioeconomic and cultural pre-eminence.

Their Boston Irish counterparts are also active agents, who

pursued self-fulfillment and self-actualization in the form of upgrading themselves into the middle-class strata of society. They replaced old furniture, household goods, clothes, automobiles, multi-storey blocks, and recreational activities, and took pride in the acquisition of modern counterparts. Many college graduates sought more exciting and challenging opportunities. Some opted to pay for childcare in order to break free from the cycle of kin obligations. Family planning was implemented to control the number of children, ensuring sufficient parental love and economic resources for each child. Many fathers strove to be with children, which had not been possible for their parents' generation. Many women gradually appropriated a national identity that is predicated on such notions as equality, freedom, and choice, rather than an ethno-religious identity that is prohibitive of abortion, homosexuality, contraception, cohabitation, and women's pursuit of careers.

Anthony Giddens (1991) postulates that modern social actors are by no means passive and powerless "narcissists" (Lasch 1978) caught in the process of social fragmentation. Indeed, my informants have assumed a rather active role in the process of social transmogrification by "playing a game" (Bourdieu 1977) with the "traditional" boundaries of their society and weaving their own life narratives and poetics. These individuals are restructuring new types of social relationships by drawing upon a divergent array of material and sociocultural resources of pre-established ways of life and by vigorously engaging with the external society rather than withdrawing from it. Simultaneously, these examples reveal that one dominant ("traditional") type of social taste (Bourdieu 1984) has been nullified, without being automatically inherited and reproduced, by the very social actors who are embedded in, and entitled to, that particular taste in their actual lives. The previous examples are antithetical to Bourdieu's presupposition that taste itself is reproduced and perpetuated by social actors who incessantly invest their symbolic capital to embody that specific taste, and thus to safeguard their place or distinctiveness in society.

The politics of culture

These two groups also manifest the dual and ambivalent aspects of modernity. On the one hand, modernity effectuates a higher level of individual autonomy, freedom, choice, opportunity, and fulfillment. On the other hand, under the existing fabric of social structures and ideologies, it confronts individuals with the possible danger of alienation and displacement in both historical and social terms. Self-fulfillment is often actualized only by defying social relations and mores, or by burning oneself out.

These two dimensions of the self, one appropriating the ideal of individualism and the other being appropriated by the reality of individualism, make the "politics of culture" salient and acute. Views concerning the state of society and individuals become more contested and negotiated. Liberals (or optimists) accentuate the positive repercussions of this process by emphasizing the individual's liberation from social dictation and the prospects for developing the real "self" that conservatives (or pessimists) would deem egoistic, deceptive, and solitary. Conservatives underscore the negative reverberations of individuation or individualism by expounding on the disintegration of context, mores, prohibitions, and continuity that liberals would see as intolerant, constraining, and moralizing. Liberals celebrate new family pluralism and the enlightened self, whereas conservatives regret the breakdown of family values and the decadence of social morality. Bellah et al. (1985) well recapitulate cultural politics on a national level:

> Liberal intellectuals, in their own minds devoted to individual freedom, sometimes caricature regional and religious groups whose traditions and communities they find ignorant and potentially authoritarian. And since liberal intellectuals have considerable influence on public policy, both through the courts and through legislation, they have on occasion forced their own enlightened views on their fellow citizens. On the other hand, some conservative groups, dismayed by rapid social change and by the social consequences of radical individualism, simplify and objectify their traditions with fundamentalist inflexibility and then condemn those of their fellow citizens who hold differing views, sometimes joining political action committees in the attempt to legislate their convictions (pp. 154–5).

[187]

The struggle for ideological hegemony has been invigorated to such an extent that neither camp has been able to dominate.[1] Various statistics indicate an American ambivalence towards both liberal enlightenment and conservative restoration, and towards both Democratic social engineering and Republican laissez-faire (Coontz 1992; Dionne 1991; Patterson and Kim 1991; Phillips 1990, 1993). In other words, American political consciousness is woven around these two divergent methodologies and ideologies.

In this context, although my informants' social worlds are becoming more diluted and fragmentary, and the sphere of personal freedom and choice has (intentionally and unintentionally) expanded, this is by no means a unilateral process. As we have seen in previous chapters, there are a multitude of counter-forces and conscious efforts, based on regret and fear of the fragmentation and dilution of social niches, to reinstate the sense of continuity and perpetuate the "overall picture" of society or "traditional values."

For instance, in the case of Brahmin families, those who do not embrace the spirit of philanthropy and the merits of *noblesse oblige* are strongly condemned by their fellows. New-money members of social clubs sometimes make themselves an object of derision by "looking back" during the meal or inquiring into other members' occupations. My informants are careful not to appear anti-social in their professions, since rumors diffuse quickly in their still-small high-society circles. Conspicuous consumption is abhorred as "bad taste," "new money," or "middle-class." There are voices and sentiments that invoke their "grand past" when "Lowells talked only to Cabots, and Cabots talked only to God."

In the case of Irish families, affirmative action (and its cousins multilingualism and multiculturalism) is strongly opposed as a form of "overprotection." Many Irish fathers do not want their sons to fight, but they also do not want their sons to be beaten up or to avoid standing up for their rights. Leaving parents alone, or staying away from kinfolk, is heavily stigmatized as selfish or spoiled, even if it is done for the sake of one's career advancement. Abortion is frowned upon as murder. Separation is often chosen instead of divorce. A child is believed to thrive poorly if left in the hands of outside childcare. There are voices and sentiments that invoke their "hometown" where "they'll take you and break you, but they'll never forsake you."

Noteworthy in the scrutiny of both groups is that the locus of old culture and tradition is highly ambiguous, sensitized, and problematic.

In the case of Brahmin families, the old culture is a source of their pride against the new-money and the no-money groups. On the other hand, tradition is something that they strive to transcend, graduate from, or defy in order to pursue lives of their own.

In the case of Irish families, tradition means the uncompromisable pride in the working-class virtues and neighborhood that saved Southie from disaster during the Depression. On the other hand, there are expectations and pressures to keep "moving up the hill" for better opportunities and higher accomplishments in the new contexts of life.

What the two groups have in common is that their social lives and realities are shaped in a process of incessant tension and negotiation between these opposing dispositions and by the struggle to synthesize contrasting principles through the conflicts of pride, the contestations of identity, and the politics of culture. Tradition and history are subject to being celebrated, invented, exaggerated, ignored, abandoned, or forgotten in the process of such endeavors and struggles.

Nurturing a context

In actual field situations, these contrasting views and sentiments are more mixed, ambivalent, and subtle – even in the mind of each informant. The expansion of women's opportunity to work outside the home is widely welcomed, but the working wives are made to feel guilty if they do not take care of sick children at home. Children's individuality is strongly advocated, but children's talking back to their parents is considered too individualistic. Discussion of sex, illness, and money is permissible, but a realistic description of these topics is tabooed. Few parents object to young adults having sexual intercourse with their lovers, but only insofar as it takes place outside of their homes. Few young people attend church, but they dream about having their weddings there. Divorce to attain self-fulfillment is understood, but it is not undertaken easily.

My informants' testimonies are, in a sense, a dialogue of their endeavor to balance these divergent and competing interpretations and sentiments. Few want to impose their opinions on others. Few want others to dictate their lives. Few want to fall into radicalism. Few want to polarize and divide their community. However, how best to accommodate this politics of culture in any balanced fashion poses challenges both epistemologically and practically. "Everything is too easy to obtain or too difficult to obtain in this society." "To keep a relationship is an extraordinary job in our society." These observations seem to epitomize how hard my informants find it to create a proper distance between themselves and others in their social lives and to secure a sense of place.

Bellah et al. (1985) suspect that this issue is more salient, problematic, and painful among those in the middle-class strata of society:

> The point is not that lower- and upper-class Americans are not individualistic, but rather that their individualism is embedded in specific patterns of social relationship and solidarity that mitigate the tendency toward an empty self and empty relationships in middle-class life. The contrast is expressed by middle-class Americans themselves when they entertain envious fantasies about more "meaningful community" among lower-class racial and ethnic groups or among (usually European) aristocrats (p. 152).

Indeed, my fieldwork exposed me to numerous occasions on which I was deeply touched by the "diffuse, enduring solidarity" of my informant families and their communities. Dinners are filled with laughter and pleasant discussions. Some informants assiduously update their genealogical charts, write their autobiographies, and organize family reunions. Most people maintain frequent contact with, and have extremely extensive knowledge about, their relatives, even those in their motherlands. Some parents plant a tree for each of their grandchildren so that they will be remembered. Many homeowners take the time to shovel an elderly neighbor's walk. Most people make strenuous efforts to support their local institutions or societies by making donations or by serving as volunteers. They can lead stable family lives without stipulating in marriage contracts who will take out the garbage, who will wash dishes, and such matters.

Many a Brahmin daughter hopes to wear a wedding dress that

her grandmother used in order to feel a sense of history. Given names are passed on to offspring for generations. It is not rare to witness a wedding party with 300 guests and a Thanksgiving family gathering with 150 members. Some Brahmin families maintain the tradition of playing football with all family members, elderly and young, after Thanksgiving dinner. Some occasionally ask their home doctors to visit and ensure their elderly neighbors' wellbeing. They all "play a game" with the state to leave the largest possible inheritance for the wellbeing of their offspring. Some select trust lawyers who are fairly young, wishing to pass down their memories to their great-grandchildren.

Many Irish parents make special efforts to take their children to hockey games early in the morning. Some start shopping for Christmas as early as summer in order to give gifts to as many of their relatives, friends, and neighbors as possible within their budgetary limits. Many Irish men are still called by their old nicknames. An Irish family places an intercom in the dining area so that they can respond immediately to an elderly woman living alone upstairs. Some corner shops still function as a kind of community center. People often drop by the Vietnam War Memorial whenever they are nearby. Intimacy, personal touch, and casual hospitality are perceived as important qualities of Irishness.

As is well known, de Tocqueville expressed his apprehension, in 1848, about the possible negative consequences of individualism in the United States: "Each man is forever thrown back on himself alone, and there is danger that he may be shut up in the solitude of his own heart" (1969, p. 508). As far as my informants are concerned, however, he would still be enchanted by the mores or "habits of the heart" that bind individuals to society in a meaningful way.

Yet what both Boston Brahmin and Boston Irish families reveal is that even these family-oriented groups – or the "meaningful community" of upper- to upper-middle class and working- to lower-middle class Americans itself – are becoming an "envious fantasy" in the process of the fragmentation of their collective history and the dilution of their cultural cohesiveness. The politics of culture is redolent of trajectories, metamorphoses, and the pull of central gravity in the way all these families are bound to society.

Katherine Newman (1988), in her study of downward mobility among middle-class Americans, points out that members of the middle class are not well equipped with rituals, symbols, and vocabularies for making sense of the painful transition to a lower social position.

In the case of Boston Brahmin families, the pain of downward mobility seems to be somewhat moderated by their still comfortable economic situation, especially among the older generation. They can still rationalize the dislocation of their social pre-eminence for the sake of the American ideals of egalitarianism and democracy, in the name of liberation from the cultural despotism of high society, and in their self-differentiation from "new money" and "no money." However, Newman's thesis will be more relevant and salient to the younger generations, whose resources, material and cultural, seem to be becoming obsolete and mediocre.

Boston Irish families take pride in their successful upward mobility. In addition, their still-active network and communication with kinfolk and neighbors provide a sense of pride against the anonymity of the middle-class culture as well as a sense of solidarity against the intrusion of outside interests. Yet many parents simultaneously relate that their children, with fewer ties to history and the neighborhood, look "lonely" and "wandering" in their quest for affluence and self-fulfillment. Many young people, on the other hand, feel compelled to run faster in order to catch up with the great expectations in middle-class America, or at least in order not to fall into the status of "parasite".

The question of how best to actualize their high expectations is becoming more urgent, especially in an age of diminishing expectations and heightened vulnerability to personal loss that is characterized by economic restructuring and political cynicism (Coontz 1992; Dionne 1991; Galbraith 1996; Johnson 1994; Krugman 1994; Newman 1988, 1993; Patterson and Kim 1991; Phillips 1990, 1993; Sorensen 1996).

My fieldwork has illuminated the tension between the process of social fragmentation and the integration of different categories and new possibilities under the logic of individualism. This dynamic relationship or dialectic contests the meaning of "tradition" and "history;" sensitizes the politics of culture, identity, and pride; and negotiates the boundaries of familial sphere, even among the family-oriented groups in a northeastern segment of American society, or the "hub of the solar system."

An individual actor in the United States has more freedom and choice for improvisation, which should make life more exciting and dynamic. However, such ad libs must be performed within the context of certain scripts in order to make sense. In what Claude Levi-Strauss (1976) terms "hot" society – where sociocultural mobility, fluidity, and change are encouraged – individuals are destined to live with uncertainty as well as an incessant tension between the self and society, and also to live with continual pressure and impediment in nurturing a context in which they can find themselves intertwined within the social web in morally meaningful ways.

Modernity and the American society and family

Modern dilemmas

The insights drawn from my fieldwork suggest wider implications for an American experiment in modernity and modernization. The industrialization of the economy reinforces, and is reinforced by, the specialization of labor and the solidification of its functional interdependence and integration. However, the interrelationships or linkages of society tend to become invisible and abstract due to the expansion of the market, the progress of the division of labor, the intensification of competition, and the complication of organizational structures. This lowered visibility of a social whole, or the fragility of such a fragmented and sequestered world, compels the individual to search desperately for his or her own security and retreat from outside forces in the name of protecting and exercising individual privacy, freedom, or rights.

However, the dearth of moral interconnectedness has a propensity to empower the legal and bureaucratic procedures that preside over this process, making the strain in the private sphere between intimacy and impersonal objectivity delicate and acute, as is well symbolized in the distinctively American provision that small children can sue their own parents. This process of what Jurgen Habermas (1984) terms the "colonization of the private sphere" further consolidates the atomization of the individual as a self-conscious, exclusive, and vulnerable entity. The harsh reality that those who can afford the best lawyers have an advantage enervates the authority of morality and ethics, and emphasizes the existential foundation of personal life (Auerbach 1976).

Many individuals rely on consumer purchases, psychic experts, romantic love, and physical and sexual distinctiveness to confirm their existence. However, such a self-identity is essentially ephemeral and fragile because these referential artifacts are all transitory.

A consumer society's preoccupation with added-value compels the individual to a never-ending quest for evanescent distinctions and insatiable desires, which ironically could trivialize the sense of personal fulfillment and actualization that they aspire to achieve (Hochschild 1983; Lasch 1978, 1984). This self-searching is vulnerable to the unpredictable conditions of the market, and particularly so since the late 1960s when the locus of the economy shifted from goods to services and information on a more global scale. The so-called "post-industrial society" (Bell 1976), "late-capitalism" (Habermas 1975; Mandel 1978; Offe 1984), or "third wave" (Toffler 1980) escalated "possessive individualism" (Macpherson 1962), or the game of achieving "distinction" (Bourdieu 1984), whether symbolic (e.g. degrees, memberships, and manners) or material (e.g. automobiles, clothing, and travel).

As contracts and transactions come increasingly to dominate our lives, psychic and emotional qualities become more emphasized as the core of self-identity. The concern for the scanning and managing of psychic conditions becomes exquisite. This is well reflected in the pervasiveness of psychology (and its related subjects such as therapy and mental health) as an academic discipline and, more importantly, as a form of popular discourse in the United States (Veroff et al. 1981a).

The prominence of romantic love stems from this cultural preoccupation with a psychic self. However, such affective sentiments are also transient, unstable, and elusive. A relationship could fall into crisis if an assumed equilibrium of give and take is called into question. Similarly, the subtle boundary between physical and sexual distinctiveness and excessive narcissism is prone to be conflated and transgressed as the individual becomes minimized (Peele 1976; Sennett 1977; Veroff et al. 1981b).

Moreover, romance and sexuality are deeply incorporated into the competitive and consumerist culture of the public domain, and as such are susceptible to the routinization of the means of expression and the homogenization of the supposedly quintessential self-identity (Cahoone 1988; Gergen 1991; Lasch 1978, 1984; Moog 1990; Sennett 1977). This paradox becomes more evident when romance and sexuality are pursued on a gender-specific basis. Stephanie Coontz critically explicates this paradox:

> The male lover tries to find a partner who represents the highest embodiment of female virtue and beauty. To be worthy of her, he must meet the highest ideals of male virtue and beauty. The paradox is this: What makes each individual unique in other's eyes is that each represents the best of a stereotype; what makes love complete is when each lover most fully conforms to the proper gender role. ... Each person loses his or her own half in the process of finding "the other half" (1992: pp. 61–2)

The fragility of identity, or the sense of rootlessness, is aggravated by the multiplication of roles and identities in a complex social organization in modern times. Bellah et al. relate this case to what they term "utilitarian" and "expressive" individualism:

> A self free of absolute values or "rigid" moral obligations can alter its behavior to adapt to others and to various social roles. It can play all of them as a game, keeping particular social identities at arm's length, yet never changing its own "basic" identity, because that identity depends only on discovering and pursuing its own personal wants and inner impulses. If the individual self must be its own source of moral guidance, then each individual must always know what he wants and desires or intuit what he feels. He must act so as to produce the greatest satisfaction of his wants or to express the fullest range of his impulses (1985, p. 77).
> ... What seems to be a self is merely a series of social masks that change with each successive situation. An absolutely autonomous self and a self determined completely by the social situation do not, then, turn out to be opposites (1985, p. 80).

Robert Wuthnow echoes Bellah et al. by arguing that:

> Rather than providing an ethical system that attaches importance to strict moral obligations, individuality seems likely to be associated with a highly relativistic outlook that focuses on inward pursuits and leaves public or collective values to be informed primarily by pragmatic considerations (1989, p. 203).

When a self is devoid of a place in the social universe and a life is reduced to a game, one is more susceptible to fragmentation, alienation, and anomie. Social and moral ecology, Bellah et al. assert, have a propensity to be "damaged by the destruction of the subtle ties that bind human beings to another, leaving them frightened and alone" (1985, p. 284) in the actual circumstances of modern life. Individual dignity is thus in danger of being invalidated and corroded, despite the modern ideal of the individual as an indivisible, enterprising, and progressive social entity.

The tragic school shootings in the United States, most notably the one at the Columbine High School in suburban Denver, Colorado, in 1999, are often interpreted as an "explosion of the self" among youths living in uncertainty, deadlock, and abstraction in a proudly free society. "Why should we not kill human beings?" A sense of the public – an imagination and empathy for others, a sense of trust and connectedness, or what Robert Putnam (1996) calls "social capital" – is enfeebled and diluted to the extent that this question can make a serious topic for discussion in classrooms and on media. It is no surprise if the dearth of such a public sense makes a hotbed of crime, violence, and discrimination and spurs the commodification of fear, terror, and danger (e.g. cop stories on TV, crime-prevention and self-defense kits, security services, guns, and gated communities). It is a pain deep-seated in the late-modern (or postmodern) America, which could be shared in other affluent and free societies. What is urgently needed today is the tolerance for – not fear of – "others" and "difference" to mitigate the moralizing, excluding, and homogenizing dimension of modernity and solidify the notion of cultural citizenship. Yet this is hard to develop in such insulated and insulating circles.

The American predicament

Amid the quandary of self-identity that is incident to the process of modernization, the twentieth century witnessed a spectacular transformation from "horse-drawn wagons to the space shuttle, from washboards to Whirlpools, from quill pens to computer keyboards" (Our Century, *US News & World Report* Special Issue, 1995, p. 60). American society has managed to ameliorate the burdens of discrimination, poverty, ill health, sexism, environmental destruction, and the inconvenience of life in general. While innumerable statistics paint grim portraits of American modernization, there are many others that contradict such dismal views and celebrate modern progress. If "history is never history but history-for" (Levi-Strauss 1966, p. 257), the past is subject to conflicting interpretations by conservatives and liberals to corroborate their ideological legitimacy.

However, there are social structures and ideologies that appear to be exacerbating the predicament of selfhood and social life in the United States of today.

The lack of investment in social capital and safety nets poses structural impediments to nurturing a sense of social reciprocity that endows individual identity with dignity and substance. John Galbraith's (1958) criticism of postwar capitalism as polarizing private opulence and public squalor points eloquently to the deficiency of governmental aid for childcare, education, housing, pensions, medical care, transportation, utilities, and other public services. Each family is compelled to think first of its own security and standard of living, spurring a vicious cycle in which mistrust of government fortifies, and is fortified by, isolation and pressure on the part of the family (Coontz 1992; Miller and Nowak 1977). Coontz critically attests to this by quoting a comment from a Chinese immigrant that "the helping resources in America are devoted only to picking people up (or disposing of them) after they have fallen off the cliff, whereas elsewhere such resources are used to prevent people from getting too near the edge" (1992, p. 230). As a matter of fact, the United States ranks far lower than most other industrial nations in its level of enforcement of educational, welfare, medical, and occupational safeguards (Hewlett 1986; Kammerman 1981; Luttwak 1993; MaFate 1991).[2] As if to counterbalance this situation, the United States has developed one of the most highly elaborated legal systems in the modern world. Privacy and personal rights are rationalized and emphasized even in the most intimate relationship, as is well exemplified in the intricate code of marriage contracts (Brill 1990).[3]

Left in an open field of self-reliance and self-help, socially insecure and vulnerable individuals are driven to pursue a niche of their own, intensifying competition, inequality, and fragmentation. According to the Census Bureau (2002), the share of national income going to the top 20 percent of earners rose from 44 percent in 1973 to 50 percent in 2000, and is 13 times that of the bottom 20 percent. The Census also found that the share of national income going to the top 1 percent of earners rose from 10 percent in 1988 to 15 percent in 1998, which is greater than that of the bottom 90 percent and the highest since the Second World War. Michele Lamont (2000) asserts that: "The dispersion of wealth is now greater in the United States than it is in several European countries, while intergenerational mobility is comparable. Yet many continue to believe that only in American can you 'be what you want'" (p. 247).

While people's faith in family commitments remains extraordinarily high, criticism and cynicism about political and economic structures and authorities have steadily increased in public opinion polls over the past three decades (Kanter and Mirvis 1989; Newman 1988, 1993; Patterson and Kim 1991; Phillips 1990, 1993). As Coontz contends, "'flight from commitment' is more pervasive beyond the family than within it" (1992, p. 275). A social structure based upon concepts of mutual obligation and reciprocity needs to be ensured in order to mitigate a crisis of social reproduction.

> When there is so little trust and commitment outside the family, it is hard to maintain them inside the family. ... [V]ery few people can sustain values at a personal level when they are continually contradicted at work, at the store, in the government, and on television. To call their failure to do so a family crisis is much like calling pneumonia a breathing crisis. Certainly, pneumonia affects people's ability to breathe easily, but telling them to start breathing properly again, or even instructing them in breathing techniques, is not going to cure the disease (p. 277).

Bellah et al. are critical of the fact that Americans "have committed what to the republican founders of our nation was the cardinal sin: we have put our own good ... ahead of the common good" (1985, p. 285). The real issue, however, is that they have little choice but to do so under the precarious and adverse circumstances prescribed by the existent fabric of society.

Family values

The predicament of selfhood and social life is further exacerbated by ideologies that do not correspond well to changing times. The call for "family values" has become conspicuous in neo-conservative discourse since the 1980s, and was appropriated even in President Bill Clinton's centrist campaign rhetoric (Stacey 1996).[4] However, the ideology of the family that culminated in the 1950s has become less feasible and relevant in actual practice.

The problem of care of the elderly reflects a demographic change during the postwar era, but it is often identified as an indication of moral degeneration or ethical breakup in contemporary society. The ideology of conjugal and gender roles in the nuclear family which culminated in the 1950s is still extant.[5] Despite a growing number of women in the labor force, housekeeping and childrearing are still widely considered the woman's sphere, and poverty is prone to be "feminized" after divorce (Brannen and Wilson 1987; Delphy 1984; Goldin 1990; Hewlett 1986). Coontz asserts that "most of the pain is caused not by the equality women have won but by the inequalities they have failed to uproot" (1992, p. 168), and expounds on this situation using the examples of divorce, work, school, and medical care:

> Accessible, low-cost divorce has been an important reform for people trapped in abusive or destructive relationships. Yet, the living standards of women and children tend to drop sharply after divorce and bitter custody disputes leave scars on all concerned, most especially on the children who may have to take sides. The majority of women who gain custody of children receive inadequate child support payments, while the children lose contact with their fathers entirely (1992, p. 205).

[199]

Work, school, and medical care in America are still organized around the 1950s myth that every household has a full-time mother at home, available to chauffeur children to doctor and dentist appointments in the middle of the day, picking up elementary school children on the early dismissal days, and stay home when a child has the flu (1992, p. 215).[6]

Sylvia Hewlett (1986) echoes Coontz by contending:

> In Europe ... there was no flowering of a cult of motherhood. As a result, European governments had no ideological hang-ups – no commitment to mother care – when it came time to set up nurseries and preschools for children. Conservative countries like France and Italy and socialist countries like Sweden have all been able to make pragmatic adjustments to the modern age and provide family support structures for working parents. America, however, remains handicapped by the fifties and its peculiar vision (p. 229).

The problem of childrearing is exacerbated by the ideology romanticizing the private, nuclear family, which is supposed to play the pivotal role in providing love and care for the child. The late nineteenth century in the United States saw a decrease in the mortality rate and the separation of women and children from labor (except among the working class). These new developments gradually deprived the family of its traditional function as the integral unit for survival and economy, and advanced a "sacralization of childhood" (Zelizer 1985) and conversely a "proletarianization of parenthood" (Lasch 1977). However, the preoccupation with parents' exclusive love and care for children made it harder to envision childrearing as a more "social" enterprise. Coontz refers to this by asserting that "[t]he debate over whether one parent can raise a child alone, for example, diverts attention from the fact that good childrearing has always required more than two parents" (1992, p. 230).

"Traditional" conjugal and gender ideologies concerning the family also have a propensity to dismay and disorient both men and women, who may even become vindictive when their actual circumstances prevent them from embodying their expected roles (May 1980, 1988; Mintz and Kellogg 1988). Several studies demonstrate that incest and sexual abuse, which are alleged to be very frequent in the United States, are most often committed by males, and that these tragedies are more likely to occur in a family where a father escalates his quest for male (paternal) dominance and authority, and a rigid boundary between the family and the outside world obstructs its moderation (Gordon 1988; Gordon and Riger 1989; Herman and Hirschman 1981; Kempe and Helfer 1980; Rush 1980; Sanday 1981). This situation becomes even more dangerous when the father's authority is undermined by unemployment (Coontz 1992).

Furthermore, these traditional "family values," just like the enlightening "progressive" doctrines, tend to impose self-righteous and antagonistic attitudes toward those who have different modes of family life for cultural or economic reasons (Barnouw 1975; Danielson 1976; Patterson 1986; Taylor 1989). If American society is becoming more divisive and polarized, it is not so much because of diversity per se but because of the intransigent imposition of anachronistic and traditionalistic ideologies that refuse to allow any possibilities for other lifestyles, or idealistic and enlightening ideologies that are detached from social realities.

The *Economist* (September 6, 2003) reports: "In 1960, 70 percent of families had at least one parent who stayed at home. By 2000, in contrast, 70 percent of families were headed by either two working parents or a working single parent" (p. 31). According to the US Census (2002), families consisting of breadwinner fathers and stay-at-home mothers account for 10 percent of all households. Married couple households have slipped from almost 80 percent in the 1950s to 50.7 percent. A third of new babies are born out of wedlock, and there has been an 850 percent increase since the 1960 in the number of unmarried couples with children. These are the realities in which a discourse of family values in the twenty-first century needs to be grounded.

This is not just an American matter. In January 2001, in his first substantive action in office, President George W. Bush reversed a Clinton policy by reinstating the funding ban for family planning programs run by agencies that also provide abortion services out of their federal funds. A year later, President Bush put a temporary hold on US contributions to the United Nations Population Fund, citing concerns over China's family planning programs. These policies are deeply rooted in the struggle, or "culture war" (Hunter 1991), to define "America" in a domestic political arena. The tradition of bi-partisan consensus on foreign affairs has faded since the end of the Cold War. Also, the boundaries between the domestic and the foreign have become less clear cut and more overlapping in the age of globalization. In such new contexts, the domestic debates and policies over values, including those over "family values," are more likely to be projected directly onto the diplomatic screen and cast reverberations on a global level. This is especially the case when the United States assumes such a conspicuous and hegemonic presence in the world of today.

How the United States deals with all the complexities of family lives in the ever-changing political, economic, cultural, demographic, and technological environments could thus have great consequences and relevance to the rest of the world and deserves our close scrutiny. For example, as I write this manuscript, the State of Massachusetts court has just ruled that a ban on gay marriage is unconstitutional. Amid mounting opposition and support, the question of gay marriage is likely to become a major campaign issue in the 2004 Presidential elections. The question of gay marriage, which has been officially approved in Belgium, Canada, and the Netherlands so far, challenges American voters and could determine who will lead the most powerful nation in the world.

At the same time, this whole issue over the family furnishes a window on the American experiment in modernity. The idealism of "modernity" has been intensively and extensively appropriated in the definition of "Americanness," or American nationalism, which facilitated and legitimatized the progress of impetuous industrialization of a "City upon a Hill" towards the "Manifest Destiny" for the "Pax Americana" in the twentieth century. The American experiment in modernity has certainly entailed moralizing, excluding, and homogenizing consequences. Yet, its inclusive, reflexive, and creative dimension has also proven itself, overcoming contradictions and re-inventing America towards the brave new future. If the tradition of America lies in the future, the future of America lies in this unfinished experiment. So could the futures of other societies that embrace the spirit of modernity. It is in this sense that I admit, as de Tocqueville did more than 150 years ago, that I see in America more than America. I want to understand it so as to at least know what we have to fear or hope from there.

Notes

Chapter 1: Introduction

1. According to several informants, it was in Oliver Wendell Holmes, Sr.'s (1809–1894) novel *Autocrat of the Breakfast Table* (1857) that the appellation "Brahmin caste of New England" was first applied to old families with long years of wealth accumulation and cultural sophistication. O'Connor (2000) states that "[w]hile their numbers may have diminished somewhat, and their financial dominance is no longer what it used to be, the Brahmin class continues to have a remarkable influence on the city's cultural and benevolent institutions" (p. 58). Even today, this appellation is a part of popular imagery, and one can occasionally come across with it in local media, if not in everyday conversations.

2. "Class" is defined here in its most general term, not in the strict Marxist sense. In such a society as that of the United States, where the "middle-class" comprises the majority of population, the Marxist distinction between the capitalist and the proletariat on the basis of the possession of productive means is less profitable for analytical purposes (Blau and Duncan 1967; Giddens 1973; Mills 1951; Pessen 1982). As a matter of fact, various studies in the United States reveal that people interpret "class" more subjectively, taking into account not only material factors but also social and symbolic ones (Blumin 1989; Hollingshead 1949; Lamont 1992, 2000; Warner and Lunt 1941). What an annual income of $25,000 means for people's lives depends on many factors, including which part of the United States they reside in, whether they own their homes or other assets, whether they have debts, how many dependents they have, whether they are healthy, what they value in their careers, what family background they come from, and how old they are.

3. References were made to Formisano and Burns, eds. (1984), Howard (1976), O'Connor (1991, 1994), and Whitehill (1959) for a general history of Boston; Baltzell (1964, 1979) for the Protestant establishment in Boston; Handlin (1941) and Ryan (1983) for Irish immigrant social history; Archdeacon (1983), DeMarco (1980), and Solomon (1956) for the experience of the "new" immigrants coming into Boston from southern and eastern Europe; O'Connor (1993) for urban renewal projects; Lukas (1985) and Formisano (1991) for the busing crisis; and the US Censuses of Population (1990, 2000) for demographic data in Boston.

4. Such recent works as Sara Payne Stuart's *My First Cousin Once Removed: Money, Madness, and the Family of Robert Lowell* (1998), George Howe Colt's *The Big House: A Century in the Life of An American Summer Home* (2003), and Jessica Shattuck's *The Hazards of Good Breeding* (2003) are insiders' narratives of the fragmentation of family saga among the Boston Brahmin families. It can be conjectured that these publications also exemplify their folk theory.

5. The names of organizations, titles, amounts of money, laws and ages are, unless otherwise noted, all those prevailing at the time of fieldwork.

6. Shorter's thesis, however, is predicated on the conflation between discourse (ideology) and practice (actual experience), as are those of Park and Burgess (1921) and Goode (1963). Further historical scrutiny is needed before we can claim that "love" was little experienced in the actual family relationship in the past when "love" was less ideologized.

7. The impetus for rationality and measurement was exemplified in the process of classification and commodification of the life course. Chudacoff (1989) illuminates how "age" came to occupy a prominent place in the public consciousness in the course of modernization. "Age" became signified as "a criterion for social status and as a norm for behavioral expectations" (p. 182). "The history of age grading shows that in a bureaucratized society, age has considerable practical advantages as an administrative and normative gauge. It is an easily measured, inescapable attribute and a quality that everyone has experienced or will experience" (p. 190).

8. Macfarlane (1987) submits that "if love can exist without capitalism, it is more questionable as to whether capitalism could have existed, or could continue to exist, without love" (p. 140).

9. As Blau and Duncan (1967) point out, heightened universalism has had profound implications for the stratification system in the United States. "The achieved status of a man, what he has accomplished in terms of some objective criteria, becomes more important than his ascribed status, who he is in the sense of what family he comes from" (p. 430).

10. This notion of "love" as an ideological apparatus for perpetuating woman's involvement in housework is expounded on by such Marxist feminists as Sokoloff (1980), Ueno (1990), and Werlhof (1986).

11. Shapiro (1986) relates this ideology to the development and prevalence of housekeepers' clubs, housekeeping/cooking magazines, cooking schools, and degree programs in domestic science (home economics) since the late nineteenth century. Domesticity became increasingly rationalized, professionalized, and commercialized.

Chapter 2: The Yankee family

1. As is indicated in Chapter 1, the name and some attributes of individuals, families, and institutions are modified in order to preserve their anonymity insofar as it does not affect analytical contexts of this book.

2. "Tradition" here follows Raymond Williams' (1977) definition as an "intentionally selective version of a shaping past and a pre-shaped present" that provides "a historical and cultural ratification of contemporary order" (p. 117).

3. None of these opinions were formed interactively, because I interviewed them separately. Since those involved in this project were sworn to absolute confidentiality regarding other informants, I have little knowledge about how much they know each other and interact.

4. Strictly speaking, "WASP" is the most general term that is applicable nationwide, while "Yankee" is more specific to the New England region and "Brahmin" to the Boston area.

5. It is often the case that these names are appropriated by local shops or corporations in order to enhance their product identities. As Marcus (2000) argues, "regenerating the dynastic legend of a family that has faded, shows just how

much that identity is a part of American middle-class desire: one of its options and one with considerable mystique" (p. 27).

6. Few offspring even apply to Harvard today, partly because they find themselves underqualified, and partly because they have more college options. One of Francis' grandchildren was accepted by Harvard but persuaded to attend another school by its lavish financial aid.

7. I begin Jonathan Shaw's story with Tomoko because he has passed away. This is her narrative.

8. Harvard's Admissions Office administers a "legacy" policy which provides an advantage to applicants whose parents (not grandparents) graduated from Harvard College (not Graduate Schools). However, this policy becomes effective only at the very final stage of selection process when there is no other factor to distinguish the equally qualified applicants. According to a senior staff member in the Office, the ratio of legacy applicants was less than 3 percent in 1996 in contrast to about 6 percent a decade ago. This decrease is, according to this informant, partly because Harvard receives more applications from a wider population, and partly because applicants tend to be more informed and self-selective in determining which colleges to apply to. The legacy applicants' acceptance rate was about 38–40 percent in 1996 in contrast to 45–50 percent a decade earlier. The entire admission rate was about 11–12 percent in 1996 in contrast to 16–18 percent in 1986 (9–10 percent in 2001–4). This staff member emphasizes that Harvard is one of the few colleges in the United States which can admit students purely on a merit basis.

No specific data were available from such renowned prep schools as Andover, Choate, Exeter, Groton, Hotchkiss, Milton Academy, Phillips Academy, Shady Hill, St. Mark's, St. Paul's, or Winsor. However, it seems that each school has its own policy concerning how much special consideration is given to the alumni/ae background of families and their contribution to the school. My informants testify that "prep" schools are still receptive to them, even though to a much lesser degree than in the past.

9. Keller (1991), in her comparison of the trajectory of two of America's emblematic families (the Kennedys and Rockefellers), also observes that "given modern society's ... stress on individual mobility and achievement, on earned over inherited status, and on the love conquers all motif, class-shaped priorities create serious dilemmas for upper class families" (p. 159). She claims: "the tension between subordinating one's self to the family group for the greater good of all and pursuing one's happiness is increasingly evident in the later generations in both families. Torn between seeing their privileges as a blessing or a curse, the later heirs seem to emphasize the emotional and spiritual costs. Though inconceivable to those who must struggle for basic necessities, the fourth generation seems to be longing for the Horatio Alger myth in reverse. ... [T]hey express a desire to be free of the showcase atmosphere that envelops them and to be connected with real life, relating to others not in terms of the family's public level but by the force of their own humanity" (p. 180).

Ostrander (1984) demonstrates "how upper-class women organize and interpret their activities primarily *within* the framework of class" (p. 153, emphasis added). Yet, what Keller's finding and my own research suggest is that those in elite society could attempt to live against the framework of class.

10. According to the 1990 US Census of Population, Beacon Hill has a total of

9,616 residents, made up of 9,040 (94 percent) Whites, 195 (2 percent) Blacks, 0 (0 percent) native Americans, 337 (3.5 percent) Asians, and 44 (0.5 percent) others. The city of Cambridge is populated by 95,826 residents, but no specific data is available in reference to West Cambridge, including its racial breakdown. While the North Shore region is inhabited by 670,080 residents in its 34 constituent communities, no specific breakdown is available concerning the "proper" spots within those communities. Considering the heterogeneity of economic composition and the spatial size of the city of Cambridge and the North Shore region (and its communities), I do not think that it would be profitable to utilize a big picture of statistics to understand a much smaller segment of society which my informants reside in and which this volume deals with. However, as far as my informants perceive (and my own observation confirms), it would not be terribly misleading to interpret the ratio of Beacon Hill as delineating an overall picture of racial balance in other "proper" spots. The 2000 US Census of Population combines Beacon Hill with Back Bay as a geographic unit, and as such no specific data is available in reference to Beacon Hill.

11. Many informants strongly repudiated a "prejudice" propagated by some outside critics that social clubs are a kind of "cartel" or "syndicate." As one informant put it: "It might be so in other social clubs in Los Angeles or in New York, but simply not true in my clubs." I have no strong evidence to prove or disapprove this statement.

12. Colt (2003) offers a reminiscent account of a century-old "big house" on Cape Cod where he spent 42 summers with his family, especially of the time when it was eventually sold off.

13. For instance, "The Frustrated Four" who, as mentioned earlier, sent a series of anonymous, harassment letters to one of my informants write: "There is a natural rhythm to Brookline life. Church of the Redeemer for Sunday School, Dexter for lower school years, learning to swim – skate – play tennis and golf – shoot skeet – first dancing school – all with your best family peers forming relationships that last a lifetime ... and all at The Country Club."

14. See Shiozaki (2001) and Benfey (2003) for the historical roots of this taste for Japanese culture and its impact on the US–Japanese relations in the nineteenth century.

15. Comparing the culture of the French and the American upper-middle class, Lamont (1992) observes that "Americans are more likely to defend cultural laissez-faire in the name of cultural egalitarianism. ... Their views on the hierarchization of cultural tastes are also more variable, and their cultural distinctions are more blurred and less stable. Consequently, American cultural boundaries are less likely to lead to objective socioeconomic boundaries, i.e. to inequality, than French cultural boundaries" (p. 178).

16. In a similar fashion, being curious about the cyclical dimensions of everyday life (the daily, weekly, and yearly routines, that would also serve to ensure a sense of collective identity), I surveyed the starting time and duration of dinner, the rotation of recipes, the day chosen for shopping and cleaning, and other miscellaneous matters. Each family has its own scheme, but it is a "rough" one which is open and subject to improvisations. My informants' overall responses revealed immense variations, contingencies, and flexibilities, defying my generalization about their distinctiveness on a collective level.

17. Keller's (1991) analysis demonstrates that even such dynastic families as the Kennedys and the Rockefellers are not exempt from this process.

18. See Marcus (1983) for the history of family trust in Massachusetts.

19. Jaher (1982), for instance, records that: "During the Second World War the president of the Federal Reserve Bank in Boston felt that New England's industrial sluggishness was partly due to Boston's inability to generate new types of manufacturing. This situation he blamed on the large amount of capital locked up in trust funds, an investment device which the banker thought kept local money in conservative, low-return governmental bonds and old industries. To rejuvenate the economy he persuaded several Boston capitalists to fund new electronics firms, founded by engineers, scientists, and professors, springing up in the metropolitan area. As in the past and contemporary Los Angeles, local capital resources and organizational and technological talent united to adapt to new conditions and thus promote the metropolitan economy. But, the Brahmins did not dominate this resurgence" (pp. 93–4).

Chapter 3: The Irish family

1. Anne Halley (1986), in her afterword to Mary Doyle Curran's novel (*The Parish and the Hill*, originally published in 1948) about Irish-American life in Massachusetts, states that "lace-curtain means middle class, especially as it points down, to difference from the shanties" (p. 232).
Shannon (1989) also expounds on the "lace-curtainism" that he observes among middle-class Irish Americans: "lace-curtain ... connotes a self-conscious, anxious attempt to create and maintain a certain level and mode of gentility ... the complex of lace-curtain values was epitomized in the cliché ... Ssh ! What will the neighbors think?" (pp. 142–5).

2. The parish functioned as the unit within which social interaction took place. Yet, Horgan simultaneously contends: "Lest this sound like the mythical village, strains should be noted. While small talk kept people informed, it also made family happenings public knowledge quickly, it worked to induce conformity of behavior, and it reaffirmed prevailing attitudes. As a result, new ideas, different values or changes in custom were slow to occur. Constraints on behavior were as much internal as external" (1988: p. 58).

3. According to the US 1990 Census of Populations, South Boston is inhabited by a total of 29,488 residents, with 28,145 (95.4 percent) Whites, 266 (0.9 percent) Black/African Americans, 447 (1.5 percent) Hispanics, 522 (1.7 percent) Asian/Pacific Islanders, 91 (0.3 percent) Native Americans and 17 (0.06 percent) others. The population was almost same as that of the 1980 Census (30,396). The number of Asians/Pacific Islanders has more than tripled from 143 in 1980, largely due to the influx of the Vietnamese immigrants. The number of Hispanics has more than doubled from 160 in 1980. In the 1990 census, almost 37 percent of the population claims to be of exclusively (i.e. unmixed) Irish ancestry, compared with 41 percent in 1980. Other significant groups were Italian (5.8 percent), Lithuanian (3 percent), Polish (2.2 percent), and English (2 percent). The 2000 Census reports that South Boston added 477 people to the population total, but with a loss of 2,818 Whites accompanied by large gains in the Hispanic (1,797), Asian/Pacific

Islander (640) and Black/African American (475) populations. According to the *Boston Globe* (October 14, 2002), over 60 percent of the Hispanics in South Boston live in public housing, and over half of the Asians in South Boston are public housing residents.

4. According to the 1990 US Census of Population, there were 561 male and 2,227 female households among a total of 6,683 family households in South Boston. The number of non-family households was 6,398. The percentage of families below the poverty level was 7.1 percent among male households, 34.6 percent among female households, and 17.4 percent among all the households in South Boston (18.7 percent in the City of Boston as a whole). The 2000 US Census reveals that there are 568 male households and 2,165 female households among 6,309 family households in South Boston. The number of non-family households (7,729) exceeds family households. The percentage of families below the poverty level is 11.5 percent among male households, 35.9 percent among female households, and 16.3 percent among all the households in South Boston (15.3 percent in the City of Boston as a whole). No data specific to the Lower End is available.

5. The *Boston Globe* (April 5, 1997), for example, reports on a local initiative taken to cope with tragedy: "Perhaps for the first time in the history of one of Boston's more patriarchal neighborhoods, the women, supported by City Councilor Peggy Davis-Mullin, are having their day. ... In living rooms and parish halls, the mothers and daughters of Southie are meeting in knots of ten and 20. Many of the faces around their kitchen tables are unfamiliar. Women from The Point are feeling out women from The Lower End. Professional women are finding common ground with women from the housing projects."

6. See O'Connor (1993) for the political background of urban renewal projects in Boston between 1950 and 1970, and Fisher and Hughes (1992) for their impacts on the West End district in Boston.

7. Bulger was President of the Massachusetts State Senate from 1978 to 1995 and thereafter President of the University of Massachusetts. In 2003, Governor Mitt Romney pressured him to resign his post, partly on account of his fugitive gangster brother James "Whitey" Bulger.

8. According to the 1990 US Census of Population, 88.5 percent of housing units in South Boston were occupied, of which 26.8 percent were owner occupied and 61.7 percent renter occupied. The 2000 Census shows that 93.4 percent of housing is occupied, of which 31.6 percent is owner occupied and 61.8 percent renter occupied. According to the 1990 US Census, the average owned home value was $153,298 in South Boston, $524,764 on the Beacon Hill, and $172,966 in the City of Boston as a whole. The average monthly gross rent was $494 in South Boston, $842 on the Beacon Hill, and $634 in the City of Boston as a whole. According to the 2000 US Census, the average owned home value is $206,433 in South Boston, $1,544,521 on the Back Bay/Beacon Hill, and $190,603 in the City of Boston as a whole. The average monthly gross rent is $668 in South Boston, $1,187 on the Beacon Hill, and $802 in the City of Boston as a whole

9. She submits that "the moral standards privileged by African Americans ('The caring self') overlap with the criteria they use to evaluate the upper half, whom they consider exploitive and lacking in solidarity, and Whites, whom they regard as domineering and lacking in human compassions" (p. 241). She

also considers that French workers take the poor as "part of us" and are far less critical of Blacks than they are of upper-middle-class and immigrants.

10. A group of local residents started *South Boston Online* as a community Web site in 1998, and developed a print version a year later when they realized many South Boston residents didn't have ready access to the Internet. This full-color newspaper, appealing especially to newcomers and young families with children, has a weekly circulation of 2,000 in print and a daily access of about 2,200 online.

11. While I have encountered this kind of discourse ("People are coming back in droves to Southie!") on numerous occasions, no official data are available on this phenomenon. As far as my informants are concerned, they can usually name a couple of friends and families but not a "drove" of them. It is possible to suspect that their claim is somewhat inflated by the strong attachment they have to the neighborhood. "Everybody knows everybody" is another example of this sort.

12. According to the statistical data published by the Election Department of the City of Boston, the 1996 Presidential Elections recorded 63 percent of the population as Democrats (Clinton and Gore), 27 percent Republicans (Dole and Kemp). On Beacon Hill, the figures were respectively 67 percent and 27 percent. The 2000 Presidential Elections recorded 62 percent as Democrats (Gore and Lieberman) and 30 percent as Republicans (Bush and Cheney) in South Boston. On Beacon Hill, the figures were respectively 62 percent and 28 percent. Recent election results demonstrate that both South Boston (Wards 6 and 7) and Beacon Hill (Ward 5) have supported Democratic candidates in races for Mayor (1997, 2001), Governor (2002) and President (1996, 2000), except that South Boston voted for the Republican candidate in the 1998 Gubernatorial race, allegedly reacting against "liberal social engineering" positions by the Democratic candidate.

13. In the 1999 City Council election, 35.7 percent of South Boston voters turned out, a higher proportion than the 24.5 percent in the city of Boston at large. The figure in the 2003 City Council election is 32 percent in South Boston and 24.6 percent in the city at large. It is widely alleged that voting rate is higher in the Upper End.

14. In 1996, a son of William Bulger was defeated by Stephen Lynch in the state's senate race. Many informants as well as various media believe this was because Lynch, who grew up on the "project," is viewed as embracing the "Southie spirit" better than his "middle-class" rival who spends summers in Cape Cod. Interestingly enough, some of my informants endorsed Bulger's son in public but actually voted for Lynch. According to them, they felt obliged to publicly acknowledge Bulger's great contributions to their neighborhood and his strong political power. However, they postulate that "people in South Boston never vote for name." In a similar fashion, the name of Tip O'Neil, a former Speaker of the federal congress, was rarely mentioned during my research, partly because he was "too liberal" and partly because he was from North Cambridge, a place which my informants consider "almost another country."

15. As O'Connor (1994) argues, the close relationship between church and state characterizes the history of the Commonwealth itself. For instance, John Powers, a former president of the state senate, and Richard Cushing, a former

Catholic archbishop of Boston, were both born and raised in South Boston and formed a lifelong friendship.

16. The series of some 15 cases of sexually abusive clergy throughout the United States since the 1990s, including the three cases in Boston between 2002 and 2003, would certainly be detrimental. The case in the Boston Archdiocese in 2003 was, in fact, the most scandalous, with 140 priests and brothers and 552 victims allegedly involved, incurring settlement payments of $85 million (*Boston Globe*, September 10, 2003).

17. According to O'Connor (1998), the number of seminarians fell from 9,000 in 1966 to 3,000 in 1990. In 1988 Boston's Cardinal Bernard Law reported an annual decline of 2 percent in regular Sunday Mass attendance over the preceding five years, and predicted a 22 percent decline in the number of diocesan priests by 2005 with the closing of 40–60 parishes by 2008 (p. 312).

18. According to the Boston Police Department's annual crime report, South Boston recorded 418 violent crime cases (4 percent of the citywide total) and 2,308 property crime cases (5 percent of the citywide total) in 1995. The number of violent crime involving firearms was 35 (2 percent of the citywide total) and the number of sexual assault incidents was 30 (4 percent of citywide total). Considering the size of South Boston's population (5.1 percent of the citywide total), these figures seem to suggest that my informants' characterization of South Boston as a "very safe neighborhood" is not excessively inflated.

19. See Lehr and O'Neill's non-fiction account (2000) of a cozy relationship between James "Whitey" Bulger and John Connolly, an FBI agent in Boston, during the 1970s and 1980s. They were old friends who grew up in the same housing project in South Boston.

20. According to the 1990 US Census of Population, 78 percent of those over 16 years old are engaged in the white-collar jobs. The citywide figure is 84 percent.

21. According to the 1990 US Census of Population, among those over 25 years old, 8 percent attained less than 9th grade, 17 percent 9th to 12th grade with no diploma, 40 percent were high school graduates, 14 percent attended some college with no degree, and 21 percent achieved college degrees in South Boston. The citywide figures were 10 percent, 14 percent, 27 percent, 14 percent, and 35 percent respectively. In the 2000 Census, the figures are 6.2 percent, 12.5 percent, 32.3 percent, 15.5 percent, and 24.2 percent in South Boston, and 9.1 percent, 12 percent, 24 percent, 14.5 percent, and 25.1 percent citywide respectively.

22. According to the 1990 US Census, 85.3 percent of workers over 16 years old who reside in South Boston use automobile or public transportation to work, and the mean travel time to work is 22 minutes.

23. According to the 1990 US Census of Population, 42.3 percent of all owners and 11.5 percent of all renters had been in their homes for more than 20 years. 58 percent of residents over 5 years old lived in South Boston in 1985, 27.8 percent in the same county, 7.4 percent in the same state, 4.3 percent in other states, and 2.5 percent abroad.

24. While no official data is available on the rate of alcoholism in South Boston, the majority of older informants testify that they have siblings or relatives who are addicted to alcohol and that few contacts are made with them. Many local churches are actively involved in providing counseling to alcoholics.

25. Hayes' collection of short stories, *This Thing Called Courage* (2002), is noteworthy in this regard in that it deals with men, including Hayes himself, coming to terms with being gay in South Boston.

26. According to the 1990 US Census of Population, median family income was $45,684 in South Boston and $43,344 in the City of Boston. It was $47,339 and $44,151 respectively in the 2000 Census. The unemployment rate was 9.3 percent in South Boston and 8.3 percent in the City of Boston in the 1990 Census, and 5 percent and 7.2 percent respectively in the 2000 Census.

27. Inheritance is much less problematized than it is among the Brahmin families. Houses, furniture, and savings are the primary form of assets. A house is viewed as a possession of the family and clan, and therefore tends to be transferred to offspring, ideally to a son. In the case of one family, the second eldest son, a fisherman now in his late forties, does not own a house of his own, and his parents, who are in their seventies, have specified the transfer of their own house (estimated at around $100,000) to him in their wills. He is also entitled to receive an equal share of his parents' savings (approximately $25,000), which will be distributed among his four other siblings. This arrangement was made several years ago after a "casual" meeting among the children, the parents, and a lawyer of their acquaintance. "It was just easy!" A couple of local lawyers relate to me that there is a growing tendency for the family house to be sold on the market, as more children live outside of South Boston with their own families and houses. As far as my informants are concerned, according the status of inheritor to a child's homosexual partner is strongly opposed or rejected.

28. Horgan (1988) generalizes the decision-making process among Irish-American families in the pre-war era as follows: "[F]athers decided when and how the family should move, buy items of furniture, purchase a car, and take a vacation. No matter how quiet, inarticulate, or unassuming the father might have been, nor how kindly he exercised his authority, he made the decisions. ... It is unfortunate that the family in Ireland and this country has sometimes been portrayed as dominated by women ... as this view hides the real difficulties of energetic and instrumental American Irish women who accepted a subordinate role within the family. One problem was that some men acted at home in an arbitrary or authoritarian manner" (p. 60).

29. As stated in Chapter 1, the probability is that I was introduced only to the families that are relatively conflict-free and socioeconomically stable. This makes it plausible to suspect that there are families that are living with more tensions and conflicts over the way in which housework is allocated and home decisions are made. A locally based family therapist, for instance, told me of a couple of "dysfunctional" cases. In one case, the husband was extremely strict with his wife's role as the housekeeper, even to the extent that he beat her for not having returned from a grocery store on time. In another case, the wife complained that her husband did not love her enough. The husband assumed that his love for the wife was sufficiently expressed by bringing his paycheck home. While these two cases are closely related to the gender ideology of modern times, many problems seem to have been caused, or aggravated, by alcoholism.

30. According to the 1990 US Census of Population, 53 percent of 1,174 female householders in South Boston (with no spouse and with related children under 18 years old) were below the poverty level, whereas 22 percent of their 141

male counterparts fell into that category. According to the 2000 US Census, 55.5 percent of 1,336 female householders in South Boston (with no spouse and with related children under 18 years old) are below the poverty level whereas 17.4 percent of their 155 male counterparts fall into that category.

31.   Horgan (1988), in her analysis of the child–parent relationship among Irish-American families before the war, reports: "Men often decided on the children's occupations and educations and, although children's abilities were taken into account, their wishes were sometimes ignored" (p. 60).

32.   An administrative staff member at South Boston High School told me in 1995 that just around a fifth of the school's students live in South Boston.

Chapter 4: Conclusion

1.   While this ambivalence is intertwined with cynicism and apathy, it is also susceptible to populism and even to radicalism.
Newman (1993) maintains: "From Jerry Brown on the left to H. Ross Perot in the middle to Pat Buchanan and David Duke on the far right, voters have turned to outsiders and political renegades, hoping they will turn the tide and bring back the prosperity that is central to the self-definition of this society" (p. 26).
Rauch (1994) also contends: "In America, the standard political model is to assure the middle class that it's being suckered by some evil other. Americans are addicted to being told that they are deprived of their fair share by 'the rich' and corporations and right-wing scrooges and the Japanese (according to liberals), by welfare cheats and pork-barrelers and left-wing social engineers and the Japanese (according to conservatives), and by 'special interests' (according to everybody). The standard message from politicians and lobbies, who earn fees on every transaction, is: you deserve more benefits and transfers than you're getting. In other words: 'Cut down some more trees.' And the public replies: Yes! Faster!" (p. 241).
Sandel (1996) criticizes the way that both conservatives and liberals pretend to be neutral by taking a non-judgmental attitude towards issues on morals and values in society. The political sphere is, according to Sandel, thus reduced to a series of empty administrative procedures and detached from the general public.

2.   For instance, Lawrence Stone, in his Tanner Lecture at Harvard University (1993), provides a long list of suggestions for coping with American society's varied problems, which includes: banning all handguns and automatic weapons; keeping schools open until 5 or 5:30 p.m.; banning violence from daytime television; putting metal detectors in the schools; locking up the 7 percent of incorrigible criminals who are responsible for 50 percent of violent crimes while turning all nonviolent criminals out of jail; federal funding of child care; promoting flextime and home employment for working parents; restricting access to divorce for parents with children; legalizing homosexual marriages; cutting back futile attempts to control the supply of illegal drugs; increasing the number of detoxification centers; garnisheeing the salaries of fathers who do not pay childcare; and cutting off welfare to mothers who continue to have more children.

3.   Such feminists as Fineman (1995) and Weitzman (1981) call for abolishing

state-granted marriage altogether and replacing it with individual contracts drawn up by each couple to marry.

4. Stone's (1993) historical research indicates that the "golden age of family life" never existed in Europe, either. He rather reveals the stifling repressiveness of the paternalistic moral code that prevailed in European society since the Renaissance. The code underscored religious piety, obedience to authority, the passive acceptance of one's lot in life, working hard in one's calling, and the repression of aberrant sexuality by shame and guilt. He interprets this repression of individual liberty as a reaction to the instability of society in those days.

5. Coontz (1992) attests: "Less than 10 percent of Americans believed that an unmarried person could be happy. As one popular advice book intoned: 'The family is the center of your living. If it isn't, you've gone far astray.' ... Nineteenth-century middle-class women had cheerfully left housework to servants, yet 1950s women of all classes created make-work in their homes and felt guilty when they did not do everything for themselves. ... By the mid-1950s, advertisers' surveys reported on a growing tendency among women to find 'housework a medium of expression for ... [their] femininity and individuality'" (pp. 25–7).

6. Michelle Conlin, however, reports in *Business Week* (October 20, 2003): "Already in Corporate American, more than 40 percent of the 500 largest companies have started to revise their marriage-centric policies, reexamining everything from subsidized spousal health care to family Christmas parties. ... Writ large, these kinds of changes could lead to more European-style systems that de-kink marital status from eligibility for social benefits" (p. 109).

Bibliography

Ahlander, N. and K. Bahr. 1995. "Beyond Drudgery, Power, and Equity: Toward an Expanded Discourse on the Moral Dimension of Housework in Families," *Journal of Marriage and the Family*, 57, February, pp. 54–68.

Alba, R. 1985. *Italian Americans: Into the Twilight of Ethnicity*. Englewood Cliffs, N.J.: Prentice-Hall.

——. 1990. *Ethnic Identity: The Transformation of White America*. New Haven: Yale University Press.

Aldrich, N. 1988. *Old Money: The Mythology of America's Upper Class*. New York: Alfred. A. Knopf.

Amory, C. 1947. *The Proper Bostonians*. Orleans, Mass.: Parnassus.

Anderson, B. 1983. *Imagined Communities: Reflections on the Origin and Spread of Nationalism*. London: Verso.

Archdeacon, T. 1983. *Becoming American: An Ethnic History*. New York: Free Press.

Aries, P. 1973 [1960]. *Centuries of Childhood*. London: Jonathan Cape.

Asad, T., ed. 1973. *Anthropology and the Colonial Encounter*. London: Ithaca Press.

Auerbach, J. 1976. *Unequal Justice: Lawyers and Social Change in Modern America*. New York: Oxford University Press.

Badinter, E. 1981. *Mother Love*. New York: Macmillan.

Bailey, B. 1989. *From Front Porch to Back Seat: Courtship in Twentieth-Century America*. Baltimore: Johns Hopkins University.

Baltzell, D. 1964. *The Protestant Establishment: Aristocracy and Caste in America*. New York: Random House.

——. 1979. *Puritan Boston and Quaker Philadelphia: Two Protestant Ethics and the Spirit of Authority and Leadership*. New York: Free Press.

Barnouw, E. 1975. *Tube of Plenty: The Evolution of American Television*. New York: Oxford University Press.

Bell, D. 1976. *The Coming of Post-industrial Society: A Venture in Social Forecasting*. New York: Basic.

Bellah, R. N., R. Madsen, W. M. Sullivan, A. Swidler, and S. M. Tipton. 1985. *Habits of the Heart: Individualism and Commitment in American Life*. Berkeley: University of California Press.

Bender, T. 1978. *Community and Social Change in America*. Baltimore: Johns Hopkins University Press.

Benfey, C. 2003. *The Great Wave: The Gilded Age Misfits, Japanese Eccentrics and the Opening of Old Japan*. New York: Random House.

Berger, P. and T. Luckmann. 1966. *The Social Construction of Reality: A Treatise in the Sociology of Knowledge*. Garden City, N.Y.: Doubleday.

Blau, P. and O. Duncan. 1967. *The American Occupational Structure*. New York: Free Press.

Bledstein, B. 1976. *Culture of Professionalism: The Middle Class and the Development of Higher Education in America*. New York: Norton.

Blumin, S. 1989. *The Emergence of the Middle Class: Social Experience in the American City, 1760–1900*. New York: Cambridge University Press.

Bott, E. 1957. *Family and Social Network: Roles, Norms, and External Relationships in*

Ordinary Urban Families. London: Tavistock.

Bourdieu, P. 1977. *Outline of a Theory of Practice.* Trans. by R. Nice. New York: Cambridge University Press.

——. 1984. *Distinction: A Social Critique of the Judgment of Taste.* Trans. by R. Nice. Cambridge, Mass.: Harvard University Press.

Brannen, J. and G. Wilson. 1987. *Give and Take in Families.* London: Allen and Unwin.

Brill, A. 1990. *Nobody's Business: The Paradox of Privacy.* Reading. Mass.: Addison-Wesley.

Brookhiser, R. 1991. "Dancing With The Girl That Brung Him," *New Yorker*, October 28, pp. 44–84.

Cahoone, L. 1988. *The Dilemma of Modernity: Philosophy, Culture, and Anti-Culture.* Albany: State University of New York.

Canavan, J. 1979. "South Boston Irish-American Social Life," *South Boston Journal*, 1 (2).

Chafe, W. 1986. *The Unfinished Journey: America Since World War II.* New York: Oxford University Press.

——. 1991. *The Paradox of Change: American Women in the Twentieth Century.* New York: Oxford University Press.

Chandler, A. 1977. *The Visible Hand: The Managerial Revolution in American Business.* Cambridge, Mass.: Harvard University Press.

Cherlin, A. 1981. *Marriage, Divorce, Remarriage.* Cambridge, Mass.: Harvard University Press.

Christopher, R. 1989. *Crashing the Gates: the De-WASPing of America's Power Elite.* New York: Simon and Schuster.

Chudacoff, H. 1989. *How Old Are You? Age Consciousness in American Culture.* Princeton: Princeton University Press.

Clifford, J. 1988. *The Predicament of Culture: Twentieth-Century Ethnography, Literature, and Art.* Cambridge, Mass.: Harvard University Press.

Colt, G. H. 2003. *The Big House: A Century in the Life of an American Summer House.* New York: Scribner.

Coontz, S. 1992. *The Way We Never Were: American Families and the Nostalgia Trap.* New York: Basic.

——. 1997. *The Way We Really Are: Coming to Terms with America's Changing Families.* New York: Basic.

Cott, N. 1977. *The Bonds of Womanhood: "Woman's Sphere" in New England, 1780–1835.* New Haven, Conn.: Yale University Press.

Crawford, C. 1978. *Mommie Dearest.* New York: William Morrow.

Crawford, M. 1930. *Famous Families of Massachusetts.* Boston: Little Brown.

Curran, M. 1986 [1948]. *The Parish and the Hill.* New York: The Feminist Press at The City University of New York.

Danielson, M. 1976. *The Politics of Exclusion.* New York: Columbia University Press.

Daly, M. 1978. *Gyn/Ecology: The Metaethics of Radical Feminism.* Boston: Beacon.

Degler, C. 1980. *At Odds: Women and the Family in America from Revolution to the Present.* New York: Oxford University Press.

Delphy, C. 1984. *Close to Home: A Materialist Analysis of Women's Oppression.* Amherst: University of Massachusetts Press.

DeMarco, W. 1980. *Ethnics and Enclaves: Boston's Italian North End.* Ann Arbor: University of Michigan Press.

D'Emilio, J. and E. Freedman. 1988. *Intimate Matters: A History of Sexuality in America.* New York: Harper and Row.

Dezell, M. 2000. *Irish America: Coming into Clover: the Evolution of a People and a Culture.* New York: Doubleday.

DiMaggio, P. 1979. "Review Essay: On Pierre Bourdieu," *American Journal of Sociology,* 86 (6), pp. 1460–75.

Dionne, E. J. 1991. *Why Americans Hate Politics.* New York: Simon and Schuster.

Donzelot, J. 1979. *The Policing of Families.* New York: Pantheon.

Dyck, A. 1994. *Rethinking Rights and Responsibilities: The Moral Bonds of Community.* Cleveland: Pilgrim.

Easterlin, R. 1980. *Birth and Fortune: The Impact of Numbers on Personal Welfare.* New York: Basic.

Edwards, J. 1991. "New Conceptions: Biosocial Innovations and the Family," *Journal of Marriage and the Family,* 53, pp. 349–60.

Ehrenreich, B. 1983. *The Hearts of Men: American Dreams and the Flight from Commitment.* Garden City, N.Y.: Anchor.

Eisinger, P. 1980. *The Politics of Displacement: Racial and Ethnic Transition in Three American Cities.* New York: Academic Press.

Eisler, B. 1986. *Private Lives: Men and Women of the Fifties.* New York: Franklin Watts.

Faderman, L. 1990. *Odd Girls and Twilight Lovers: A History of Lesbian Life in Twentieth-Century America.* New York: Columbia University Press.

Fardon, R. 1990. *Localizing Strategies: Regional Traditions of Ethnographic Writing.* Edinburgh: Scottish Academic Press.

Fineman, M. 1995. *The Neutered Mother, the Sexual Family and Other Twentieth Century Tragedies.* New York: Routledge.

Firth, R. 1965 [1936]. *We, The Tikopia: A Sociological Study of Kinship in Primitive Polynesia.* Boston: Beacon.

——. 1951. *Elements of Social Organization.* London: Watts.

——. 1959. *Social Change in Tikopia: Re-Study of a Polynesian Community After a Generation.* London: Allen and Unwin.

Fisher, S. and C. Hughes. 1992. *The Last Tenement: Confronting Community and Urban Renewal in Boston's West End.* Boston: Bostonian Society.

Flandrin, J.-L. 1979. *Families in Former Times: Kinship, Household, and Sexuality.* New York: Cambridge University Press.

Formisano, R. 1991. *Boston against Busing: Race, Class, and Ethnicity in the 1960s and 1970s.* Chapel Hill, N.C.: University of North Carolina Press.

Formisano, R. and C. Burns, eds. 1984. *Boston, 1700–1980: The Evolution of Urban Politics.* Westport, Conn.: Greenwood.

Foucault, M. 1977. *Discipline and Punish: The Birth of the Prison.* New York: Pantheon.

——. 1978. *The History of Sexuality.* New York: Pantheon.

Friedan, B. 1963. *The Feminine Mystique.* New York: Dell.

Galbraith, J. 1958. *The Affluent Society.* Boston: Houghton Mifflin.

——. 1996. *The Good Society: The Humane Agenda.* Boston: Houghton Mifflin.

Geertz, C. 1973. *The Interpretation of Cultures.* New York: Basic.

——. 1988. *Works and Lives: The Anthropologist as Author.* Stanford: Stanford University Press.

Gelfand, M. 1998. *Trustee for a City: Ralph Lowell of Boston.* Boston: Northeastern University Press.

Gellner, E. 1988. "The Stakes in Anthropology," *American Scholar,* 57 (1), pp. 17–30.

Gergen, K. 1991. *The Saturated Self: Dilemmas of Identity in Contemporary Life.* New York: Basic.

Gerson, K. 1985. *Hard Choices: How Women Decide About Work, Career, and Motherhood.* Berkeley: University of California Press.

Giddens, A. 1973. *The Class Structure of the Advanced Societies.* New York: Harper and Row.

——. 1979. *Central Problems in Social Theory: Action, Structure, and Contradictions in Social Analysis.* Berkeley: University of California Press.

——. 1984. *The Constitution of Society: Outline of the Theory of Structuration.* Cambridge: Polity.

——. 1991. *Modernity and Self-Identity: Self and Society in the Late Modern Age.* Stanford: Stanford University Press.

Gjessing, G. 1968. "The Social Responsibility of the Social Scientist," *Current Anthropology,* December, pp. 397–402.

Goldin, C. 1990. *Understanding the Gender Gap: An Economic History of American Women.* New York: Oxford University Press.

Goode, J. 1963. *World Revolution and Family Patterns.* New York: Free Press of Glencoe.

Gordon, L. 1988. *Heroes of Their Own Lives: The Politics and History of Family Violence, Boston, 1880–1960.* New York: Viking.

Gordon, L. and S. Riger. 1989. *The Female Fear.* New York: Free Press.

Gullestad, M. 1996. "From Obedience to Negotiation: Dilemmas in the Transmission of Values Between the Generations in Norway," *Journal of the Royal Anthropological Institute,* 2 (1), pp. 25–42.

Gupta, A. and J. Ferguson. 1992. "Beyond 'Culture': Space, Identity, and the Politics of Difference," *Cultural Anthropology,* 7 (1), pp. 6–23.

Haber, S. 1954. *Efficiency and Uplift: Scientific Management in the Progressive Era, 1890–1920.* Chicago: University of Chicago Press.

Habermas, J. 1971. *Knowledge and Human Interests.* Boston: Beacon.

——. 1975. *Legitimation Crisis.* Trans. by T. McCarthy. Boston: Beacon.

——. 1984. *The Theory of Communicative Action.* Trans. by T. McCarthy. Boston: Beacon.

Halberstam, D. 1972. *The Best and the Brightest.* Greenwich, Conn.: Fawcett.

Hall, P. 1982. *The Organization of American Culture, 1700–1900: Private Institutions, Elites, and the Origins of American Nationality.* New York: New York University Press.

Handlin. O. 1941. *Boston's Immigrants.* Cambridge, Mass.: Harvard University Press.

Harrison, C. 1988. *On Account of Sex: The Politics of Women's Issues, 1945–1968.* Berkeley: University of California Press.

Hartmann, S. 1982. *The Home Front and Beyond: American Women in the 1940s.* Boston: Twayne.

Hayes, J. G. 2002. *This Thing Called Courage: South Boston Stories.* New York: Harrington Park.

Herman, J. and L. Hirschman. 1981. *Father–Daughter Incest.* Cambridge, Mass.: Harvard University Press.

Herzfeld, M. 1985. *The Poetics of Manhood: Contest and Identity in a Cretan Mountain Village.* Princeton: Princeton University Press.

Hewlett, S. 1986. *A Lesser Life.* New York: Warner.

Higham, J. 1974. "Hanging Together: Divergent Unities in American History," *Journal of American History*, 61, pp. 3–28.

Hochschild, A. 1983. *The Managed Heart: Commercialization of Human Feeling.* Berkeley: University of California Press.

Hollingshead, A. 1949. *Elmtown's Youth: The Impact of Social Classes on Adolescents.* New York: John Wiley.

Hooyman, N. and A. Kiyak. 1988. *Social Gentology: A Multidisciplinary Perspective.* Boston: Allyn and Bacon.

Horgan, E. S. 1988. "The American Catholic Irish Family," in *Ethnic Families in America: Patterns and Variations* (Charles H. Mindel and Robert W. Habenstein, eds). New York: Elsevier.

Howard, B. 1976. *Boston: A Social History.* New York: Hawthorn.

Hunter, J. 1991. *Culture Wars: The Struggle to Define America.* New York: Basic.

Illich, I. 1981. *Shadow Work.* Boston: M. Boyars.

Jaher, F. 1982. *The Urban Establishment: Upper Strata in Boston, New York, Charleston, Chicago, and Los Angeles.* Urbana, Ill.: University of Illinois Press.

Jameson, F. 1987. "On Habits of the Heart," *The South Atlantic Quarterly*, 86 (4), Fall, pp. 545–65.

——. 1991. *Postmodernism, or The Cultural Logic of Late Capitalism.* Durham: Duke University Press.

Johnson, H. 1994. *Divided We Fall: Gambling With History in the Nineties.* New York: Norton.

Kammerman, S. 1981. *Child Care, Family Benefits, and Working Parents: A Study in Comparative Policy.* New York: Columbia University Press.

Kanter, D. and P. Mirvis. 1989. *The Cynical Americans: Living and Working in an Age of Discontent and Disillusion.* San Francisco: Jossey-Bass.

Keller, S. 1991. "The American Upper Class Family: Precarious Claims on the Future," *Journal of Comparative Family Studies*, 22 (1), pp. 159–82.

Kempe, C. H. and R. E. Helfer, eds. 1980. *The Battered Child.* Chicago: Chicago University Press,

Kessler-Harris, A. 1982. *Out to Work: A History of Wage-Earning Women in the United States.* New York: Oxford University Press.

——. 1992. "Cultural Locations: Positioning American Studies in the Great Debate," *American Quarterly*, 44 (3), pp. 299–313.

Kett, J. 1977. *Rites of Passage: Adolescence in America, 1790 to The Present.* New York: Basic.

Krugman, P. 1994. *The Age of Diminished Expectations: US Economic Policy in the 1990s.* Washington, D.C.: Washington Post Co.

Lamont, M. 1992. *Money, Morals, and Manners: The Culture of the French and the American Upper-Middle Class.* Chicago: University of Chicago Press.

——. 2000. *The Dignity of Working Men: Morality and the Boundary of Race, Class, and Immigration.* New York and Cambridge: Russel Sage Foundation and Harvard University Press.

Landsman, G. 1995. "Negotiating Work and Womanhood," *American Anthropologist*, 97 (1), pp. 33–40.

Lasch, C. 1977. *Haven in a Heartless World: The Family Besieged.* New York: Basic Readings.

——. 1978. *Culture of Narcissism: American Life in an Age of Diminishing Expectations.* New York: Norton.

——. 1984. *The Minimal Self: Psychic Survival in Troubled Times*. New York: Norton.

Leach, E. 1954. *Political Systems of Highland Burma: A Study of Kachin Social Structure*. London: London School of Economics and Political Science.

Lehr, D. and G. O'Neill. 2000. *Black Mass: The Irish Mob, The FBI, and A Devil's Deal*. Oxford: Public Affairs.

Levi-Strauss, C. 1963. *Totemism*. Boston: Beacon.

——. 1966. *The Savage Mind*. Chicago: University of Chicago Press.

——.1976. *Structural Anthropology, vol. 2*. Trans. by M. Layton. Chicago: University of Chicago Press.

Lieberson, S. and M. Waters. 1988. *From Many Strands: Ethnic and Racial Groups in Contemporary America*. New York: Russell Sage Foundation.

Loftus, P. 1991. *That Old Gang of Mine: A History of South Boston*. South Boston: TOGM-P.J.L. Jr.

Louv, R. 1990. *Childhood's Future*. Boston: Houghton Mifflin.

Lukas, A. 1985. *Common Ground: A Turbulent Decade in the Lives of Three American Families*. New York: Alfred A. Knopf.

Luttwak, E. 1993. *Endangered American Dream*. New York: Simon and Schuster.

Lynd, R. 1939. *Knowledge for What? The Place of Social Science in American Culture*. Princeton: Princeton University Press.

MacDonald, M.P. 1999. *All Souls: A Family Story from Southie*. New York: Ballantine.

Macfarlane, A. 1987. *The Culture of Capitalism*. Oxford: Blackwell.

MacIntyre, A. 1981. *After Virtue*. Bouth Bend, Ind.: University of Notre Dame Press.

Macpherson, C. B. 1962. *The Political Theory of Possessive Individualism: Hobbes to Locke*. Oxford: Clarendon.

MaFate, K. 1991. *Poverty, Inequality and Crisis of Social Policy: Summary of Findings*. Washington, D.C.: Joint Center for Political and Economic Studies.

Mandel, E. 1978. *Late Capitalism*. Trans. by J. De Bres. London: Verso.

Marcus. G., ed. 1983. *Elites: Ethnographic Issues*. Albuquerque: University of New Mexico Press.

Marcus, G. 2000. "The Deep Legacy of Dynastic Subjectivity: The Resonances of a Family Identity in Private and Public Spheres," in *Elites: Choice, Leadership and Succession* (J. de Pina-Cabral and A.P. de Lima, eds). Oxford and New York: Berg.

Marcus, G. and M. Fischer. 1986. *Anthropology as Cultural Critique: An Experimental Moment in the Human Sciences*. Chicago: University of Chicago Press.

Marcus, G. and P. Hall. 1992. *Lives in Trust: The Fortunes of Dynastic Families in Late Twentieth-Century America*. San Francisco: Westview.

Marquand, J. 1937. *The Late George Apley: A Novel in The Form of A Memoir*. Boston: Little, Brown, and Company.

Marx, K. 1947 [1867–1894]. *Capital*. Trans. by D. Torr. New York: International.

Matthews, G. 1987. *"Just a Housewife": The Rise and Fall of Domesticity in America*. New York: Oxford University Press.

May, E. T. 1980. *Great Expectations: Marriage and Divorce in Post-Victorian America*. Chicago: University of Chicago Press.

——. 1988. *Homeward Bound: American Families in the Cold War Era*. New York: Basic.

Maybury-Lewis, D., ed. 1979. *Dialectical Societies: The Ge and Bororo of Central Brazil*. Cambridge, Mass.: Harvard University Press.

McLaughlin, S. D., B. Melber, J. Billy, D. Zimmerle, L. Winges, and T. Johnson, 1988.

The Changing Lives of American Women. Chapel Hill, N.C.: University of North Carolina.

Medick, H. and D. Sabean. 1984. *Interest and Emotions: Essays on the Study of Family and Kinship.* New York: Cambridge University Press.

Milkman, R. 1987. *Gender at Work: The Dynamics of Job Segregation by Sex During World War II.* Urbana, Ill.: University of Illinois Press.

Mills, C. W. 1951. *White Collar: The American Middle Classes.* New York: Oxford University Press.

Miller, D. and M. Nowak. 1977. *The Fifties: The Way We Really Were.* Garden City, N.Y.: Doubleday.

Mintz, S. and S. Kellogg. 1988. *Domestic Revolutions: A Social History of American Family Life.* New York: Free Press.

Moog, C. 1990. *"Are They Selling Her Lips?" Advertising and Identity.* New York: Morrow.

Moore, S. 1987. "Explaining the Present: Theoretical Dilemmas in Processual Ethnography," *American Ethnologist*, 14 (4), November, pp. 727–36.

Moskowitz, F. and R. Moskowitz. 1990. *Parenting Your Aging Parents.* Woodland Hills, Calif.: Key Publications.

Needham, R. 1971. "Remarks on the Analysis of Kinship and Marriage," in *Rethinking Kinship and Marriage* (R. Needham, ed.). London: Tavistock.

Newman, K. 1988. *Falling from Grace: The Experience of Downward Mobility in the American Middle Class.* New York: Free Press.

——. 1993. *Declining Fortunes: The Withering of the American Dream.* New York: Basic.

Oakley, A. 1974. *Woman's Work: The Housewife, Past and Present.* New York: Pantheon.

O'Connor, T. 1991. *Bibles, Brahmins, and Bosses.* Boston: Boston Public Library.

——. 1993. *Building a New Boston: Politics and Urban Renewal, 1950–1970.* Boston: Northeastern University Press.

——. 1994 [1988]. *South Boston: My Home Town.* Boston: Northeastern University Press.

——. 1995. *The Boston Irish: A Political History.* Boston: Back Bay.

——. 1998. *Boston Catholics: A History of the Church and Its People.* Boston: Northeastern University Press.

——. 2000. *Boston A to Z.* Cambridge, Mass.: Harvard University Press.

——. 2001. *The Hub: Boston Past and Present.* Boston: Northeastern University Press.

Offe, C. 1984. *Contradictions of the Welfare State.* Cambridge, Mass.: MIT Press.

Ortner, S. 1984. "Theory in Anthropology Since the Sixties," *Comparative Studies in Society and History*, 26 (1), pp. 126–66.

Ostrander, S. 1984. *Women of the Upper Class.* Philadelphia: Temple University Press.

Park, E. and E. Burgess. 1921. *Introduction to the Science of Sociology.* Chicago: University of Chicago Press.

Parsons, T. and R. Bales. 1954. *Family Socialization and Interaction Process.* Glencoe, Ill.: Free Press.

Patterson, J. 1986. *American Struggles Against Poverty, 1900–1985.* Cambridge, Mass.: Harvard University Press.

Patterson, J., and P. Kim. 1991. *The Day America Told the Truth: What People Really Believe about Everything that Really Matters.* New York: Prentice Hall.

Peele, S. 1976. *Love and Addiction.* New York: Signet.

Pessen, E. 1982. "Social Structure and Politics in American History," *American Historical Review*, 81, pp. 101–12.

Peterson, P. 1993. *Facing Up: How To Rescue the Economy from Crushing Debt and Restore the American Dream.* New York: Simon and Schuster.

Phillips, K. 1990. *Politics of Rich and Poor.* New York: Randam House.

———. 1993. *Boiling Point: Republicans, Democrats, and the Decline of Middle-Class Prosperity.* New York: Random House.

Pleck, E. 1987. *Domestic Tyranny: The Making of Social Policy Against Family Violence from Colonial Times to the Present.* New York: Oxford University Press.

Putnam, R. 1996. "Democracy in America at Century's End," in *Democracy's Victory and Crisis: Nobel Symposium, No. 93.* Cambridge, England: Cambridge University Press.

Ragone, H. 1994. *Surrogate Motherhood: Conception in the Heart.* Boulder, Colo.: Westview.

Rauch, J. 1994. *Demosclerosis: The Silent Killer of American Government.* New York: Times Books.

Rothman, E. 1984. *Hands and Hearts: A History of Courtship in America.* New York: Basic.

Rotundo, E. 1993. *American Manhood: Transformations in Masculinity from the Revolution to the Modern Era.* New York: Basic.

Rush, F. 1980. *The Best-Kept Secret: Sexual Abuse of Children.* Eaglewood Cliffs, N.J.: Prentice Hall.

Ryan, D. 1979. "Monsignor Denis O'Callaghan: The Unmeltable Irishman," *South Boston Journal,* 1 (2).

———. 1983. *Beyond the Ballot Box: A Social History of the Boston Irish, 1845–1917.* Rutherford, N.J.: Fairleigh Dickinson University Press.

Ryan, M. 1975. *Womanhood in America: From Colonial Times to the Present.* New York: Franklin Watts.

———. 1981. *Cradle of The Middle Class: The Family in Oneida County, New York, 1790–1865.* Cambridge: Cambridge University Press.

Sahlins, M. 1976. *Culture and Practical Reason.* Chicago: University of Chicago Press.

Sanday, P. 1981. *Female Power and Male Dominance.* Cambridge, England: Cambridge University Press.

Sandel, M. 1996. *Democracy's Discontent: America in Search of A Public Philosophy.* Cambridge: Belknap Press of Harvard University Press.

Sangren, S. 1988. "Rhetoric and the Authority of Ethnography: 'Postmodernism' and the Social Reproduction of Texts," in *Current Anthropology,* 29 (3), pp. 405–35.

Satkewich, C. 1979. "St. Vincent's Church and the Irish," *South Boston Journal,* 1 (2).

Scanzoni, J., K. Polonko, J. Teachman, and L. Thompson. 1990. *The Sexual Bond: Rethinking Families and Close Relationships.* Newbury Park, Calif.: Sage.

Schneider, D. 1968. *American Kinship: A Cultural Account.* Chicago: University of Chicago Press.

Segalen, M. 1983. *Love and Power in the Peasant Family.* Oxford: Blackwell.

Sennett, R. 1977. *The Fall of Public Man.* New York: Knopf.

Shannon, W. 1989. *The American Irish: a Political and Social Portrait.* Amherst: University of Massachusetts Press.

Shapiro, L. 1986. *Perfection Salad.* Toronto: Collins.

Shattuck, J. 2003. *The Hazards of Good Breeding: A Novel.* New York: W. W. Norton.

Shiozaki, S. 2001. *Amerika "Chinichiha" no Kigen* (The Origin of "Japanologists" in the United States). Tokyo: Heibonsha.

Shorter, E. 1975. *The Making of the Modern Family*. New York: Basic.

Skolnick, A. 1991. *Embattled Paradise: The American Family in an Age of Uncertainty*. New York: Basic.

Smelser, N. 1968. *Essays in Sociological Explanation*. Englewood Cliffs, N.J.: Prentice Hall.

Social Register Association. 1993, 1994, 1995. *Social Register*. New York.

Sokoloff, J. 1980. *Between Money and Love: The Dialectics of Women's Home and Market Work*. New York: Praeger.

Solomon, M. 1956. *Ancestors and Immigrants: A Changing New England Tradition*. Cambridge, Mass.: Harvard University Press.

Sorensen, T. 1996. *Why I Am A Democrat*. New York: Henry Holt.

Stacey, J. 1990. *Brave New Families: Stories of Domestic Upheaval in Late Twentieth Century America*. New York: Basic.

——. 1996. *In the Name of the Family: Rethinking Family Values in the Postmodern Age*. Boston: Beacon.

Stack, C. 1974. *All Our Kin: Strategies for Survival in a Black Community*. New York: Harper.

——. 1996. *Call to Home: African Americans Reclaim the Rural South*. New York: Basic.

Stone, L. 1993. "'Family Values' Past and Present" (The Tanner Lecture on Human Values, Harvard University). Unpublished Manuscript.

Story, R. 1980. *Harvard and the Boston Upper Class: The Forging of an Aristocracy, 1800–1870*. Middletown, Conn.: Wesleyan University Press.

Strathern, M. 1992. *After Nature: English Kinship in The Twentieth Century*. Cambridge, England: University of Cambridge Press.

Strauss, L. 1953. *Natural Right and History*. Chicago: University of Chicago Press.

Stuart, S. P. 1998. *My First Cousin Once Removed: Money, Madness, and the Family of Robert Lowell*. New York: Harper Perennial.

Taylor, E. 1989. *Prime-Time Families: Television Culture in the Postwar America*. Berkeley: University of California Press.

Thernstrom, S. 1973. *The Other Bostonians: Poverty and Progress in the American Metropolis, 1880–1970*. Cambridge, Mass.: Harvard University Press.

Tocqueville, A. de. 1969. *Democracy in America*. Trans. by G. Lawrence. New York: Doubleday, Anchor.

Toffler, A. 1980. *The Third Wave*. New York: Morrow.

Trachtenberg, A. 1982. *The Incorporation of America: Culture and Society in the Gilded Age*. New York: Hill and Wang.

Ueno, C. 1990. *Kafuchousei to Shihonsei* (Patriarchy and Capitalism). Tokyo: Iwanami.

US Census of Population. http://eire.census.gov/popest/estimates.php

Van Horn, S. H. 1988. *Women, Work, and Fertility, 1900–1986*. New York: New York University Press.

Veeder, N. 1992. *Women's Decision-Making: Common Themes – Irish Voices*. Westport, Conn.: Praeger.

Veroff, J., R. Kulka, and E. Douvan. 1981a. *Mental Health in America: Patterns of Help-Seeking from 1957 to 1976*. New York: Basic.

——. 1981b. *The Inner American: A Self-Portrait from 1957 to 1976*. New York: Basic.

Vincent, J. 1986. "System and Process, 1974–1985," *Annual Review of Anthropology*, pp. 99–119.

Warner, L. and P. Lunt. 1941. *The Social Life of a Modern Community*. New Haven: Yale University Press.

Warren, C. 1987. *Madwives: Schizophrenic Women in the 1950s*. New Brunswick: Rutgers University Press.

Weber, M. 1976 [1904–5]. *The Protestant Ethic and the Spirit of Capitalism*. New York: Charles Scribner's.

Weiner, L. 1985. *From Working Girl to Working Mother: The Female Labor Force in the United States, 1820–1980*. Chapel Hill, N.C.: University of North Carolina Press.

Weitzman, L. 1981. *The Marriage Contract: Spouses, Lovers and the Law*. New York: Free Press.

Werlhof, C. von. 1984 [1986]. "Schattenarbeit oder Hausarbei?" Trans. by M. Maruyama as "Shadou Waku ka Kajiroudouka" (Shadow Work or Housework?), in *Kajiroudou to Shihonshugi* (Housework and Capitalism) (M. Maruyama, ed.), 1986. Tokyo: Iwanami.

Whitehill, W. 1959. *Boston: Topographical History*. Cambridge, Mass.: Belknap Press of Harvard University Press.

Wiebe, R. 1975. *The Segmented Society: A Historical Preface to the Meaning of America*. New York: Oxford University Press.

Will. G. 1992. *Restoration: Congress, Term Limits and the Recovery of Deliberative Democracy*. New York: Free Press.

Williams, R. 1977. *Marxism and Literature*. Oxford: Oxford University Press.

Wilson, W. J. 1996. *When Work Disappears: The World of the New Urban Poor*. New York: Alfred A. Knopf.

Wood, G. 1992. *The Radicalism of the American Revolution*. New York: Alfred A. Knopf.

Wuthnow, R. 1989. *Meaning and Moral Order: Explorations in Cultural Analysis*. Berkeley: University of California Press.

Yanagisako, S. 1985. *Transforming the Past: Tradition and Kinship among Japanese Americans*. Stanford: Stanford University Press.

Yanagisako, S. and J. Collier, eds. 1987. *Gender and Kinship: Essays Towards a Unified Analysis*. Stanford: Stanford University Press.

Yanagisako, S. and C. Delaney, eds. 1995. *Naturalizing Power: Essays in Feminist Cultural Analysis*. New York: Routledge.

Zelizer, V. 1985. *Pricing the Priceless Child: The Changing Social Value of Children*. New York: Basic.

Index

Adams family, 35, 99
  Charles Francis, 99
  John, 65
  Samuel, 29–32 *passim*, 37, 78
affirmative action, 37, 38, 133, 136, 188
Ahlander, N., 168–9
Aldrich, N., 52–3, 54, 61–2, 74, 100, 180
American Party *see* Know-Nothings
Amory, C., 36, 51
Anderson, B., 34, 64, 182
Appleton family, 28, 35, 93
  Diana, 31, 32
  Theodore Lowell, 28–32 *passim*, 34, 65, 93
Aries, P., 20
Auerbach, J., 194

Badinter, E., 20, 21
Bahr, K., 168–9
Bellah, R., 21, 131, 183, 187, 190, 195, 196, 199
birth control, 89, 138, 162, 163–4, 168, 185, 186
Boston
  "Athens of America," 9
  Beacon Hill, 28, 39, 43, 54–9 *passim*, 62, 91, 105, 126, 127, 132, 153, 180
  ethnic makeup, 10, 106, 205n10, 207n3
  history, 6–9
  "hub of the solar system," 6
  languages in, 10, 123
  number of colleges/hospitals, 9
  population, 6, 7, 8, 10, 117
  see also Brahmins; Irish; South Boston
Boston Evening Transcript, 64
Boston Globe, 10, 64, 110, 113, 129, 135, 136, 139, 140, 141, 207n3, 208n5, 210n16
Boston Herald, 110
Bott, E., 13
Bourdieu, P., 25, 26, 35, 50, 53, 59, 99, 129, 180, 183, 186, 194

Brahmins, Boston
  and art, 11, 39, 41, 43, 45, 72, 74, 75, 78, 102, 103, 157
  "Boston disease," 41, 53, 71, 185 (*see also* WASP Rot Syndrome)
  changing culture, 31, 34–5, 39, 42, 44–5, 47, 50, 53, 62, 86, 95
  childhood, 37, 40–1, 45, 72, 89–92
  conservative/liberal, 18, 32, 34, 42, 45, 46, 47, 77, 187
  declining influence of, 7, 12, 28, 30, 32–3, 35, 180, 36–50, 52, 99–100, 179–80, 191–2
  education, 36, 38, 40, 43, 44, 47, 48, 71, 73, 90, 91, 92, 100
  family continuity, 41, 43, 45–6, 49, 50, 64–5, 66, 78, 93–4, 95, 101
  family trusts, 44, 48, 50, 97, 98–101, 103, 155, 191, 207n19
  financial decline, 28, 37, 38–9, 42–6 *passim*, 48, 50, 51, 60, 67, 88, 90, 191–2
  identifying traits, 35–6, 50
  incomes, 41, 44, 48, 54, 70, 71, 97–8, 99, 100
  inheritance, 52, 60, 99, 101–4, 180
  marriage, 31, 36–7, 38, 40–4 *passim*, 47, 50, 62, 65, 79, 80, 81–2, 86, 87, 101, 102
  meals, 61, 76, 93–4, 95, 188
  names in, 46, 51, 54, 65, 87, 93
  origin of term, 203n1
  and "outsiders," 29, 34, 37–8, 42, 43, 44, 46, 47–8, 55, 61, 62–3, 64, 68, 79–80, 104
  pessimistic/optimistic, 32, 187
  philanthropy, 37, 39, 59–60, 70, 72, 77, 188
  and politics, 58, 68, 77
  pre-nuptial contracts, 83
  recreation, 76–7, 79, 80
  rejection of tradition, 30, 31, 37, 39, 40, 41, 43, 45, 53, 63, 89–90, 185